INTERCONNECTIVITY, FLOW, AND BALANCE

A Values-Based Framework for
Achieving Sustainable Growth in Uncertain Times

YVETTE BETHEL

ORGSOUL INTERNATIONAL

Interconnectivity, Flow, and Balance

A Values-Based Framework for Achieving Sustainable Growth in Uncertain Times

Organizational Soul
P.O. Box N-511
Nassau, Bahamas

Email: info@orgsoul.com

ISBN: 978-0-578-20266-2

Printed in the United States of America
First Edition Printing: 2018

DEDICATION

This book is dedicated to the movement of beneficial disruption that is afoot.

CONTENTS

ACKNOWLEDGMENTS

Creating a book takes a village, so it is important for me to acknowledge the contributions made by the extraordinary people who helped make this book a reality. I have to start with my mother, Jacqueline Bethel, for always expecting high standards from me and providing unwavering support. Helen Klonaris helped me walk my talk, Christine Moore helped my active voice to come through, and Aden Nichols for polish. Ally Machate and your team of editors, I deeply appreciate your editing talent, your candor, and your dedication to helping me make this book the best possible representation of my ideas. Peter Bowerman, your wit, generosity, and talent are appreciated.

Dr. Showalter Johnson and Terry Fountain: thank you for your support. My thanks to Tyrone Fitzgerald, Chandler Sands, Royann Dean, Craig Symonette, Katherine Hamilton, D'Adra Smith, Melissa Minns, Keshala Knowles, and Wellington Hepburn for your participation in focus groups that helped me fine-tune the material and my thinking. Thank you to Michelle Vandepas, and Karen Curry-Parker for your sage advice during this book-writing journey.

I am especially thankful to Joshua Freedman, CEO/COO of Six Seconds (the largest global *emotional intelligence* network), who invited me to present at an emotional intelligence conference in Boston in 2013. That presentation was the catalyst for this book.

You all contributed to this book by sharing your precious time and your genius. For this, I am eternally grateful!

INTRODUCTION

*A mind once stretched by a new idea never
regains its original dimensions.*

— Oliver Wendell Holmes American physician,
poet, and humorist

One of the overarching goals of this book is to stretch your thinking and invite you to perceive your organization through new eyes. New perspectives bring fresh insights you can use to resolve mundane, as well as dramatic, unconventional challenges.

This book introduces a framework that functions like the operating system of a computer. The operating system is the most important software on your computer. It connects and communicates with hardware and other software, and while it operates quietly in the background, it makes your experience seamless. Once you know the ground rules, the operations they facilitate become routine. When your operating system malfunctions, you may experience interruptions, delays, or worse — a crash.

Similarly, the *Interconnectivity, Flow, and Balance Model* (IFB) is an operating system that functions in the background of your organization. Like computer operating systems, IFB is ever present, not always perceived, and prolific. It arranges your organization's internal ecosystem around inherent rules of behavioral and other systems that guide daily activities, meaningful change, and innovation. When IFB malfunctions, the organization can still operate but there can be disruptions, unintended results, or delays.

The IFB Model is an evolving, multipurpose tool that can stimulate the growth of your organization and give it the flexibility it needs to succeed in increasingly uncertain times. It is a model that takes the whole organization into consideration, balancing the development of leaders and teams with strategic needs. The model better equips leaders to enhance *collaboration*, improve internal communication, strengthen performance, and inspire innovation.

Another invaluable use of the IFB Model is to improve *engagement*. The 2017 Gallup State of the American Workplace report found that 67 percent of American workers are either not engaged or are actively disengaged. Internationally, 87 percent of workers fall within these two categories.

In response to low engagement numbers and the risks associated with this trend, organizational decision makers are paying closer attention to engagement levels because they understand the intricate link between engagement and team performance. Gallup research indicates companies with engaged employees outperform their competitors by an impressive 147 percent. This is useful because during volatile times an engaged workforce is more important than ever, especially as leaders seek to create a competitive advantage through their people.

Engagement is linked to trust, and together they create a powerful driver of performance. The IFB Model is values based, centered on trust. Edelman's 2018 Trust Barometer points out that in 2017, the world faced a global crisis of trust because of the combined and cumulative actions of the media, government, and corporations. As a result, a battle to find the truth has emerged, making trust an increasingly valuable commodity.

Leaders need to find ways to make use of people's natural talents that seek expression within organizations. It takes time to develop and refine the skills required to create a *change-based organization*, powered by IFB. A change-based organization treats change as a constant, and this is an inherent trait of the IFB Model. IFB is not an instant fix that will solve all your challenges, but it can transform your organization when used effectively.

The IFB Model keeps change at the top of mind, treating it as a constant, perpetual state that requires deliberate balancing; it includes discrete change initiatives but is not limited to them. While this book is primarily designed for organizational decision makers seeking meaningful change, others can use it effectively as well. For example, it can be used as a resource by middle managers expected to implement changes using IFB principles. The more your team members understand and embrace the concepts of interconnectivity, flow, and balance, the more likely it is that they will commit themselves to developing the skills needed for successful IFB implementation.

Who Can Benefit from This Book

Although the IFB Model has applications that extend beyond the boundaries of organizations, this book targets business owners, executives, and other decision makers who work within organizations of all sizes—from scrappy startups to multinational corporations. These organizations include for-profit and nonprofit organizations, churches, and governments. The IFB Model can be used by consultants as a tool kit that can offer fresh insights into clients' organizations and by training companies for differentiating their tutorial offerings.

This book also serves as a resource for professors of university-level business courses; it encompasses an evolving body of ideas that can better prepare students for thriving and leading within evolving workplace and industry dynamics.

You can use the IFB Model to help reduce risks within your organization by improving engagement, addressing persistent challenges, and reversing flagging performance. It was created with useful longevity in mind, supporting ongoing healthy organizational evolution. The model embraces the reality that there will always be imbalances within the workplace, some more pronounced than others—but not every imbalance deserves your attention. This book provides tools you can use to decide which tensions should be treated as high priorities.

HOW TO USE THIS BOOK

The secret of getting ahead, is getting started.

— Anonymous

The IFB material can be used in multiple ways: to facilitate cultural change, to enhance the outcomes of your strategy, to turbocharge your talent development strategy, or to facilitate restructuring initiatives. This is a transformative model that highlights people and structural considerations, so it can be used whenever you're planning and executing change. Another possible use is to examine cultural compatibilities when organizational leaders are considering a merger, acquisition, or joint venture; it can also be helpful during the integration phase(s).

The IFB framework can be applied within these and other contexts to facilitate innovation; that is, problem-solving that addresses chronic challenges like corruption, or the introduction of new products or services. From a structural perspective, the IFB material can assist decision makers with restructuring initiatives and help improve operational efficiencies. The IFB Model is also a useful workforce development tool that can shine a light on the need for updated skillsets within your organization.

The *Pillar of Trust* concept is introduced in Part II. It represents the core values that are built into the model. While competencies related to the value of trust are important, the IFB Model also encompasses the skills needed to sustain interconnectivity, flow, and balance.

In summary, IFB tools can support organizational leaders in a variety of contexts — mergers and acquisitions, restructuring exercises, innovation, problem-solving, strategic planning, efficiency studies, and cultural change projects, to name a few. They are flexible enough to be used wholly or in part by organizational leaders, consultants, and trainers who are seeking sustainable change.

Getting the Most from This Book

Part I introduces you to the IFB Model. Admittedly, these concepts are deep, but they are very worthy of your serious study. Learning to apply the IFB Model can help you perceive your organization differently so you can resolve the challenges that keep you up at night. This book is useful as a guide, so reading (or re-reading) it when you are anticipating or undergoing a change initiative can be rewarding.

Parts I and II delve into conceptual frameworks that focus on developing your understanding of the IFB Model. More specifically, Part I deepens your understanding of the concepts of interconnectivity, flow, and balance, outlining theories and tools you can use to support the application of the IFB Model.

The IFB Model operates as intended when employees at all levels have built and sustained their individual and collective Pillars of Trust. Part II is dedicated to exploring the components of trust, providing insights into the trust-building competencies required for teams. Decision makers can use it as a *competency*-building framework for themselves, other leaders, and frontline employees who are expected to exhibit competencies based on trust. While Part II focuses on trust, it is not the only core value resident within IFB organizations. Other compatible values can also be integrated.

Part III is the practical section of the book, providing you with tools and processes you can use to integrate IFB into the day-to-day operations of your organization; it takes you through each dimension of the model and provides guidelines for diagnosing, envisioning, designing, planning, implementing, and sustaining IFB.

When leaders decide to implement the IFB framework, initial implementation should be considered a strategic priority and integrated into the plan. Over time, IFB practices should become part of your daily operational and cultural activities. This means that at the post-implementation stage, the practices should become an integral part of your organizational activities.

There are features of this book that were included to support you with better understanding the material. These features include diagrams, tables, and case studies, as well as the glossary at the end of the book. The glossary defines IFB and business vocabulary. Words in the glossary are italicized the first time they appear in the text to let you know you can find the definition at the end of the book.

The diagrams and tables provide perspectives about the *organizational ecosystem* that illustrations can better express. The case studies were included for readers who learn better from real-world examples of the principles under consideration.

Part I:

Understanding the IFB Model

The Interconnectivity, Flow, and Balance Model is an integrated framework that can help change-makers transform institutions into change-based organizations; it offers multiple benefits, depending on your goals. In Part I, we will explore concepts and examples that will prove useful in Part III, which is dedicated to supporting you with implementing the IFB framework. To help you understand the model, the concepts are outlined sequentially, but remember that the three dimensions of the IFB Model operate simultaneously.

CHAPTER 1

SETTING THE STAGE

If you create the stage setting and it is grand, everyone who enters will play their part.

—Morris Lapidus, architect

A change-based organization is a fluid operation. It's not perfect, but it is responsive. Leaders in these organizations know when to absorb changes or protect themselves against shifts within their internal and external environments, preferably without drama or losses. Leaders and employees alike recognize the value change brings to their organizations, whether the change was effectively executed or not.

Everyone in change-based organizations perceives change as part of their everyday interactions and they know what level of constant change will create instability based on the unique qualities of their respective *cultures*. In change-based organizations, one of the fundamental operating principles is *change is constant*—it encompasses costly initiatives and everyday, incremental change journeys.

Change as a constant is one of the premises of the IFB Model. If properly constructed, the framework can absorb internal and external shocks to the organizational ecosystem, shortening response time, minimizing adverse effects, and preparing for future challenges.

The IFB framework is intentionally flexible. It can improve the potential for successful change by strengthening aspects of your existing culture or transforming it into something quite different. Leaders who use the IFB Model can take what's productive and healthy within their organizations and improve on it. The IFB Model also highlights unhealthy systems of operation and behavior that can be eliminated or transformed.

Change-based organizations powered by IFB are built on a foundation of integrity and trust, and these qualities should permeate all activities. The presence of trust is vital for an organization to achieve IFB standing, and IFB status is in turn a powerful tool for helping organizational leaders to achieve their goals. These goals range from establishing long-term sustainability to creating a competitive advantage through innovation, disruption, or *social responsibility*.

The IFB framework is compatible with different types of cultures; it can help organizational leaders orchestrate cultural shifts in sustainable ways. For example, some organizations are strongly oriented toward stability and *control*, but leaders sometimes want to integrate elements of innovation without transitioning to a full-fledged innovative organization. The IFB Model can be used to make a shift and sustain the desired state. On the other end of the spectrum, decision-makers within some innovative cultures prefer only enough structure to allow them to maintain their innovative identity.

Chapter 1 introduces the core elements of the IFB framework, providing an overview of the model by developing the concepts successively. Interconnectivity is at the *heart* of the model, and the configuration of this IFB component contributes to the quality of flow and decision-makers' ability to orchestrate balance.

A Closer Look at the IFB Framework

The IFB Model is specifically designed to transform human eco-systems by harnessing naturally occurring dynamics. It keeps the organizational ecosystem at the forefront of leaders' minds, so they can proactively strengthen their own performance as well as that of their team, setting the stage for long-term sustainability. While other human ecosystems — such as families, sport teams, and cities — can benefit from the IFB principles, this book provides insights into how to implement the principles within organizations.

Even though the components of the IFB Model — interconnectivity, flow, and balance — are described sequentially in this book, they do not operate in a linear fashion. The three dimensions operate as layers that are integrative, constantly interacting with each other.

We are all interconnected, even if we perceive ourselves as solitary islands in a vast ocean. As part of multiple interconnected networks, individuals need to be able to execute effectively and take actions that lead to the greater good of their teams.

Interconnectivity is about building quality *relationships*. Flow competencies can be used to observe externally occurring flows so leaders can use this information to modify organization-centric, internal flows to remain relevant. The quality of interconnectivity affects a variety of flows including workflows, the flow of information, and more. *Balance* can be quantitatively or subjectively defined by leaders based on strategic priorities, including their organization's vision, mission, and core values.

Once leaders define the states of interconnectivity and flow required for organizational balance, they can become more effective at identifying imbalances, addressing them proactively. The dynamism between interconnectivity and flow requires nonstop observation when balancing priority tensions within an organization. Therefore, once implemented, the IFB Model becomes a perpetually activated asset.

Around the world, distrust is reaching pandemic proportions. With the emergence of increased polarization, the lack of clarity between what's real and what isn't, and the exposure of corruption, sexual harassment, and multifarious scandals, it is becoming increasingly important for businesses to be trusted by their employees, clients, and other *stakeholders*. For these reasons and more, the IFB Model is built on a Pillar of Trust, comprising the competencies of *integrity*, *self-mastery*, and a "we" disposition.

How IFB Can Help Leaders

One benefit of improving your understanding of the IFB framework is that it allows you to manage undercurrents and overt actions within your organization rather than allowing those forces to hijack decisions. Market and other external forces should provide information that you and your team of decision-makers can also use as you chart your course.

IFB can also affect the capacity and success of your organization. Your internal capacity can improve with the right leadership, competent employees, effective communication, clear *policies and procedures*, and an effectively planned and executed strategic plan.

The IFB Model is more likely to be successful if the entire organization is committed to its implementation. Half-hearted commitment to implementation may lead to improvement, but if some departments are not committed to or displaying collaborative behaviors, IFB sustainability is questionable. Implementing IFB within only a single department violates a basic tenet of the model: all parts of the organization are interconnected.

When strategic decision-makers develop a plan for an organization, the IFB Model can affect how things are done and, by extension, the sustainability of an organization. The framework is geared toward positioning organizations for both short-term results and long-term growth. It manages the health of the organization from the inside-out.

The Nuts and Bolts of the IFB Model

Interconnectivity, flow, and balance are dynamic, sometimes unpredictable, and constantly in motion. Whether IFB dynamics are managed effectively by decision-makers or not, activity is ongoing.

Figure 1.1 illustrates the IFB Model and how it operates. No part of this model takes precedence over another—each component is inextricably entangled with the others. As you master the skills you need to operate the IFB Model, each element should evolve with the others.

Starting on the left of Figure 1.1 is the Pillar of Trust. The IFB Model operates on the premise that interpersonal connectivity is strengthened when the Pillar of Trust is structurally sound. The Pillar of Trust has three components: integrity, self-mastery, and a "we" disposition (inclusivity).

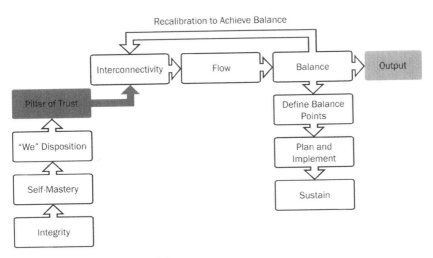

Figure 1.1   *The IFB Model*

Interconnectivity within an organization includes, but is not limited to, interpersonal relationships; most people, processes, policies, and strategies are interconnected. Once perceived, these connections may be understood, and that information can inform decisions. When they remain hidden, connections can lead to unproductive outcomes for a team, especially if the purpose of the relationship is counterproductive to team goals.

Connections may therefore be evident or hidden. If the former, interconnectivity can be harnessed to support your vision and mission; if, on the other hand, these connections are hidden, your vision and goals could be compromised.

As you transition from left to right in Figure 1.1, the next component in the IFB Model is flow. Flow is facilitated by the quality of relationships, the competence of team members, the relevance of *organizational structure*(s), and the capacity of leaders to execute strategic plans. The *drivers of flow* emanate from either dysfunctional interactions or trust-based collaboration. The difference between low- and high-quality flow drivers become clearer over time, as low-quality drivers can be less sustainable in the long term.

Balance is dynamic by nature. Regardless of whether trust is evident, external factors impinge upon balance. Despite the source of imbalance, when trust is present—in conjunction with competence and other quality interconnective factors—it supports decision-makers in their attempts to maintain equipoise, recover from crises, and grow business sustainably.

While the terms "interconnectivity," "flow," and "balance" are not typically referred to or considered in an integrative way, it is common to refer to the individual concepts. We hear interconnective phrases like "the weakest link," "We are stronger together," and "Let's create synergies"—indicating an existing awareness that we are interconnected. Similarly, we hear flow terms like "workflow," "flowchart," and "streams of income." The idea of balance emerges in corporate jargon, too: "balanced scorecard," "balance sheet," and "Let's weigh the alternatives." The IFB Model brings these three familiar concepts together as an integrative filter through which you can view your team or organization differently.

Interconnectivity

Interconnectivity refers to the structure of the *relationship* network that makes it possible for flow of all varieties to occur. Numerous types of interconnective structures are possible, including interpersonal relationships, which create organic, living, interconnective structures.

Interconnectivity also occurs within nonpersonal relationships. Nonpersonal relationships exist between *policies and procedures,* or even strategic goals and policies. They provide structures that enable productivity, whether or not employees have access to the necessary resources. As you consider the interconnective infrastructure, remember that even though nonpersonal relationships are connected and affect each other, human interaction is required for these relationships to be activated.

In some organizations, policies and procedures have an interesting relationship with each other. Policies can be formal or informal. Ideally, formal policies should be aligned with documented procedures. Informal policies are accepted, undocumented practices that can sometimes contradict formal policies and processes, thus creating potential for imbalances. In circumstances like this, a leader may make decisions based on formal policies, but because the informal policy is really in effect and there is no effort to bring the two into alignment, the resulting outcome may be unexpected or unwanted.

The strength of all types of interconnection affects the sustainability, quality, and outcomes of flow. However, leaders should realize that a strong relationship may not necessarily serve the greater good of the team; this is because strong connectivity and flow can divert resources and impair outcomes in ways that benefit one person or a few stakeholders at the expense of the team.

This can happen when a relationship exists to support the *power* ambitions of a single person or a select few. Under such circumstances, the focus is on fulfilling personal agendas, resulting in undermining the needs of the team.

Leaders who are consumed by the need for power often deploy team resources in ways that serve one, a few, or all in the power network, but not the greater good of the team. When using the IFB Model to assess relationships, leaders should look beyond the surface of interpersonal relationships and pay close attention to why they exist and how they affect the whole team.

The Pillar of Trust

As in buildings, some elements of the Pillar of Trust may be structurally sound, providing strong support to the overall edifice. A structurally sound Pillar of Trust is essential to healthy organizational ecosystems for multiple reasons. Namely: it enhances response time in ambiguous, complex circumstances; improves engagement levels; enhances the customer experience; and it is directly linked to retention. Studies reveal that the higher your trust levels, the more likely performance levels will display a growth pattern.

Your organizational ecosystem is constantly evolving. Relationships strengthen and weaken, moods shift, leaders make mistakes and sometimes correct them, so your environment is always changing. While all this is happening, your Pillar of Trust should always be there to support the entire ecosystem.

Change has a natural rhythm. It can take organizations two steps forward and one step back, progressing in a nonlinear pattern. Leaders who operate according to IFB principles should possess adaptive skills moving in tandem with rhythms and cycles, anticipating next moves, in a perpetual dance.

When leaders establish their own Pillars of Trust from the inside-out, they start at the individual level, developing themselves so they can demonstrate trustworthy behaviors and contribute to the growth of team trust levels. Leaders are not the only ones who should improve their trustworthiness and willingness to trust others. The team Pillar of Trust is sturdiest when most team members are dedicated to building it.

The Pillar of Trust comprises three competency areas: *integrity*, self-mastery, and a "we" disposition. These three competencies support your organizational ecosystem by strengthening relationships and networks. They have the power to transform how people relate to each other: stimulating respectful conversations, mending damaged relationships, and sparking creativity.

The Pillar of Trust ensures all interpersonal interactions are grounded in trust, respect, inclusion, and *self-regulation*. Without it, interconnectivity and flow can coexist with the appearance of balance because of symptoms of success. Success is a subjective concept which can be achieved without the presence of trust.

Another consideration when it comes to trust building is that millennials are now the supermajority, and they communicate differently than other generations. Effective communication practices are an essential component of engagement and trust, and with lowered engagement levels around the world, is key to organizational sustainability. When implementing IFB, leaders should take the time to become aware of what each generation needs and take the steps necessary to address these emerging preferences.

Different surveys provide various perspectives of the needs of millennials, but regardless the generation, trust is recognized as a basic team-building block. For instance, a survey highlighted in the *Harvard Business Review* identifies the top three things millennials want at work as the same top three that Baby Boomers and Generation X'ers want—they are: making a positive impact, solving social and environmental challenges, and working with a diverse group of people. All these preferences require trust as a foundation.

Regardless of the generation, when most of your team members embrace the concept of trust, it has the *power* to deepen existing relationships, heal estranged ones, and create new connections. Not only does trust contribute to higher-quality relationships between individuals, it can be used to dismantle *silos*—close-knit groups of people that have the potential to create complex challenges within organizations.

Flow

For our purposes, flow refers to the movement of information, work, and decisions, as facilitated by the performance of people and systems. Different types of flow can coexist, moving simultaneously or sequentially along various paths. Sometimes flow is steady and sometimes not, so there may or may not be a discernible rhythm.

For example, a production department may only be able to produce intermittently because the workers do not have the resources they need for continuous production. The flows they facilitate may be arbitrary, with no real rhythm, or they may follow patterns that lead to or support balance.

When it comes to individual experiences, flow can refer to a state achieved when a person slips into a kind of organic sense of creative harmony, unaffected by external white noise. But within organizations, the IFB Model refers to flow as it relates to the movement of work, information, and so forth through an interconnective structure—much the way water flows through a network of pipes where flow can be obstructed in some channels and free in others.

Flow can be brought about by *force* or orchestrated fluidly by an engaged team that activates it naturally. The drivers of these flows can either benefit or disadvantage an organization, with the prevailing outcomes depending on the intentions and competencies behind the drivers.

For instance, some leaders coerce coworkers to comply with their wishes using fear and intimidation to further their career agendas. Although strong short- to medium-term results are sometimes possible under these circumstances, imbalances can occur when top performers eventually burn out and opt to leave.

Within any organization, multiple drivers operate simultaneously, sustaining or impairing flow. For instance, some organizations operate with trust as a driver within some departments and fear as a driver in others. When this happens, one may become dominant or they may cancel each other out. To reconcile either of these situations the priority driver(s) need to be identified. If the priority driver is to be trust, it should be instilled within the team.

Being aware of flow drivers is critical to understanding overall flow within your organization. The same importance applies to the ability of leaders to recognize patterns of flow, whether steady, unsteady, or blocked. Each distinct pattern, with its own rhythm and pace, can be either appropriate or unsuitable, depending on whether it fulfills the strategic priorities and core values of your organization.

Balance

Balance occurs when leaders and team members harness interconnectivity to enable optimal flow, contributing to the maintenance of a healthy equilibrium. However, "healthy equilibrium" doesn't mean all dimensions of the organization are in balance. In fact, the goal is not to get rid of all imbalances; some may be necessary or inconsequential.

Managing balance involves identifying the current state and acting deliberately to bring about a new state or maintain an existing one. Decision-makers who are adept at balancing aspects of their businesses are not only attuned and responsive to extreme changes within their organizations but also able to discern nuances that can pose risks. Therefore, decision-makers should focus on the dimensions that can reduce risks and improve performance while sustaining a state of balance.

When balancing, decision-makers should identify priority tensions. As is true of interconnectivity and flow, balancing main concerns should be based on the vision, values, strategic goals, existing strengths, weaknesses, and other organizational factors. One organization may emphasize integrity, engagement, and inclusion to achieve balance. Another may have recently strengthened trust, so leaders focus on revenue generation and innovation to improve profitability and remain viable.

Balance doesn't have to involve sacrificing operating from the outermost edges of a spectrum to lead from the middle. In fact, balance can exist in an organization that has chosen to operate from the furthest ends of a spectrum. An example of this is when leaders decide to significantly reduce output of a product line to balance supply with decreasing market demand.

Balance manifests differently within every organization. Leaders of organizations may consider their institutions to be in balance when they are generating profits. When profitability is generated in a trust-based environment, it can be created by orchestrating balance between effective leadership, relevant training, and a team that feels valued.

Alternatively, decision-makers can create the appearance of balance when there is team dysfunction, fear, a constrictive policy structure, and coercive leadership. Decision-makers who lead using these strategies may think their organization or department is in balance because they are meeting or exceeding their goals. Unfortunately, significant tensions are more than likely lurking in the shadows.

Regardless of the strategic vision for your organization, achieving balance using the IFB Model applies to your capacity to facilitate equilibrium using your unique mix of desired and undesired cultural traits. Achieving balance doesn't necessarily mean your organization will be able to transform undesired cultural characteristics. What it means is that leaders can achieve balance by managing them, which sometimes entails neutralizing unproductive cultural traits with balanced decisions.

If decision-makers take the time to establish interconnectivity, flow, and balance but do not achieve equilibrium, the first thing to do is revisit the Pillar of Trust to see if the steps they took to strengthen the *interconnective infrastructure* are working. If not, the relationships contributing to unwanted outcomes need to be better understood so leaders can take alternative steps to strengthen the infrastructure. When higher levels of trust are required, leaders should recalibrate; this could mean getting better at modeling trustworthy behaviors.

Connecting Change–Based Operations and the IFB Model

Leaders in change-based organizations use the IFB Model to support planned and unexpected changes in their ecosystems, taking appropriate action as needed. For example, inertia is one characteristic that can appear in ecosystems. Inertia refers to the lag time between an event and an organization's response to it. Inertia can be anticipated and planned for, but it may be difficult to predict its extent.

There can be beneficial or damaging events both within and outside an organizational ecosystem and sometimes the response time is slow, other times there's virtually no delay. Different organizational ecosystems respond differently to the same types of events and one reason for this variation is culture.

Sometimes the events causing change are linear and predictable, so leaders can attempt to use this information to prepare. But there is so much uncertainty in our environments that it is increasingly difficult to foretell events. As a result, nonlinear change is the norm and change skills and systems need an upgrade.

This is why the IFB Model is more important than ever. When used effectively, IFB skills can be established at individual and team levels. As a result, leaders and employees can individually improve their relationships and networks, enhance flows, and create balance within their lives. Collectively, the same skills can strengthen team performance once founded on the Pillar of Trust.

Therefore, establishing IFB at the personal level helps facilitate team IFB, which then enables organizational IFB. Individual IFB refers to a person's ability to create and sustain a network of trust-based relationships that benefit the team by enabling connection, flow, and balance. Developing the skills needed to build and sustain quality relationships between individuals contributes to the capability of teams to connect with each other, collaborate, and deliver results.

Regardless the size of a team or network of teams, at the individual level, employees need to be aware of dynamics between themselves and the people in their immediate environments. It also helps if they acknowledge the dynamics that exist between others within their relational networks, as this also affects workflows and output.

Healthy relationships within and between teams enable higher performance. They are also integral to maintaining change-based organizations. When IFB is functioning effectively and change is being treated as a constant, the silo effect begins to be resolved. Everything about silos contradicts the principles that support IFB organizations, so if silos already exist within your organization, you can use the same skills required for strengthening the Pillar of Trust to improve team unity.

Constructive individual connections are a prerequisite for team interconnectivity and networking. Strong connections help organizational ecosystems facilitate flows into and from external environments in a variety of ways. When individual and team interconnectivity and flow are not operating as planned, the underlying reasons need closer attention. While some organizations immediately invest in resources to correct unanticipated flow states, others underestimate the effects of unsteady or blocked flow and statements like, "They just need to learn to get along," or "If it ain't broke, don't fix it," are indicative of undervalued risk.

Here is an example of how unhealthy relationships can lead to unsteady or blocked flow: Apex Inc. is experiencing an extraordinary year. Financially, its performance is exceeding expectations and because of the company's sustained results over five consecutive years, the organization is in the process of vertically integrating, purchasing one of its suppliers, with the intention of maintaining two separate executive teams.

Despite positive revenue streams, there are silos at Apex Inc. They were caused by the executive team members' inability to communicate effectively with each other. Instead of collaborating, they are in competitive mode, vying for the role of CEO. As a result, they conceal important information from each other, spread rumors, and do whatever it takes to position themselves as the most valuable players. This organization can use the IFB Model to help decision-makers address nonbeneficial cultural practices. Leaders will need to strengthen the Pillar of Trust, so they can build healthy relationships and deconstruct silos.

IFB can exist within a department at the micro level, within an entire organization, and between an organization and various communities it serves. As you shift upwards from the departmental level, more and more stakeholders are part of the ecosystem, but the size of a team or number of stakeholders is not necessarily an indicator of complexity.

IFB and Culture

When I started writing this book, I thought of framing IFB as a type of culture. I even went as far as considering coining the term "IFB Culture." But while exploring the possible applications of the model, I realized the IFB Model transcends culture. It has cultural applications but is not limited to describing it.

So what is "culture"? Various authors describe it in different ways. One definition of organizational culture is a system of shared values, assumptions, beliefs, and practices that provides a framework for how coworkers interact with each other and perform. Characteristics of culture include policies, procedures, rituals, social norms, technology, strategy, language, leadership styles, artifacts, and symbols.

Leaders in IFB organizations should pay close attention to culture because they cannot consider IFB without contemplating culture. Culture is important because it is an increasingly relevant component of success; more and more organizations recognize it as an opportunity to create a competitive advantage, especially if the qualities of culture are difficult to replicate.

The importance of culture was highlighted in 2016 when 82 percent of the respondents who participated in the Global Human Capital Trends Survey indicated culture was important. The results also suggested that few factors contribute more to the success of a business than culture. This finding makes it necessary for decision-makers to recognize how critical it is for everyone, including leaders, to take ownership of, and become more deliberate about the evolution of their respective organizational cultures.

The term *"climate"* is sometimes used interchangeably with "culture." Clearly, the two concepts are connected, but some authors distinguish between them describing *culture* as how the organization works and climate as how the organization feels. When implemented as designed, the IFB Model should have a positive effect on both culture and climate, assuming the efficacy of the IFB plan and the organization's capacity to execute it.

You can use a variety of tools to diagnose the quality of relationships in your organization and help your culture evolve. One well-known framework diagnosing workplace relationships is Maslow's Hierarchy of Needs. According to the theory, if people in your organization are preoccupied with job security, you will probably hear comments like "I'm looking out for number one!" If they are self-actualized, leaders may be more inclined to work toward strengthening individual and collective Pillars of Trust.

To build deep trust, lower level needs must first be satisfied, otherwise they will hijack attempts to strengthen trust and engagement. To get to deep trust, teams need to progress through each level of the *hierarchy*, starting by satisfying safety and security needs before they can move to higher, more actualized levels, where belonging, esteem, and self-actualization can happen. As teams evolve through this process, improved engagement, effective leadership, empowered teams, and collaboration are all possible. It takes patience, vision, courage, and of course IFB to get there.

CHAPTER 2

INVESTING IN YOUR INTERCONNECTIVE INFRASTRUCTURE

We cannot live only for ourselves. A thousand fibers connect
us with our fellow men; and among those fibers, as sympathetic
threads, our actions run as causes, and they come back
to us as effects.

— Herman Melville, author and poet

W hen we think about connectivity in organizations, we tend to call to mind work relationships, or how the sequence of a production line operates. In the former example, interconnectivity is interpersonal, demonstrated in the quality of relationships; in the latter, it exists within or between processes. The quality of multiple types of interconnectivity is based on the strength of the Pillar of Trust. We often think of trust in terms of how it impacts interpersonal relationships, but it also affects the quality of processes, enhancing them or causing deceleration.

Leaders in change-based organizations powered by IFB rely heavily on people and connections. Without interconnection, there is no framework to support flow and balance. Connectivity is critical — clearly — but it also makes sense to ensure that connections are of a high caliber because of the benefits of healthy connectivity. You can detect the quality of relationships by observing team members and how they interact. The output of your processes may be another useful indicator of how strong or weak your connections are.

Interconnectivity is not limited to an organization's infrastructure. It extends to the way people think, permeating *mindsets*. It refers to the team's ability to connect the dots—to perceive connections or the lack of them. An interconnective mindset is useful because it ensures we do not fall into the trap of creating silos as we redesign our organizational infrastructures.

Multiple layers of interconnectivity exist within any organization. Interpersonal relationships, communication channels, *organizational structure*, strategy, and policies all make up the interconnective infrastructure. No layer can exist or operate separately because each part of the overall structure connects with and supports the others, either directly or indirectly. Figure 2.1 provides an illustrated view of the layers of interconnectivity within organizations.

This chapter introduces the Model of Interconnective Infrastructure, exploring the multiple overlays of connection that exist within the workplace: both what they are and how they work together. The chapter covers topics specific to interpersonal relationships and networks, establishing the building blocks for Chapter 3, which is about building your *relationship architecture*. Chapter 4 expands the definition of relationships beyond interpersonal interactions, highlighting nonpersonal relationships that affect performance.

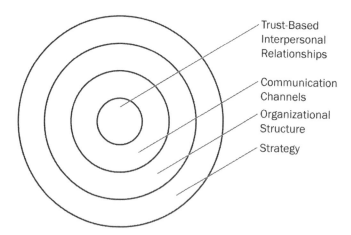

Trust-Based
Interpersonal
Relationships

Communication
Channels

Organizational
Structure

Strategy

Figure 2.1   *The Model of Interconnective Infrastructure*

Why Interconnectivity Is Important

Connection is the foundation of the IFB Model. When you can establish healthy interpersonal and nonpersonal relationships within your organization, you have a base that allows you to build a competitive advantage. Getting there is a journey, because healthy interconnective infrastructures are not easy to pull off.

If you are aware of how interconnectivity works within your organization, you can use this information to understand how it is beneficially or harmfully affecting the performance of your organization and its capacity to change. An example of an unproductive influence is when an executive—let's call her Sarah— has an informal network of frontline employees who have direct access to her. This type of connectivity can have negative effects when undetected negative biases coming from employees inform Sarah's future decisions in an unbalanced way.

By tapping into her informal network, Sarah thinks she's keeping her ears to the ground. While this is probably true, she discounts the fact that the managers being circumvented also have valuable perspectives, which may invalidate or clarify information coming from her frontline network.

When leaders take the time to understand how interconnectivity works within their respective domains, another benefit results: they can begin to discover hidden relationships that, if strengthened or harnessed, can contribute to improved team performance.

The Model of Interconnective Infrastructure

The Model of Interconnective Infrastructure places relationships at the center of the framework (refer to Figure 2.1) because individual development and the quality of interpersonal relationships affect every type of connectivity. Progressing from the inside-out, relationship quality is one indicator of the effectiveness of communication channels. Communication skills are another primary indicator. Together, quality relationships combined with healthy communication habits can positively affect engagement, performance, and growth potential.

Organizational structure refers to nonpersonal elements of the interconnective structure. These tools provide the framework for connections. For example, organizational charts illustrate the reporting structures that affect work flows, communication, and overall productivity. Structures are not limited to organizational charts, they include policies and procedures, delegated authorities, and other tools we will explore in Chapter 4. Collectively, their configuration affects cultural norms and, by extension, the quality of connectivity.

Strategy is transformative and should be all encompassing. Even though it is on the perimeter of the model, it has the potential to change components of the interconnective structure from the outside-in. Strategy can lead to new workflows and can drive restructuring that helps organizations to better serve their goals. Changing or implementing a strategy may mean forging new communication channels or improving existing ones. And ultimately it can lead to new hires and relationships because it highlights the need for collaboration and a stronger Pillar of Trust. So, the Model of Interconnective Infrastructure works from both from the inside-out and the outside-in.

The overlays of interconnectivity depicted in Figure 2.1 facilitate flow both within each layer of the model and between layers. As a result, the layers are not discrete; they are all interconnected and permeable. This model can help decision-makers form an initial diagnosis about the quality of interconnectivity. Then you can dig a little deeper, asking questions like why is this working the way it does, what is not apparent on the surface, and what are the opportunities and risks in the current state? Observing your interconnective infrastructure from the inside-out and the outside-in can also provide worthwhile perspectives.

When using this model, leaders should determine what causes connection and disconnection, taking care to avoid singling out a layer. Instead, they should consider all layers of the interconnective infrastructure conjunctively because the cause(s) of connectivity or disconnection may become apparent when you least expect them. The objects within Figure 2.1 are further developed below to help you apply the principles to IFB diagnosis and planning.

Interpersonal Relationships

Interpersonal relationships, the nucleus of your interconnective infrastructure, directly affect the quality of your communicative infrastructure. Communication practices form part of your overall infrastructure and are a reflection of the quality of relationships within your organization. Without both trust-based relationships and effective communication practices, the other interconnective layers will not perform optimally.

Trust-based relationships are founded on honesty, consideration, and open communication channels. Communication channels can close when someone has something to hide or when leaders only want to hear information that aligns with how they think. They open optimally when trust, transparency and respect are part of everyday interactions.

The Pillar of Trust is the glue within the interconnective infrastructure and as already noted, it is made up of three distinct elements: integrity, self-mastery, and a "we" disposition. Together, self-mastery and the "we" disposition rest on a foundation of integrity, so trust can be both possible and sustainable.

There are multiple combinations of strong and weak components of the Pillar of Trust that make up this metaphorical glue, some stronger than others. Together, they can be tested by external elements. Leaders should pay close attention to the Pillar of Trust since it defines the quality of relationships, an important driver of organizational success.

The foundation of trust is integrity; integrity refers to a person's ability to be honest and to demonstrate alignment between their words and their actions, especially when they are under external pressure to deviate from a strongly held personal position. Integrity is an important element of credibility.

The layer above integrity is self-mastery. When building an engaged team is a priority, knee-jerk reactions can compromise efforts to establish team safety and trust. Self-mastery helps team members interact respectfully at all times, especially in supercharged, emotional situations.

Integrity and self-mastery are building blocks for the "we" disposition. Demonstrating a "we" disposition important because coworkers want to feel you care about them, and a leader's ability to actively demonstrate that he genuinely cares about coworkers helps to anchor team trust.

When the Pillar of Trust is securely established within an organization, it sets the stage for employees to be predisposed to maintaining connective relationships. This is especially useful when challenging situations arise. Alternatively, when trust is compromised it becomes a potential cause of failure of collaborate. At times like this, employees should be attuned to how important maintaining or restoring balance is, and they should be empowered to resolve team challenges.

We have already established that when trust is absent from work relationships, this deficiency can compromise other layers of connectivity. So, if trust is diminished while IFB is being implemented as a goal achievement tool, leaders should invest time in reconstructing it before moving forward.

Whether trust is present or conspicuously absent, relationships in the workplace exist to facilitate performance. *High-performing relationships* require collaboration to deliver results. *Low-performing relationships* can show up in different forms, exhibiting circumventive (although this means there is no relationship), antagonistic, or self-interested characteristics.

The Shifting Nature of Interpersonal Relationships

Unexpected and predictable change happens within change-based organizations. One example of unexpected change that can happen is when interpersonal relationships shift in reaction to conflict. This can have a ripple effect on a single department or worse, an entire organization. An example of expected change is a planned change in leadership after a manager retires. Even though the change is planned, when a person assumes a new position, connections may shift, unexpectedly reconfiguring some of the relationship dynamics.

Whether a leader is appointed because of a succession planning process, or a talent acquisition exercise, changes can occur. Internally appointed leaders tend to rely heavily on their existing network of relationships, the ones they cultivated over time that form a comfort zone. Even team members may be familiar with a newly appointed leader, this is no guarantee that the culture of the team will remain intact. Leaders coming from outside the organization or team are inheriting a network and culture built by the previous incumbent. These leaders can bring something new to the culture and change it, fit in seamlessly with it, or become changed by it.

Shifting allegiances can also happen in the context of power and politics. Power dynamics result from the use of various types of power by people within an organizational or other context. When leaders and coworkers compete for power, they tend to demonstrate political behaviors that seek to influence outcomes through the behaviors of others.

If political dynamics are embedded within an organization, political leaders and other employees constantly seek to reinforce their personal power agendas. Thus, relationships are built on loyalty and obligation, not trust or deep connection.

Operational changes within an organization can create shifts within relationship networks for a variety of reasons. Workflows may change and separate people from those they used to work with, shifting them into new relationships. Another type of operational change that alters in how people interact occurs when leaders modify work routines that are highly transactional into strategic ones. When this happens, mindsets and conversations change from finding ways to accomplish the work to recommending strategic solutions and taking ownership.

Some relationship changes may be beneficial to organizations, creating potential for collaboration and high performance. Others may be detrimental, decreasing trust and compromising productivity. Whatever the case, relationships will inevitably shift and as a result, leaders should have the capacity to detect the potential effects of changes on relationships and prepare for them because unfacilitated relationship changes can lead to unproductive dynamics.

Characteristics of Interpersonal Relationships

When analyzing interpersonal *relationship architecture* (teams and networks) in the context of the IFB Model, leaders should clearly define relationships, so they can develop and implement accurate strategies to address relational deficiencies.

Interpersonal interconnectivity that emerges organically does not always serve the greater good. Instead it can show up depending on a variety of individual agendas. Healthy interconnectivity is determined by the organization's ability to balance productive inputs (from its vision, mission, purpose, and goals) with counterproductive ones (such as personal agendas, *office politics*, and dishonesty). The following list is not an exhaustive one, but it gives you an idea of the various ways you can characterize interpersonal interconnectivity:

Stable	Stable interpersonal connections are steady and durable. When interconnectivity stable, connections are based on trust, respect, credibility, and integrity. Stable interconnectivity is useful regardless of the quality of or intent behind flow. However, stable interpersonal connections do not guarantee any particular type of flow because of other variables. A stable connection may be due to a personal friendship, a healthy work relationship, or loyalties that support, divert, or suppress flow. Therefore, when diagnosing and designing flow, decision-makers should not assume a stable connection automatically indicates healthy flow.
	Stable interconnectivity does not refer only to interpersonal relationships. Any type of stable link, such as

the link between policies and procedures can potentially facilitate or impede flow.

Compromised Compromised connectivity refers to a weakened state of relationship; deterioration can be attributable to personality clashes, emotion, unfair policy decisions, obstacles, leadership challenges, power, control, and other frustrations. When interconnectivity is compromised, linkages might still exist, but they can be weak, ungrounded associations at best. Fear or another emotion can force a connection to remain intact, but the link can also be abandoned when compromised, disabling flow or causing it to be rerouted.

In environments characterized by fear, dishonesty, hostility, control, or competition, productivity is still possible. In fact, some of these workplaces can achieve results classified as high performing, even though deep interpersonal rifts exist. As a result, true balance is not present because these characteristics can lead to social stratification, which creates a class system separating the chosen or assertive few from the marginalized masses. Divisiveness is the antithesis of team building and IFB. It destabilizes the team and threatens agility and the sustainability of results.

Interconnectivity is possible under suboptimal conditions, but the glue between already weak relationships can be further compromised when put under pressure.

Compromised relationships can result from employees who feel marginalized or threatened, they may bond with others who feel the same way, creating a subculture. Others may enter into self-preservation mode to ensure their own survival, sacrificing their relationships. Healthy, actualized, and collaborative relationships are not usually evident in these environments.

As precautionary note, sometimes strong alliances form for the wrong reasons, hindering team performance. Therefore, while a single relationship may be stable, it can undermine an entire team if its purpose is to obstruct.

Situational   One type of situational interconnectivity happens during temporary assignments. It can be project-based where people may or may not know each other before a project begins and have a finite period to optimize relationships and produce results. You can optimize relationship quality on a temporary assignment if team members are capable building the Pillar of Trust.

Another type of situational relationship involves personal agendas being pursued as a higher priority than team goals; this causes shifting alliances. For example, a coworker could attempt to force loyalty if they possess damaging evidence that can destroy another coworker's career or network; that coworker may agree to comply with the proposed alliance, but possibility for trust is irrevocably damaged.

When power shifts alliances can also shift, this happens when situational relationships are based on political ambitions. Power shifts have the potential to change cultures and disrupt performance. When unproductive power shifts occur frequently, the resulting shifts in alliances can lead to unsustainable team results and maintaining a healthy Pillar of Trust can be difficult.

Situational relationships can also operate as long-term connections. Circumvention is one example of this phenomenon. Circumvention occurs when a relationship that should exist does not, so team members find themselves maneuvering around a colleague. Perhaps the formal connection defined by the *organizational chart* is weak and a new one is created to work around the ailing relationship. Sometimes leaders attempt circumvention when they lack confidence in a coworker's competence or allegiances.

Too New   Sometimes a relationship is too new to determine its potential. This can happen when a person is new to a role — say a well-known team member is promoted and their behavior at the new level is not yet established. Whether a recently appointed person is new to a team or not, how they relate to their coworkers should align with The Pillar of Trust.

Formal/   Formal relationships exist based on the prescribed
Informal   organizational structure and standardized engagement procedures. Informal relationships exist outside the framework of the formal structure. They operate as an informal web that is active behind the scenes. Whether they are detected or not, informal relationships can help or hinder an organization.

For instance, in a family-owned business, relationships are formally defined by an organizational chart, but informal familial relationships still exist. Informal relationships can also materialize when people who worked in the same department in the past maintain close relationships, even though they now work in different departments or locations.

Internal/   Internal relationships include relationships between
External   employees, management, business owners, executives, and the board. These relationships are internal to the organization and can add value to, detract from, or have no discernible impact on it.

External relationships include (but are not limited to) clients, regulators, unions, the local community, and vendors. They can enhance or undermine an organization; they are not controllable, though they may be subject to influence.

Inclusive/
Exclusive

Inclusive relationships are open, nondiscriminating, and respectful. These relationships are based on trust and encourage people to interact with each other. When a team operates as an inclusive unit, most people — if not everyone — feel like they are a part of the team.

Exclusive relationships form for various reasons. For example, some exist to monopolize power. These types of relationships can be based on a number of expectation, one of which is quid pro quo: giving something valuable to one person with the expectation of reciprocation.

Exclusive relationships are closed and can organize in a variety of ways. Whereas some self-organize in such a way that no one outside the relationship is aware of the existence of the relationship, others are openly exclusive.

Loyal/
Disloyal

Loyalty results from being devoted to someone because they are reliable, or charismatic. Loyalty can also exist when a person is afraid of the consequences of being disloyal. It can be value-based or blind; it can be founded on a sense of obligation or even guilt. Where blind loyalty is present, a person may be willing to override their internal *value system* to execute a directive. Blind loyalty can lead to polarities within an organization causing employees to feel compelled to take a side.

Being labeled as "disloyal" can mean different things. Perhaps a person is not trusted to be loyal to another person or a cause because they are perceived as lacking integrity. Conversely, the label of disloyalty may also be assigned to those who won't sacrifice their personal integrity to show loyalty to a person or a cause that conflicts with their values.

Entire networks within organizations can be formed based on loyalties, strengthened by informal reward systems related to power. These networks can be used to undermine others, supporting personal agendas.

Nonexistent A nonexistent relationship may sound counterintuitive, but it is worth considering because it can result from a damaged relationship. The lack of a relationship sometimes occurs when an organizational chart indicates there should be a relationship, but in actuality, the designated people are in conflict and the relationship is impaired. This does not necessarily mean there is no flow — like the flow of water, organizational flows can find alternate, sometimes less effective channels to enable movement.

Reconstructing relationships that have deteriorated due to a toxic history is difficult, since deep rebuilding efforts call for the establishment of authentic connections based on integrity and trust.

Sometimes a relationship does not exist simply because no one perceived the need to create one. Alternatively, a person may perceive the opportunity for interconnectivity but be uninterested in making a meaningful connection.

Even if a relationship is nonexistent, someone who values courteous interaction can decide to communicate respectfully, on an as-needed basis, but this approach limits contact. This is a superficial work relationship that only exists for expedience. This is not true connection, though it does expedite the work.

Essential / Some relationships have a more profound effect on
Nonessential a business because of perceived potential and risks. Essential relationships are defined by strategic and other priorities and can evolve or collapse over time. When considering both essential and nonessential relationships in the context of IFB, decisions will be made to sacrifice some relationships and pursue others.

Examples of Low-Performing Relationships

A low-performing relationship can be a damaged one, characterized by impaired trust. If potential exists for strengthening, it can improve results if other environmental factors allow it. There are multiple low-performing relationship dynamics, three of them are explored in this section. They are:

- circumvention
- the ivory tower
- power and relationships

Circumventive Relationships

Circumventive connections are those that maneuver around weak relationships. Sometimes circumvention develops to work around a person who is an acknowledged expert but has a manner that is blunt, impatient, and generally difficult. These behaviors can potentially affect engagement and compromise the performance of a team.

Ideally, leaders should determine how best to work with circumvented experts, especially if only having one such authority means there is no backup, exposing an organization to increased risk. Correcting this type of situation involves intervening with the expert and those who are circumventing them, and facilitating trust building while clearly establishing interactive accountabilities for persons involved.

Circumvention can happen when persons are perceived as difficult. Researcher Peter Tyrer of the Imperial College in London found that "the overall prevalence of personality disorders is in the order of 10% in the community, but if you also include personality difficulty (a sub-threshold condition below the status of a disorder), this rises to nearly 30%, as a very large proportion of people have some problems with personality function when placed in certain settings."[1] Thus, the potential for encountering personality disorders within the workplace exists, and such people are likely to be found in the midst of circumventive, compromised, or even toxic circumstances.

When circumvention happens because a coworker lacks required technical competencies, the team can still perform, but the impaired performance of one coworker means other team members are doing more than their fair share of the work. If unfair work distribution continues over an extended period, it can lead to burnout and declining engagement levels — especially when the underperforming employee is highly regarded and compensated.

Case Study: Circumvention at Its Worst

Mike is a technical expert who works for a government agency. None of his coworkers adequately comprehend the scope and complexity of his work; therefore, they can only superficially assess the effect he has on the department and the communities they serve. This is compounded by the fact that Mike and his supervisor, Ryan, have an antagonistic relationship. Despite this, Mike genuinely wants to contribute positively to the goals of his department.

In meetings, Mike and Ryan get into heated arguments. Ryan finds Mike's confrontational communication style to be hostile. Mike has difficulty respecting Ryan because he feels Ryan is arrogant, often making misinformed statements that Mike refuses to tolerate.

Because of the impaired relationship, Ryan circumvents Mike. One way he does this is by declining Mike's requests to attend relevant international conferences where his expertise and skills are critical to making meaningful contributions to the business both internationally and locally. Instead, Ryan circumvents Mike and send John, a junior employee who lacks the relevant technical expertise, to attend these conferences. John is selected because he caters to the agenda of senior management and the trip is a reward for his compliance.

From the vantage point of senior management, sending a stand-in ensures representation at the international meeting, which they think is important for stakeholder optics. However, it creates a superficial system that is intended to give the appearance of connection but all it does is to create deep disconnection. The inexperienced alternate cannot adequately represent his team, and therefore is unable to forge meaningful relationships with international participants who can potentially support local programs.

Additionally, John (the substitute attendee) is unable to articulate the needs of his agency at international conferences, so knowledge and performance gaps remain unaddressed. What makes matters worse is John usually produces reports outlining details of the meetings, but he does not understand the highly technical conversations, so the value of the reports is questionable at best.

The situation is further compounded: Mike, in being circumvented by his supervisor, cannot perform his duties optimally because he was not exposed to new methodologies introduced at these conferences. John is unable to clarify the technical discussions for Mike or answer his questions. Although Mike knows John is only following directives, the dynamics of the situation also contribute to a strained relationship between John and Mike.

Using the list of Characteristics of Interpersonal Relationships to analyze this case, Ryan has a formal relationship with Mike as defined by the organizational chart. By using his position power, Ryan created a hybrid, informal position for John which has both formal and informal qualities. Ryan's decision to circumvent Mike compromised the entire team because by excluding the expert, the department cannot truly succeed. Even though this is the case, Ryan continues to reward John because the rewards (travel opportunities) are not only for past loyalty, they are to ensure John's future allegiance.

A View from the Ivory Tower

Another relationship dynamic—the *ivory tower*—is also worthy of exploring. When an ivory tower exists within an organization, executives or managers create a dynamic that disconnects them from the rest of the team. Separation can be physical, emotional, or a combination of both. Ivory towers often find opportunities for expression in hierarchical structures with multiple layers. Leaders can consciously or unconsciously establish ivory towers — sometimes with another goal in mind.

Executives in ivory towers are unable or unwilling to connect directly with their team members. However, their separation is not total. These decision-makers rely on one or more informants to provide information they need for decision-making. Sometimes intelligence obtained from informants is accurate, but there can be risks when it cannot be tested for accuracy or when the information is incomplete.

Despite their isolation, executives who are in an ivory tower make decisions that directly affect frontline employees. This means these employees have to execute decisions that are based on insufficient or incorrect information. Additionally, depending on the reason for isolation and the agendas of the informants, emotion can also distort their decisions.

To implement the IFB Model, leaders should first appreciate how remaining in their ivory towers can negatively affect their results. Armed with this information, they can equip themselves with skills they need to establish healthy connections. Unfortunately, simply deciding to improve relationships does not guarantee these leaders will think or behave differently, especially if they perceive themselves as losing power during the process. Transformative action should be prudently orchestrated because ivory towers tend to be hardwired to political dynamics.

Relationships and Power

In work environments where power and status are highly valued, political undercurrents and overtones saturate interactions. Various types of power emerge in political environments and as a result, several types of relationships coexist:

- relationships that circumvent
- relationships that strengthen or weaken different types of power

- relationships that get work done
- relationships or networks based on ambitions and status seeking
- relationships that exist among those marginalized by power players

Power games don't fade because leaders decide to change the culture. Without authentic commitment to intrinsic change, a vision of the desired state, and a cultural change plan, unproductive political activity will continually reinvent itself.

Dismantling Power Structures

Given the potential volatility of power dynamics, leaders should sustain balance while dismantling *power structures*. In an IFB world, trust building is the first step. Another strategy change leaders can use to achieve balance when dismantling power and creating an *empowered* team is to implement a new code of conduct. The intended changes will more likely be successful when leaders meaningfully develop themselves as well as their team members and adhere to the standards.

The following are examples of conduct guidelines you can consider using to dismantle power structures. Keep in mind that your circumstances are unique, so you may need to modify these guidelines for your organization.

- No relationship is untouchable. Leaders should seek to understand as many interpersonal connections as possible and the associated distribution of power.
- Leaders should exhibit *empathy* and forgiveness especially in the face of damaged relationships.
- Ensure the system of reward is merit based.
- Disassembling power structures should not degenerate into a witch hunt. To avert this, the Pillar of Trust should guide change activities.

Dismantling unproductive power structures is no easy proposition. Despite your best intentions, this activity can create fluctuations in team climate because some leaders at the top of the power hierarchy will attempt to protect their power at all costs.

Dismantling power and political team dynamics requires leaders who are not only resilient, they need to be willing and able to perceive their own contributions to the unproductive patterns. These leaders then need to build or strengthen the behaviors they need to be perceived as trustworthy. They can achieve and sustain this is by shifting *mental models* that no longer serve them and by attaining emotional self-mastery.

Despite a leader's commitment to a vision of empowerment, it is not easy to dismantle an entire system of political behaviors. Implementing new systems of interaction involves many people and requires them all to commit to exhibiting the new behaviors consistently, over time.

How to Move from Low-Performing to High-Performing Relationships

Restructuring low-performing relationships into high-performing ones involves identifying and disabling traditional power dynamics. These dynamics get in the way of strengthening interpersonal relationships highlighted in the Model of Interconnective Infrastructure. Understandably, immobilizing detrimental systems of power and control is not an easy process, as attitudes of entitlement and emotions (such as fear) can activate valiant resistance, both passive and otherwise.

Instead of wielding power over others as a form of enticement or threat, leaders should empower as many of their team members as possible. When employees are empowered and their displays of integrity are supported, they can tap into their networks, exhibit creativity, and make inclusive decisions. As a result, accountability can become second nature because people are more likely to be intrinsically motivated to take ownership.

Whether there are destabilizing power dynamics or other causes of workplace relationship challenges, high-performing relationships can overcome disruptive actions caused by challenging personalities. This is possible when people within those relationships are respectful in their conduct and understand the consequences of their actions.

High-Performing (Interpersonal) Relationships

The foundation of a high-performing IFB relationship is built on the qualities that make up the Pillar of Trust. Integrity is a foundational component of the Pillar because it lends itself to building deeply connective relationships. High-performing relationships are also characterized by competence, effective communication, and leadership skills. When relationships are low performing, it can affect the accomplishments of an entire team, especially when workflows depend on damaged or nonexistent relationships.

High-performing relationships do not require team members to accept each other's values as a prerequisite for providing meaningful support. Persons in high-performing relationships operate from a foundation of shared goals; they communicate respectfully, are willing to discuss difficult or controversial subjects, focusing on solutions. While no relationship is perfect, these individuals know that work associations require deliberate cultivation, just like any other kind of relationship, so they are willing to invest quality time and commit to making adjustments that support collaboration.

CHAPTER 3

RELATIONSHIP ARCHITECTURE

*It you believe business is built on relationships, make building
them your business.*

—Scott Stratten, author and speaker

rchitects design physical structures. Similarly, leaders can
be "relationship architects." They can embrace workforce
design by learning about how relationships configure themselves into networks and then considering how to harness the beneficial qualities of networked relationships while minimizing the effects
of unproductive ones. This involves recognizing:

- which relationships exist
- why they exist
- which relationships are formal, which ones are not, and
  which ones are both formal and informal
- the power structures
- whether connections are strong or weak, appropriate or
  inappropriate
- where opportunities for growth exist

Relationship architecture refers to the configuration of relationship
networks that exist within an organization. A single relationship
network may consist of two or three people, or groups of people —
or many more. These networks expand and contract depending on
internal and external circumstances, and they may support team

goals or disrupt them — or they can exist for personal reasons that are not immediately discernible.

Usually, your relationship architecture is formally configured in an organizational chart. However, while organizational charts capture formal workplace relationships, they do not portray the informal, social relationships that coexist, nor do they identify the nature of those social relationships. As a leader, collecting and analyzing data that adds dimension to your understanding of your relationship architecture can enrich your decision-making, organizational design, planning, and IFB implementation processes. It can also introduce biases, so you need to be self-aware.

Flexible relationship architecture in work networks allows people to come and go. It can shift to accommodate change because it is a form of open architecture that enables interconnectivity, flow, and balance both within an organization and externally. This permits new or improved opportunities for collaboration between individuals.

Flexible relationship architecture also allows coworkers to manage their own relationships. For instance, a member of a team of predominantly entry-level employees is promoted to the role of supervisor and has to lead the team she was previously a part of. The new supervisor understands that her relationships with individual members of the team need to change, so she takes deliberate actions that sustain trust while making the transition. To achieve this, she needs the relationships to be flexible enough to accommodate changes in how she relates, so she can facilitate the achievement of team goals.

Conversely, unshakeable allegiances and profound resistance to change are symptoms of an inflexible, closed architecture designed to maintain the status quo. Sometimes at any cost. This is an obstacle to implementing IFB and leaders will need to examine the situation so they can make decisions that will maintain, create, or restore balance.

Chapter 2 introduced the Model of Relationship Infrastructure and explored various Characteristics of Relationships. This chapter expands the discussion to relationship networks and provides tools you can use to assess the relationship architecture (networks) within your organization so you can make better informed decisions or co-design a new relationship network if necessary.

In this chapter, we will explore an expanded definition of relationship architecture and provide examples of how yours can be mapped to illustrate both internal and external relationship networks. This chapter also introduces a tool that will help you prioritize relationships to determine which are most important to the execution of your plans and the well-being of your organization. Chapter 4 completes the explanation of the Model of Relationship Infrastructure introduced in Chapter 2. It explores communication and different types of nonpersonal relationships.

Why Understanding Relationship Architecture Is Important

Relationships are a critical part of the IFB Model and essential to successful implementation of change initiatives. Mapping the current configuration of relationships provides insights so the barriers to, and facilitators of, change and performance can be appropriately addressed. The long-term goal of mapping relationships is for leaders to develop more accurate perceptions of relationships, which will allow them to optimize their networks in different ways.

Decision-makers should take the time to understand relationship architecture, identifying the growth potential and limitations embedded within internal and external networks. For instance, two top performers with complementary skills are not collaborating because neither one perceives the benefits of such a connection. If leaders can identify the hidden potential and orchestrate a connection by assigning them to a joint project, the resulting bond can lead to future results that were not previously possible. As with many things, there are risks, but if you identify these risks and design the project in a way that mitigates these risks, you can improve the potential for long-term, beneficial connection.

When leaders can make the right connections, engagement levels can grow, and the likelihood of losing top performers can be reduced. For these and other reasons, understanding your relationship architecture is important. Therefore, if you can accurately identify the potential for creating or strengthening relationships, you can facilitate collaboration and performance more effectively.

Characterizing Relationships

Chapter 2 highlights a partial list of relationship characteristics, but there are more. For example, relationships might be open or closed, carefully orchestrated or haphazard, self-regulated or externally influenced — to name a few additional descriptors.

When assessing your relationship architecture, it is important to recognize you may not know the real reason a relationship or network exists, either because this information is deliberately hidden or because even the people within the relationship are not conscious of its purpose.

While decision-makers can (and should) attempt to identify the known purpose(s) of relationships in their respective organizations, they should not fall into the trap of assuming they know all there is to know about a relationship; such assumptions can lead to grossly misinformed decisions.

When loyalty or romantic involvement exist within a network, those involved may be intent on hiding the relationship for a variety of reasons. If the existence of an intimate personal relationship remains undetected in a work environment, there are multiple implications, depending on policies, politics, and placement of those persons in the organizational chart.

Networks can be open or closed, or a combination of these qualities. Let's take a look at a typically closed network that can sometimes have open qualities. Cliques are exclusive groups of people with similar interests and ways of thinking. People in a clique may be bonded together by shared characteristics or experiences. They can be fiercely loyal to each other unless a member does something perceived as offensive to members of the clique. Because cliques tend to be closed, members may be reluctant to share information about each other with someone outside the group, while at the same time they may be open to gossip, allowing information about nonmembers to flow in and out of the clique.

When you assess your relationship architecture, you should characterize the relationships within your organization but avoid applying fixed labels. As much as possible, leaders should characterize relationships using fact-based information, otherwise bias can prevail. For example, a relationship can be labeled as "dysfunctional," or it can be described as having the capacity to be antagonistic or harmonious, depending on the circumstances. Refraining from drawing premature conclusions helps leaders perceive relationships from a more productive perspective. This is especially useful when designing social architecture to better meet your strategic priorities.

Reinventing Relationship Architecture

Your relationship architecture can be visually diagnosed using relationship-mapping software. You can also use a manual approach as presented later in this chapter. Diagnosing your relationship architecture involves observing existing networks from multiple perspectives. You may create your own descriptors and use the ones outlined in this section along with the list of characteristics introduced in Chapter 2. Once you map your relationship architecture and identify opportunities for change, you can start your reinventive design and planning processes.

Reinventing your relationship architecture can be useful when leaders detect risky interpersonal imbalances and decide to restore or establish team equilibrium. One situation where you can use mapping to reinvent your relationship architecture is in the aftermath of a merger. Another reason you may choose to map and reinvent relationships is when toxic power dynamics manifest within your team, compromising productivity.

Sometimes reinvention is needed when your relational architecture is operating effectively within the parameters of your current goals. In cases like this, your existing configuration of relationships supports short-term growth, but maintaining the current architecture may make it impossible for your team to achieve long-term goals. This can happen because team members can develop blind spots that do not allow them to identify opportunities for change, even when current team performance meets or exceeds existing goals.

For instance, a single department operates in two different locations after outgrowing its original physical space. After additional office space was provided in the second locations, the department lost much of its cohesion because it never occurred to decision-makers that the location split would negatively affect the quality of the relationship architecture, and the associated work flows. On the surface, the relationship architecture seemed to be operating adequately because team members created the appearance of balance by using work-arounds — but the circumventive work and information flows were not sustainable in the long-term.

If relationship reinvention is your goal, integrity, self-mastery and a "we" disposition are critical; leaders cannot allow a state of busyness to obscure their ability to notice their own miscalculations and overlooked opportunities. Instead, they should be tuned into to their own behaviors and how they affect members of their teams, particularly since building and sustaining trust are important goals in any IFB implementation.

Reinventing relationship architecture sometimes requires developing a new purpose for or way of engaging your relationship network. If this is the case, gaining agreement from members of your network ensures they will own the new norms and commit to changing behaviors that are not congruent with the envisioned culture.

When your intention is to build cohesive relationships, it is quite conceivable that you can miscalculate during the reinvention process. In other words, people have minds of their own and the connections you are attempting to facilitate may not happen. If your plan is not working just be honest about it: acknowledge your miscalculation as soon as you can and course correct. This is the beauty of the IFB framework, it has built-in features that facilitate responsiveness and adaptation.

In addition to skills mentioned in this chapter — including ones associated with establishing the Pillar of Trust — there are other skills and strategies leaders can develop and utilize when reinventing relationships or strengthening interpersonal interconnectivity. They include:

- demonstrating awareness of others and caring about the members of your team
- leveraging the strengths of others
- replacing punitive, disciplinarian reactions with responses based on positive reinforcement
- thinking positively (change is as simple or as difficult as you make it)
- demonstrating the capacity and willingness to identify and respectfully confront circumstances that require attention
- being intellectually curious (willing to ask powerful questions, listen, learn about yourself and others, and question your biases)
- building *morale*
- being attuned to gaps

Because of the variety in relationship quality and strength, leaders should approach each relationship using adaptive leadership skills. Adaptation allows executives to interact with coworkers appropriately, both individually and collectively, in ways that help build and maintain relationships.

Where Relationships Do – or Do Not – Exist

When considering relationship architecture, you should respect why relationships exist and how they operate. To shift the way relationships and networks operate, you can support a mindset shift among those in the relationships. A conscious relationship strategy, in which relationship architects consider the real reason(s) for the relationship before taking action, might be achieved through coaching (where practicable).

You should also take the time to identify why relationships have not developed. Is it because of latent conflict, the lack of opportunity to connect with a key person, or something else? It is also important to understand why potentially critical relationships have not taken root and blossomed.

If a relationship does not develop because there was no perceived reason to connect or because the people once in the relationship drifted apart from lack of proximity, you may be able to stimulate the connection (if all parties are open to it). However, if a relationship was damaged in the past and has not been restored, it may not be possible to make meaningful connections.

Where Relationships Are Devolving

Decisions to attempt to salvage disintegrating relationships should depend on why they are deteriorating and the mutual openness of all parties to reconcile. Decision-makers should not attempt to facilitate rehabilitation of all fractured relationships as this is a daunting pursuit that can potentially throw organizations off balance in the long-term. Instead, they should identify at-risk, critical relationships and pursue restoration based on the organization's strategic priorities, impact assessments, and the willingness of the people in those impaired relationships to reconcile.

For instance, an at-risk relationship may exist between a supervisor and his team. A supervisor, Wesley, is in a critical departmental role but he was promoted before he was properly developed and even though he was a top performer in his previous role, he is overwhelmed by the work and is the source of the bottlenecks in his department. Despite this, Wesley maintains a positive attitude and continues to work toward improving his turn-around time.

The management team needs to acknowledge their decision to prematurely promote Wesley, reassess the situation, and give him appropriate support to improve his productivity so he can strengthen his relationship with his new team. If the management team and Wesley decide to take this route, the managers also need to openly demonstrate support for Wesley so members of his team can give him the space and assistance he needs to clear up the bottlenecks and improve his turn-around time.

Coordinating Relationships

Relationship coordination occurs when teams synchronize their activities based on mutual respect, as well as shared knowledge and goals. It builds morale and allows team members to respond rapidly to new information without layers of bureaucracy interfering in decision-making. *Relational coordination* is another way designers and planners can convert unproductive interconnective structures into empowered networks. This practice is also useful for strengthening already healthy connectivity.

At Southwest Airlines, their commitment to relationship coordination led decision-makers to create an organizational structure that requires a higher ratio of supervisors to line staff than in competing organizations. Their supervisors are facilitative, spending a higher percentage of their time coaching and engaging their teams. Not only are they trained to *coach*, they are also proficient in their own duties as well as those of their team members. This allows them to fill in for and work side-by-side with frontline employees when necessary. Working side-by-side lessens the workload, and at the same time serves as a developmental opportunity, because supervisors are modeling desired behaviors.

The executive team at Southwest Airlines emphasizes building high-performance relationships because they recognize that relationship coordination is the best way to create customer value and competitive advantage. As a rule, when something goes awry, their management team preserves relationships by avoiding finger-pointing, opting instead to consciously focus on why something went wrong and how it can be resolved at its point of origin.

Connectors

In Malcolm Gladwell's book, *The Tipping Point*, he describes a person who facilitates networking as a "connector." According to Gladwell, connectors have extensive people networks and can make connections naturally. Therefore, there is no need for them to be aggressive or overly friendly. Instead, they are authentic and tend to like people. Connectors are skilled at identifying new opportunities for relationships and understanding which relationships they can revive.

Connectors don't rely solely on the past to inform their decisions to connect. They don't even have to know the people they meet or introduce to one another because they are adept at using their instincts. They may also possess the *critical thinking* capacities to use information about current conditions and future needs to make beneficial connections and avoid establishing contacts when they perceive high risks for themselves or others.

When implementing the IFB Model, trusted connectors can be an invaluable resource. They can help build and reinforce the existing relationship architecture; they can identify potential employees, vendors, and other stakeholders who are most likely the right fit for the organization; and they can use their skills to help relationship architects identify hidden connections or build bridges. Their skills are invaluable; especially when building healthy teams and networks is an essential component of enhancing and sustaining employee engagement and performance.

Connectors may occupy formal hiring or sales roles, but you should also be aware of your informal connectors for they can be powerful influencers. Wherever they exist in your organization, once you identify them, you can think about how to incentivize them to use their natural skills to develop others and support building robust relationship networks within your organization.

Types of Relationship Networks

As we have already established, leaders can construct relationship networks on foundations of loyalty, trust, or need (or some combination of the three). Sometimes loyalty-based networks do not support the goals of the team, but rather individual agendas, causing people to value loyalty over integrity. These networks can also be based on an expectation of reward for those offering their loyalty or a sense of indebtedness for favors.

Different types of professional relationship networks appear in both internal and external environments and depending on the organization, personal and professional networks may overlap. When this happens, leaders can find themselves in circumstances where they are building strategic networks with coworkers who are also their friends or even family members.

These relationships can foster collaboration or lead to unconventional approaches. They can also cause tension when mismanaged. When relationship networks overlap in ways that create potential for risks, leaders should remain attuned to their teams and related risks, exercise objectivity, and be prepared for the possible need for speedy decision-making and action.

The need to innovate work relationships has become particularly pertinent because of the growth of the millennial demographic and the increasing need for organizational agility. Therefore, learning to perceive traditional versus progressive and formal versus informal relationships is especially necessary when diagnosing relationships using the IFB framework.

Conceivably, informal networks within your organization could extend to other organizations. This is especially evident when someone leaves one employer for another organization while maintaining strong ties with former coworkers. These enduring relationships can allow previous team members to continue to influence decisions. This dynamic is a risky one because past employees are no longer part of the evolving environment within their previous workplaces. At best, their recommendations may be inadequately informed because they are unaware of new developments; at worst, they may be completely out of touch.

Unproductive Networks

When networks are unproductive, relationships may not support the shared goals of the team. They can appear to, but the overriding driver may be personal ambition. Sometimes unproductive networks endure because their counterproductive qualities are imperceptible.

At other times, they persevere because leaders lack the skill — or the will — to transform these systems.

Unproductive relationships can nullify IFB leaders' attempts to achieve meaningful change. Even when new processes are put in place, familiar behavioral dynamics can emerge, reestablishing outmoded patterns. Unproductive networks can be difficult to detect because they can be exclusive, closed to new members. In some cases, membership might be somewhat open, with decision-makers selecting people who are simpatico with those already in the network.

The organizational silo is one type of unproductive network. Silos exist when a department or team decides to isolate themselves from other departments. Work will continue to flow in circumstances like this (particularly routine flows that require limited interaction). However, transactions that require problem solving tend to get stuck because of underdeveloped or impaired communication practices.

People can comfortably work within silos especially when they typically operate in protectionist mode. When life has taught them that this is how they should be, they may feel that what they are doing is appropriate. Team members like this can be so motivated to protect their turf that they are unable or unwilling to perceive the consequences of operating this way.

Silos operate in the same way as self-absorbed individuals. When a department functions as a silo, its team members tend to care only about the goals of their own department. All other work is secondary, so it can be delayed or ignored because nothing is more important than the department's results.

Because of such an inwardly focused orientation, employees in siloed departments lack the capacity to see the big picture or willingness to care about it. As a result, they become adept at perceiving the immediate goals of their team but may not fully understand how those goals fit into the larger picture.

Another form of unproductive network is one that exists solely for building or reinforcing undermining power structures. These informal networks are webs of relationships that overlay the formal structure and can span multiple departments and stakeholders. They can be built and sustained by employees—at any level—who have ambitions of amassing or supporting power and influence. This applies to both formal and informal leaders.

Productive Networks

Productive networks operate based on shared goals. People within these networks have earned the trust of their coworkers and they collaborate with others. These coworkers are committed to sustaining a cohesive team and seek ways to grow as a unified entity, propelling each other beyond perceived, individual limits. In productive networks, team members define success individually and collectively, ensuring appropriate balance between the two.

By their very nature, productive networks can neutralize silos and recalibrate political networks, but achieving productive interconnectivity requires deep shifts in mental and emotional models and strategies. Recalibration strategies should include reward systems that incentivize employees better than the reward systems that drive siloed behaviors.

There are high-performing teams that produce superlative results but are not cohesive. This can happen in some instances when leaders reward competitive behaviors. In cases like this the team can perform if one or a few high performers produce extraordinary results, individually.

Another example of high-performing teams delivering strong results in the absence of collaboration is when members of the team have a compelling need to safeguard their job security. They may cooperate based on fear and survival, but not in service of the goals of the team.

Further Categorizing Your Networks

Networking skills are essential to IFB implementation, so leaders need to hone the skills they need to deliberately cultivate healthy networks. From the employee's perspective, they need to be adaptive because they are most likely part of multiple networks and change is inevitable.

The following are four types of productive and unproductive networks that are present or can emerge when building an IFB relationship structure. These four types are closely related so overlap is possible, even probable. As you consider them, keep in mind the awareness that networks are not limited to relationships within your organization:

Operational Networks   Building an operational network to support your productivity is useful whether you own a business or work in a corporation. Operational networks that facilitate interconnectivity, flow and balance will help you get work done efficiently and effectively and can bring about increased sales opportunities, enhanced performance results, and multiple other benefits.

Empowering Networks   Political players tend to associate networks with having a power base. In an IFB organization, team members shift from using networks to reinforce a position of power for a single person or powerful few to sharing power thought the network in ways that empower the entire team. Empowered networks support and develop members, allowing them to fully engage their strengths and talents. In addition to cultivating empowered members, this kind of network can be an adaptive, co-creative entity.

Developmental Networks   A developmental network supports the personal and career evolution of its members by offering coaching, training, education, or *mentoring*. Its purpose is to provide ongoing opportunities for development. While developmental plans can focus on training or educational pursuits, they can be expanded to include mentoring, coaching, *stretch projects*, membership in professional networks, and alliances with people who possess specialized knowledge or connections.

Personal *Networks* Your work life should be part of a holistic life plan. Therefore, it is especially important to cultivate your personal networks, so you and your team members can achieve balance. As a leader, your personal and professional networks can overlap, but you shouldn't allow this to put the relationships you want to maintain at risk. Personal networks support different aspects of your life: fun, spirituality, finance, etc.

Mapping Internal Relationship Architecture

Understanding the nature of the relationships within your networks is central to implementing IFB principles. A clear understanding sets decision-makers up to create well-informed plans for enhanced sustainability in the long term and agility in the short term.

Mapping the current and future relationship architecture (networks) of your organization is a useful learning and planning exercise. Maps of your existing architecture can inform future decisions and plans. Maps of your desired relationship architecture, if implemented successfully, can have an empowering effect when unity, engagement, and cohesion are embedded within the future map. Your *relationship map* should include all departments within your organization, and over time extend to your connections with external stakeholders, since those relationships will also provide insights into your internal relationship architecture.

As you start to map your current relationship networks, you will notice that a person can serve different roles as a member of multiple networks. Keep in mind your aim is not to identify every single relationship that affects your team; some will remain undiscovered. Therefore, as far as possible, identify the ones that are important because of your strategic direction.

Mapping your relationship architecture not only provides clarity regarding organizational networks, but it can also be used to analyze relationships and plan constructive disruption. Constructive disruption is the act of challenging conventional wisdom and structures (like networks). It allows leaders to innovate new ways of being and doing.

Constructive disruption can be an unwelcome change methodology; like any other change, there is potential for conflict and chaos. When leaders are adept at using disruption constructively while reworking relationship architecture, they are powerfully and positively introducing appropriate change to networks by opening new, desirable, and beneficial pathways to relationships, supporting the resolution of existing relational challenges, and strengthening already healthy relationships.

How to Map Your Relationship Architecture

In Figure 3.1, *Team A* represents the executive team, *Team B* represents the operations team, and *Team C* represents the sales team. Within each cluster is an executive or senior manager is responsible for the department, and the employees clustered around the managers are the team members in a department.

The proximity of each employee to their managers represents the closeness of the relationship between the manager and their team members; similarly, the proximity of the employees in a cluster to each other represents the closeness of the relationships between team members.

Case Study: Mapping Internal Relationship Architecture

In Figure 3.1, *Team A* is the executive team. In this company, the CEO works very closely with vice president AD (Ann Dougherty), but the relationships between the CEO and the other vice presidents are less intimate. Ann is viewed as the heir apparent for the role of CEO. Vice president AA (Alexander Abbott) and vice president AC (Andrew Crane) are also interested in the position of CEO, so their relationships with Ann are shallow at best.

Compounding these dynamics, Ann and Andrew oversee departments that work closely together.

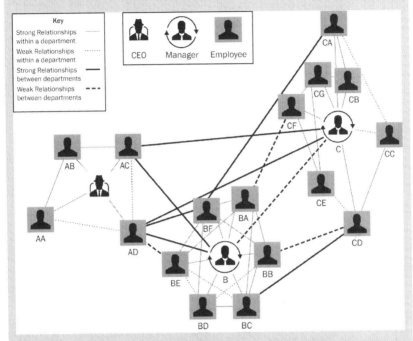

Figure 3.1   *Map of Internal Relationship Architecture*

Team B, responsible for operations, is productive, with strong problem-solving and *self-management* competencies. Employees in *Team B* have healthy relationships with senior manager and some, or all, of their coworkers. The senior manager is adept at harnessing diversity and effectively confronts issues that threaten connectivity, so this manager takes corrective action at the first sign of a relationship becoming vulnerable.

According to the map, weaker relationships exist between employees BE (Bruce Evans) and BD (Brenda Doyle), BC (Barry Clapper) and Bruce, and BB (Beth Brown) and Brenda. They are receiving coaching and training, so they can learn to self-manage more effectively. Thanks to a unified vision and a supportive senior manager, members of *Team B* share the goal of productive and respectful work relationships, so they can forgive past indiscretions. They genuinely view stabilizing the network of relationships as everyone's goal and a shared responsibility.

Teams B and *C* operate as silos because the senior managers of these two teams have a strained working relationship. *Team B*'s senior manager (Becky) is willing to do what it takes to repair the relationship. Becky understands the importance of demonstrating collaboration because she cultivates this behavior within her team and wants to be perceived as consistent. Unfortunately, the senior manager (Chuck) of *Team C* is not interested in resolving the relationship challenges. As a result, communication between Becky and Chuck is intermittent at best, but would be nonexistent if it was left to Chuck.

Team C is the sales team. They rely on the operations team (*Team B*) to process sales data in time for commissions to be paid, but things don't always work out as planned. Thus, there is tension not only between the senior managers but also between the teams at the junior level. Within *Team C*, competition is rewarded, although there is strong connectivity among CE (Carol Evans), CF (Cole Farnum), and CG (Clare Galt). CC (Caitlin Cadwell), however, is a high performer who alienates coworkers with her ruthless behavior. Despite the reporting relationship, even the senior manager of *Team C* (Chuck) has trouble communicating with Caitlin because of her behavior.

In the example of relationship architecture in Figure 3.1, intra- and interdepartmental relationships are affected by the quality of leadership, the mix of personalities and interpersonal behavioral skill levels, accountability to healthy communication practices, and the modeling of desired behaviors by leaders. It would be naive to think all relationship dynamics can be observed, but understanding relationships that you deem critical to the success of the team can get you through the mapping process, focusing especially on high risk and opportunity. Here are a few resources that can help you uncover important relationship dynamics:

- observation
- the grapevine (use with caution, as you tend to have to share information to receive it)
- focus group sessions
- interviews
- 360° multi-rater assessments
- relationship mapping surveys
- network mapping
- organizational charts and work flow information

Decision-makers should remain flexible about conclusions they draw about workplace dynamics, as coworkers and the networks they form have multiple facets that can change depending on the circumstances. This can result in leaders misreading relationships and using that information to attempt to strengthen engagement and achieve other strategic results.

Mapping External Relationship Architecture

Just as individuals do not function in complete isolation, organizations do not operate in a vacuum. Therefore, every employee who interacts with employees from other institutions should be equipped to develop and preserve heathy external relationships. The responsiveness of external stakeholders is key to overall business performance.

Trust improves relationship quality and can serve as the catalyst for sharing information that would remain hidden when connections are superficial. Generally, decision-makers should create effective communication channels both internally and externally. To improve the overall quality and reliability of information moving through these channels, team members who connect with external stakeholders should continuously seek to understand and manage the quality of their relationships within the industry and community. They should also know how to interact with regulators and take steps to understand the competition.

Case Study: Team Disunity

At Team Disunity, recruiters hire employees for what they perceive the successful candidate's proven technical knowledge, skills, and abilities to be. Unfortunately, these recruiters do not pay the same kind of attention to the candidate's potential cultural fit, so while new employees are hired according to the time-to-fill guidelines established by HR and its business partners, multiple challenges can emerge.

When employees are hired who are a close technical match for their roles but not the right fit for the culture, collaboration can be difficult to achieve. Despite this, some teams can find ways to meet deadlines because of intense applied pressure. In such circumstances, morale is understandably low, and conflict can remain latent. Although intermittent or superficial communication supports some degree of intra- and interdepartmental flow, when pressure is intense, workflows are mechanical because people are forced to cooperate under less than optimal conditions. In essence you have people working together whose survival instincts are perpetually amplified, a recipe for retention risk.

Members of Team Disunity have relationships with long-time suppliers who are also negatively affected by the team's internal dynamics. Ineffective communication of important information, slow response times, and conflicting instructions put a strain on external relationships.

While members of Team Disunity think they are perceived in a better light, internal challenges are obvious to their external stakeholders — in fact, sometimes suppliers take advantage of the team's perceived weaknesses. This is a concern because depending on the magnitude of the challenge, impaired relationships between an organization and its stakeholders can lead to conflict, legal action, and unnecessary costs.

Figure 3.2, the Map of External Relationship Architecture, is an example of the configuration of relationships and networks both inside and outside an organization. Analyzing these relationships is beneficial to the IFB process since reviewing internal and external stakeholder relationships can result in better informed strategic planning and execution. The Relationship-Strengthening Potential Tool, illustrated in Figure 3.3, applies to both internal and external relationships, and therefore can serve as an additional tool to assess interconnectivity.

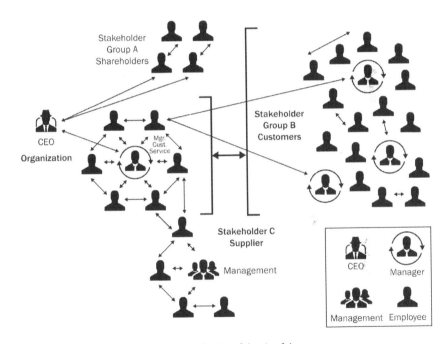

Figure 3.2   *Map of External Relationship Architecture*

Balancing both internal and external interconnectivity supports healthy engagement. Figure 3.2 expands the web of relationships beyond the boundaries of the organization. This simplified map illustrates relationships within an organization, which can be beneficial, non-beneficial, or somewhere in the middle. These relationships connect the team with shareholders, customers, and suppliers.

The internal networks that extend outside the organization establish their own standards for interaction and determine whether people on the inside will accept (or offer) high- or below-standard exchanges. When corruption is afoot, coverup and deceit are the yardsticks. When the relationships are constructive and based on trust, the transparency individuals practice enriches their interactions.

Figure 3.2 also introduces a dynamic that occurs during daily activities. External stakeholders connect with internal stakeholders as well as other external stakeholders, enabling multiple channels for flow. When connections are constructive, flow ensures that the right information moves throughout the organization and, where appropriate, to and from external stakeholders.

Work flow is another type of flow that can occur between internal and external stakeholders. In manufacturing organizations, production can begin in one country while final assembly is completed in another. Despite this, all production activities are interconnected and require coordinated communication between entities involved in the process from end to end. Once sold, these products may be consumed or they may flow back to the organization if there are defects. If handled properly, this cycle results in process improvements that enhance future workflows.

As you can see, understanding your internal and external relationship networks can provide you with information that can clarify multiple dynamics that may be negatively affecting team performance. Relationship and network dynamics have the power to facilitate change and results, delay them, or even bring them to a standstill. Therefore, when using the IFB Model, leaders should define relationships to the extent possible and, in a disciplined way, integrate relationship considerations into strategic planning and execution processes.

Creating a Relationship Map for Your Organization

As previously mentioned, there are software applications that can provide you with a deeper understanding of the complex relationship networks that operate within your organization. However, leaders can create a simplified map of relationship architecture using the organizational chart as a foundation. Figure 3.3 offers an example of a do-it-yourself organizational chart/relationship map that can support your conversations about internal networks. You can superimpose lines, icons, and descriptors to illustrate the informal relationship network and the nature and effects of these relationships.

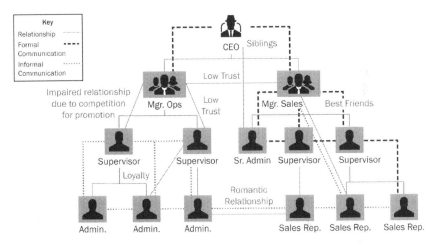

Figure 3.3 *Mapping Your Relationship Architecture*

In Figure 3.3, the CEO, Christine, has a challenged work relationship with the manager of the sales team (Patti). Despite this, Christine and Patti meet regularly but the conversations are guarded. Christine has a similar relationship with the manager of operations, Cameron, and though she communicates through formal channels, she is not happy with the performance of Cameron's team. The problem is rooted in low trust levels between Cameron and the supervisors within his team; Cameron doesn't disseminate information from Christine, nor is information from entry level employees in the operations team communicated upward.

Cameron was recently promoted because he was ruthlessly ambitious. He used merciless political strategies to get ahead, so his actions damaged his closest relationships, alienating him from his team. As a result, informal communication occurs among his supervisors and administrative staff—in fact they formed a clique that excludes him so they are not adequately informed about organizational priorities.

Even though the operations team provides some support to sales through routine work flows, it functions as a silo because the two managers, Cameron and Patti, do not trust each other. The only relationship between the two teams is a romantic one between two entry-level employees, Allison and David. From the CEO's perspective, both teams are getting work done, but productivity is challenged because of the silos and the two teams need to work together on an upcoming project to upgrade sales processes.

Within the operations team, there is a bond of loyalty between a supervisor, Hillary, and one of the administrators, Vicky, so they conceal each other's mistakes, causing underperformance to remain undetected by the manager.

The CEO's brother, Roy, is a senior sales administrator on the sales team and he is sometimes privy to his brother's decisions before they are communicated. This undermines Patti, and because Patti's best friend Lynn is a supervisor on the sales team, Patti confides in her. But Lynn is part of a grapevine that channels Patti's private thoughts about the CEO to Roy. This happens because Roy is perceived as a power broker and the supervisors want to remain in his good books.

Christine uses this manual mapping process to help her make decisions. She realizes that she needs to deconstruct the silos before she can experience any success with her planned changes. You can create a similar graphic to illustrate the connections within your organization. Feel free to add external stakeholders to the organizational chart to more clearly illustrate the quality of relationships between people and organizations connected with members of your team. Knowledge of your external stakeholders and the environment they operate in can help you to problem-solve at the root cause level.

Using the Relationship–Strengthening Potential Tool

When designing your relationship architecture, multiple relationship patterns are possible. To avert an overwhelmed or confused state that can lead to immobility, leaders need a tool to determine which relationships are critical to the success of the team and prioritize them for potential recalibration.

The Relationship-Strengthening Potential Tool was created to provide important insights into which relationships you should focus on to achieve the best possible results. This will save time in implementing IFB because knowing which relationships can offer the greatest benefit is essential to your planning. When thinking about prioritizing relationships, and strengthening them is the goal, consider:

- your criteria for prioritizing relationships
- what you will do if the people don't respond to cues to strengthen their relationships (a contingency plan)
- why relationships exist, fail, or are not initiated
- the purpose of strengthening relationships
- if there is potential to strengthen relationships (Are people in those relationships open to change?)
- how relationships strengthen or detract from team engagement and productivity
- how priority relationships affect other relationships (second and third tier relationships), intra- and interdepartmentally

Using the Tool

Once leaders define internal and external relationships using relationship maps, the next step is to consider how these relationships affect flow. To do this, you need to determine how strong the relationships are, and which can be fortified so you can identify the ones that currently or potentially affect flow positively, and negatively. If you take this approach, the next step is to define how these networks affect productivity.

Figure 3.4, The Relationship-Strengthening Potential Tool, can be used to determine if opportunities exist for coworkers to strengthen relationship interconnectivity build building or strengthening the Pillar of Trust, and if so, which relationships have the most potential positively affecting the entire team.

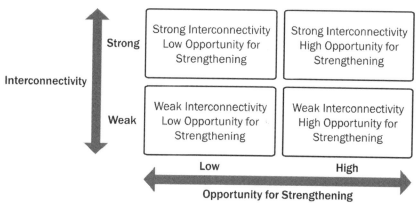

Figure 3.4   *The Relationship-Strengthening Potential Tool*

Using the Relationship-Strengthening Potential Tool, you can determine if connections need to be enhanced to achieve strategic goals, or if the status quo should be maintained. You can use it to decide if changes need to be made to a relationship (strong or weak), if power structures need to be shifted, or if relationships should be allowed to crumble. The tool can also be used to compare relationships between groups, allowing prioritization so decision-makers can determine if a relationship needs to be addressed and who will facilitate corrective steps.

Weak Interconnectivity with Low Opportunity for Strengthening
The bottom left quadrant represents weak interconnectivity with low opportunity for strengthening. Weak interconnectivity can occur

when there is low trust among team members. Relationships in this quadrant may be profoundly damaged with low likelihood of turnaround. Alternatively, the relationship may not be damaged but just superficial, because bonds were never properly established. If this relationship in this quadrant has the potential to impact team performance significantly, the circumstances may be further investigated to determine the potential for strengthening.

Some relationships in this category offer more opportunities for strengthening than others. Consider your strategic priorities and how essential each relationship is to the plan. With this information, decision-makers can determine if they need to act to strengthen trust, and by extension connectivity. This can be achieved either by seeking opportunities to support transformation of relationships or by transitioning employees who willfully resist team building.

If a relationship that is characterized by weak interconnectivity and low opportunity for strengthening is critical to the performance of the team, and the probability of interconnectivity continues to be low after attempts have been made to strengthen it, it's time to develop a strategy to ensure that the weak relationships do not negatively affect the entire team.

Strong Interconnectivity with Low Opportunity for Strengthening

Strong interconnectivity can be beneficial to an organization, though in some cases it may not be. If relationships are already based on trust and respect, they may have low opportunity for strengthening. However, sustaining trust takes effort, so there still needs to be commitment to maintaining strong relationships. Where appropriate, this commitment can be one of sustaining versus strengthening. Also note that the existence of strong relationships does not guarantee healthy interconnectivity, flow, or balance, because this is dependent upon other factors—such as why the relationships exist in the first place.

High trust levels can exist within different types of relationships in an organization—between management and staff, managers, or among entry-level employees—creating loyalties that can be either beneficial to organizational goals or counterproductive. Therefore, it is important to view strong interconnectivity with low opportunity for strengthening from a macro perspective. In circumstances where the strength of the relationship is contributing to dysfunction, another type of relationship modification strategy may be required.

If existing relationships are unproductive and there is low opportunity for strengthening, decision-makers can transfer employees to change the relationship dynamics (where appropriate). Change may temporarily or permanently weaken the impact of these relationships, but it can also significantly enhance them and the unproductive dynamics they generate. Therefore, you should not assume that a relationship that falls within this quadrant is risk free. The reason for the relationship, considered in light of the goals of the organization, should determine how risky it is and what can and should be done.

Weak Interconnectivity with High Opportunity for Strengthening

Relationships characterized by weak interconnectivity and high opportunity for strengthening fall into several categories: they might be relationships damaged over a long term, ones where circumstances recently changed, or new relationships. As already mentioned, some relationships that were impaired over a protracted period may be strengthened if the people in the relationships are amenable to working together—shared goals may be used as a step toward trust. A recently reestablished relationship in which trust is growing also presents an opportunity for strengthening if those in the relationship are open and can learn the skills they need to grow and sustain their relationship (Pillar of Trust).

New relationships can emerge after changes in staff or modifications to workflows that reorganize the people interactions. With effective self-management being practiced by all participants in relationships, the potential for relationship strengthening remains high. When a relationship falls within the bottom-right quadrant of the chart *and* is critical to the team, you may be able to seek opportunities to strengthen it.

Strong Interconnectivity and High Opportunity for Strengthening

When relationships fall within the top-right quadrant, a team can be high performing and cohesive with shared goals and additional capacity to grow. Strong interconnectivity with high opportunity for strengthening those bonds can also exist in a team in which political games created dubious patterns of loyalty that resulted in a divided team. For these teams, strengthening can happen if members contributing to division are developed or transferred and leaders who model trust-building, inclusive behaviors are at the helm.

Healthy interconnectivity sets the stage for flow but doesn't guarantee it. Other variables like decision-making skills, resource availability, and constantly shifting priorities can all enhance or weaken potential for connectivity. As with the other three quadrants, if the relationship is classified as critical, leaders still need to understand why it exists, so they can decide whether to refocus an already strong relationship.

Using the Relationship-Strengthening Potential Tool

Placement of relationships in any of the quadrants doesn't automatically indicate the need for action or that a relationship is a priority for strengthening, connection, or maintenance. The Relationship-Strengthening Potential Tool can be used in conjunction with the strategic *action plan* to determine priorities and the likelihood of the effectiveness of the plan if low-performing relationships are allowed to get in the way. Because relationship dynamics can make or break an organization's success (they are an indicator of engagement), the goals, relationship map(s), and other tools that illustrate the current state of relationships should be consulted before and during IFB planning and decision-making.

Case Study: Defining Relationship–Strengthening Potential

Figure 3.5 provides an example of how relationships can be plotted on the Relationship-Strengthening Potential Tool. Two relationships are mapped: Charles (C) is the manager of the sales team, and CeCe (CC) is a high-performing salesperson. This relationship is critical because it is a primary driver of the performance of a small department. It is also difficult to replace because the salesperson has a long-term, close working relationship with the manager.

CeCe is a top performer in a department of five, bringing in 75 percent of total revenue. Despite Charles' best efforts to develop the entire team, other salespeople have not been able to deliver a higher percentage of the revenue.

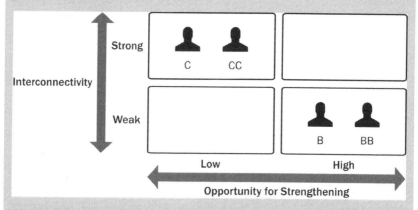

Figure 3.5   *Example of Relationship-Strengthening Potential*

Both Charles and CeCe perceive low opportunity for strengthening their relationship because it is trust-based and already strong. From a strategic perspective, decision-makers need to determine how much risk this relationship represents because the rest of the department is not performing at the same level as CeCe. These leaders recognize the potential for achieving better results if the rest of the team is performing. They are also uncomfortable with the reality that if CeCe decides to resign with short notice, there is very high financial risk.

This team relationship, in its current configuration, is a very high priority. The executive responsible for the sales department can intervene and work with Charles to understand the causes of the performance trends and create a plan to strengthen the entire department. Depending on the underlying causes, the plan might be to refocus the departmental development plan, work to repair relationships, or transfer or terminate team members who are not the right fit. If Charles and his reporting executive are unable to strengthen the sales performance of other members of the team, Charles' role as a manager may also come under scrutiny.

The second relationship illustrated in Figure 3.5 is one in which Ben (B), a supervisor from the operations department, has an underdeveloped working relationship with Barbara (BB), who is new to the department. Barbara was a top performer in her previous department and expectations are high. At this early stage, Ben and Barbara need to build their relationship as the foundation for supporting her future performance. Ben can lead the process by:

- adequately onboarding and coaching Barbara
- establishing a development plan for Barbara
- setting clear goals for Barbara's performance (technical and behavioral)
- providing Barbara with the resources and any other support she needs

Decision-makers deemed both relationships in Figure 3.5 as having potential for strengthening and as being of value; therefore, strengthening both is a high priority. While this is an oversimplified example, it provides insight into how the exercise can work holistically.

Reconstructing Relationships

Once decision-makers complete the diagnostic phase and priority relationships are identified, one of the next steps is to create an IFB plan that configures relationships to better support the organization. Reconstructing relationships can involve transferring people into and out of departments. It can also mean changes in authorities, coaching, training, modified workflows, and so on.

Employees cannot be forced into relating with each other; rather, they should be intrinsically motivated. Therefore, as you saw in the exploration of the relationship-strengthening tool, mapping existing and future relationships can only take you so far. The intent behind mapping is not to have leaders act as puppeteers while employees do whatever they are told; it is to set the stage for building high impact, mutually beneficial relationships that employees are intrinsically motivated to build and sustain.

Case Study: Reconstructing Relationships

Mark, a new frontline employee, described a time when he went the extra mile to help his employer resolve a potentially difficult client situation. Mark works in the back office of a bank. A wealthy client needed a transaction facilitated after the deadline passed because of an emergency. To complicate matters, the approving officer (Lori) went home early for the day. So despite policy guidelines that prohibit transferring large sums of money without the approval of a senior officer, Mark used his discretion and facilitated the transaction. He thought he was doing the right thing.

When he returned to work the following day, Mark was excited about helping his team avert a risky client situation and anticipated some form of recognition. Unfortunately, because the situation exposed a pattern of Lori's lack of adherence to work hours, Mark was met with her displaced fury—even though it wasn't his fault. Mark was surprised to be on the receiving end of his supervisor's wrath and felt deflated. This was the defining moment for Mark's disengagement. He decided to never take the initiative again, and because the confrontation happened in a common area, everyone else in the department got the same message.

Soon after Lori's meltdown, organizational leaders decided to improve engagement and initiated relationship mapping and prioritization exercises. They decided that Mark and Lori's relationship falls within the weak interconnectivity, high opportunity for strengthening quadrant. They also decided the relationship was essential to the performance of the team. Hence they identified it as a high-priority relationship and decided to support its restoration. Their rationale for identifying this relationship as a priority is that they thought if they could restore the relationship, they could help the entire team start trusting Lori again.

To reconstruct the relationship between Mark and Lori, the pair will have to accept this proposition. Lori will have to commit to developing leadership skills defined by the Pillar of Trust. In the short term, she can apologize to Mark and the rest of the team for how she addressed the situation. If Mark is open to her apology, Lori can acknowledge Mark's resourcefulness. Mark's actions indicate he may be capable of taking on increased responsibility so, if appropriate, Lori can also explore opportunities for his development.

CHAPTER 4

EXPANDING THE DEFINITION
OF RELATIONSHIPS

If you want to understand function, study structure.

—Francis Crick, co-discoverer of the structure
of the DNA molecule

Interpersonal relationships are at the heart of the interconnective infrastructure, and the quality of relationships can potentially deconstruct or contribute to trust and flow. Up to this stage in our exploration of Interconnectivity, relationships referred to connections between two or more people, but as we have pointed out, the scope of relationships at work extends to:

- relationships between different components of workflows (how a process connects from end to end through different departments)
- relationships between the vision, mission, and values
- relationships between policies and the people who interpret and apply them
- relationships between organizations and outside stakeholders like the media

Because we can have relationships with such a wide variety of people, guidelines, structures and institutions, IFB designers should identify and understand both personal and nonpersonal relationships in their quest to determine which ones require attention, upgrades, facilitation, or discontinuance.

This chapter provides further insight into the rest of the interconnective infrastructure. We explore how to open communication channels to facilitate connection and how organizational structure and strategy also contribute to flow.

Why Expand the Definition of Relationships?

Because decision-makers tend to define relationships as interpersonal, their definition may limit their perceptions when it comes to problem-solving. The IFB Model helps leaders understand the nonpersonal elements of the interconnective infrastructure, and how nonpersonal aspects of the infrastructure relate with each other. This provides them with new perspectives they can use to clearly view their organizations.

Communication Channels

While both external and internal communication channels coexist, this book is inward focused because we are taking an inside-out approach to the IFB Model. Internal communication channels are critical components of interconnectivity. They facilitate the flow of information and productivity. They can also be used to improve morale and decision-making by allowing quality information to move in multiple directions using modes of communication such as:

- meetings
- surveys
- focus group sessions
- newsletters
- video messages and podcasts
- emails
- the internet and intranet
- social media
- the grapevine

In an organization characterized by trust-based relationships, employees trust senior staff members to share information when needed and frontline staff trust management to escalate their responses to executives, ensuring that channels remain open and functional.

When communication happens between two people, one person formulates and sends a message, while the other receives it. The sender creates the message based on their worldview, and the receiver translates the message through their unique filter before formulating a response.

The same principles apply when communicating a message through an entire organization. Once communication channels are open and operating effectively, leaders can craft messages that move through formal and informal networks using communication modes such as meetings, newsletters, or podcasts.

However, simply sending a message through various channels does not constitute IFB connectivity. For authentic connection to occur and channels to remain open, coworkers need to trust each other and deliberately craft their messages to ensure the right information is going to the right people using an appropriate tone.

When communication channels are compromised, it is sometimes because low-quality communication framework is in place; it can also happen when people are communicating without connecting. Such an outcome can transpire when:

- People are frustrated with each other.
- Coworkers have a lot to say but there is not much substance.
- People fear punitive action if they say what they really think.
- Coworkers are not competent and have little value to add but feel compelled to say something.

When coworkers communicate without connecting and compromise the communication channels, decisions might be based on insufficient information, leading to unexpected risks and perpetuating low trust levels.

Case Study: How Communication Affects Teams

Ted and Fiona work for the same company and lead teams that should work closely together. They used to have a collegial working relationship, but their relationship was damaged by an incident that occurred five years ago. While Ted and Fiona remained on speaking terms after the incident, the quality of their conversations deteriorated. Now, when Ted contacts Fiona about processing work, Fiona will speak with him, but because she doesn't trust him, so she only answers the questions asked.

Ted and Fiona limit their conversations to asking and answering questions, sharing only superficial or necessary information. The openness they once shared no longer seems possible, which puts their company at risk because in their positions as leaders, Ted and Fiona need to speak freely with and challenge each other if the business is to continue to grow.

This compromised communication pattern also affects the morale of other members of their teams. For instance, Fiona relentlessly interrogates members of her team who communicate with Ted or his team members about routine work flows without going through her first. Now Fiona's team members are reluctant to speak with Ted's cohort (and vice versa) because of the perceived consequences of having these conversations.

In this case, the *channels of communication* are blocked even though workflows between the teams must be maintained. Because of tense relations, emails are the preferred mode of communication, and even emails are closely monitored by Fiona and Ted.

Channels of communication—which are made up of human beings—facilitate movement of information throughout an organization vertically, horizontally, and even diagonally. For example, a top-down channel can start with the CEO, who distributes a message to executives; those executives ensure that information is sent to management, which disseminates the information to frontline staff.

To facilitate flow, employees at all levels should participate in managing channels of communication to ensure that little to no relevant information is obstructed. Unfortunately, despite some decision-makers' best efforts to create connections and unrestricted channels of communication, the quality of information flow might still be unstable.

Blocked Communication

Blocked communication happens when information is not flowing through the organization. This can be due to negligence, inconsistency, the absence of a plan, incompetence, power plays, or too many competing priorities. Figure 4.1 illustrates a layer of managers receiving information from executives and staff, but not taking time to facilitate movement of information in either direction due to any of the reasons we've discussed, or because quality communication practices are just not a priority.

Managers in Figure 4.1 also receive feedback from staff that should be communicated to executives. Such a bottom-up information flow can be blocked for the reasons mentioned or for one or a combination of the following reasons:

- Managers do not possess adequate problem-solving skills.
- Managers want to cover up important information that exposes their failings.
- Executives are not interested in what non-management employees have to say.
- Managers put a spin on employee sentiments to protect themselves and members of their teams.

When flow is blocked, important information is buried or forgotten until an urgent situation arises that forces an exchange. Leaders in cultures that fail to put accountabilities in place for multidirectional communication, tend to only force efficient operation of top-down channels when a situation requires urgent attention. Under duress, when information moves up these channels it is in response to requests for information. If the culture is one that features blame, the responses can be incomplete or laced with excuses and other forms of deflection.

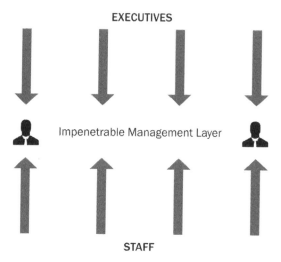

Figure 4.1   *Blocked Communication*

When employees lack representation through their managers, they may attempt to find other ways to get messages to their desired destination. Some employees inappropriately vent in general staff meetings, while others may use their relationship networks to circumvent the impenetrable layer of managers; still others become frustrated and resign.

Case Study: The Intent to Mislead

Abbey doesn't trust her manager, Pete. During her most recent interim performance review, Pete surprised her with a below-average performance rating. Abbey reacted negatively to the rating and even though she attempted to justify a higher score, Pete refused to consider her point of view.

A week later, Pete followed up with Abbey about a project that was almost due. Abbey knew she wouldn't be able to deliver on time, but she assured Pete the project was progressing as expected, secretly hoping she could organize last-minute support. Abbey deliberately misled Pete because she didn't want him to hold the missed deadline against her.

Unfortunately, Abbey never received the extra support and missed her deadline. A day later, Pete followed up with her and she gave Pete what she felt were convincing reasons for not submitting the report. However, Pete thought the deadline was an important one and missing it was also a reflection on him, so no excuse was acceptable to him.

In this case, the communication channel was open and used by Pete and Abbey, but the messages Abbey communicated misrepresented the true status of the project. When a message is delivered with the intent to mislead, the channel is available but no longer effective.

IFB leaders need to identify where obstructions or message distortions exist in each communication channel within a network. They need to monitor communication quality regularly since relationships fluctuate in strength and purpose.

Formal and Informal Communication Channels

Your formal communication channels should operate based on reporting lines defined by your organizational chart. Designing formal communication channels requires vision for what they should look like when operating optimally, identifying the communication modes that would be most effective, and defining the quality of relationships. The design might be based on the strategic needs of the business, or if you have the resources, a communication audit that clarifies the effectiveness and appeal of existing communication channels and modalities being used within your organization.

Informal channels of communication are just as significant as formal ones, but sometimes they can be more difficult to identify and manage. They exist both within formal connections and outside the chain of command defined by the organizational chart. In fact, informal channels operate within open or closed networks that may have a very differently defined hierarchy than the organizational chart. Adding to the complexity of informal channels is the reality that information flowing through them can be difficult to verify because the identity and credibility of sources can be concealed.

The terms "informal" and "unofficial" channels are sometimes used interchangeably. Office gossip is one type of information that flows through unofficial channels; and the network that facilitates gossip is called the grapevine. As a conduit, the grapevine can distort information because there tends to be less diligence with fact-checking in informal networks.

In light of the potential for distortions, it behooves decision-makers to pay attention to the grapevine when managing information through formal channels. While the grapevine can have a positive effect as well, it can yield information that adversely affects morale. However, even though information conveyed through the grapevine may not have an initial "feel-good" effect, IFB leaders who are paying close attention to morale know how to take balancing action to address dips.

Informal channels can be limiting or facilitative. They can stimulate trust or cause distrust, so depending on the situation, you may decide to avoid or engage them. If you attempt to silence an informal channel, you may just end up forcing it into hiding, amplifying fact distortions.

A potentially limiting dynamic can emerge when informality degenerates into a casual interchange. Over-familiarity can support or inhibit flow. When someone is so relaxed that they become desensitized to the urgency of their coworkers' needs, they might neglect to provide timely support. A casual attitude in a close relationship can result in downgrading the priority of the work because friends may anticipate automatic forgiveness for minor infractions. Friendships may also cause coworkers to make excuses and attempt to cover up for each other's unresponsiveness, but delays caused by overfamiliarity can have deeper ramifications.

Opening Communication Channels

Active listening is essential to opening channels of communication. Listening enables flow, allowing information to move through various channels unimpeded. Effective leaders understand that authentic listening is a non-negotiable skill.

Maintaining respectful verbal communication and body language requires self-awareness (as well as awareness of others) when deciding which conversations to facilitate or redirect. Unproductive conversations contribute to low trust levels and undermine the effectiveness of communication channels. The following anecdote is likely apocryphal, but it demonstrates practical application of a filtering process that can help keep communication channels open.

Triple Filter Test

In ancient Greece, Socrates was reputed to hold knowledge in high esteem. One day an acquaintance met the great philosopher and said, "Do you know what I just heard about your friend?"

"Hold on a minute," Socrates replied. "Before telling me anything I would like you to pass a little test. It's called the Triple Filter Test."

"Triple Filter?"

"That's right," Socrates continued. "Before you talk to me about my friend, it might be a good idea to take a moment and filter what you are going to say. That is why I call it the Triple Filter Test. The first filter is truth. Have you made absolutely sure that what you are about to tell me is true?"

"No," the man said. "Actually, I just heard about it and..."

"All right," Socrates interrupted, "so you don't really know if it is true or not."

"Now let's try the second filter, the filter of goodness. Is what you are about to tell me about my friend something good?"

"No. On the contrary..." the man began.

"So," Socrates interjected, "you want to tell me something bad about him, but you are not certain it is true. You may still pass the test because there is one filter left. The third filter is usefulness. Is what you want to tell me about my friend going to be useful to me?"

"Not particularly," the man admitted.

"Well," concluded Socrates, "if what you want to tell me is neither true nor good nor even useful, then why tell it to me at all?"

This Triple Filter Test supports trust and open communication channels. It facilitates integrity, self-mastery, and a "we" disposition — all parts of the Pillar of Trust. By transforming conversations into constructive exchanges; the Triple Filter Test can help to open closed or underperforming communication channels.

Another filtering system that helps build trust is to ask yourself and anyone who is gossiping or complaining, "How can we help this person?" or "How can we contribute to turning this situation around?" While these questions may not always be appropriate, they can be used to transform your mental model from one that features criticism, gossip, or frustration to one that fosters collaboration.

Southwest Airlines opened its internal communication channels by establishing a role called *boundary spanners*. Persons in these roles are responsible for seeing that all employees receive the information they need to perform their duties. Boundary spanners also manage communication flows to ensure people receive appropriate information through established channels. Southwest Airlines has a unique culture that is difficult to replicate, so if a similar role cannot be established within your organization effectively, the coaching and communications responsibilities reflected in a role like this can be integrated into existing supervisory roles.

Multidirectional Flow of Communication

Figure 4.2 illustrates the concept of multidirectional flow. This is an ideal state in which many channels are open and being utilized optimally. Considering the dynamism of human relationships, channels need to be monitored and understood so that if one is blocked, it can be cleared, and if this is not possible, alternative channels can be created or used to prevent imbalances.

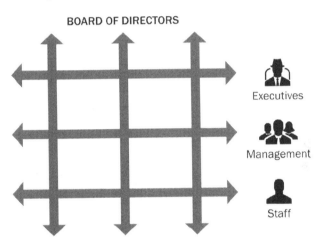

Figure 4.2   *Multidirectional Communication Flow*

Case Study: Reopening Communication Channels

Consider this example of what happens when multidirectional information flow is impaired. Steve, a manager, is currently at odds with his reporting executive, Todd. They do not communicate effectively, and this is obvious because Todd is frequently sarcastic toward Steve. Todd makes statements like, "We all know who created this problem," or "Some managers need to go back to university." Consequently, Steve does everything he can to avoid interaction with Todd.

This is a recent development: Steve and Todd were on amicable terms until a recent performance assessment, where Todd surprised Steve with a less-than-satisfactory performance rating. Steve expressed his disappointment, stating that he thought Todd was not coaching him effectively. Todd was taken aback by Steve's accusation and the relationship changed.

The CEO noticed the deterioration of the relationship because Steve used to be a top performer who was in constant communication with Todd. However, communication between them was now intermittent at best, and Steve is now demoralized by Todd's insulting comments. One day, the CEO was prompted to step in and referee, encouraging Todd and Steve to rehabilitate their relationship because Steve's performance was continuing to deteriorate. To make matters worse, the tension between Todd and Steve was beginning to negatively affect the entire team.

In this case study, the conflict between Todd and Steve obstructed top-down, lateral, and bottom-up channels of communication because Steve stopped communicating effectively with Todd, his peers, and those reporting directly to him. The CEO wanted to inspire restorative action. By addressing unproductive behavioral changes by both Steve and Todd, the CEO can work toward supporting them with rebuilding trust, so they can reopen weak communication channels.

Top-Down Communication Channels

When top-down communication is the primary or only direction of information flow, decision-makers are unable or unwilling to access information from the frontline through formal channels. A potential challenge with this is that if they only access information informally, it may not be subjected to rigorous tests to determine accuracy. On the other hand, it may be that the unfiltered information is closer to the truth, and this can be advantageous.

Top-down communication as the dominant direction of flow can imply leaders' lack of interest in the ideas, suggestions, and feedback of employees. This is one way to perpetuate ivory towers. Despite the dominance of the top-down orientation, it is still possible for informal, bottom-up channels to operate under these circumstances.

Bottom-Up Communication Channels

Bottom-up communication channels are pathways that facilitate the flow of information from the bottom of the organization (entry level) to the top (executives and board). These channels give *voice* to employees at the lower levels so their suggestions and needs can be communicated and addressed.

When both bottom-up and top-down communication channels are open and operational, IFB implementation can be very effective. But you first need:

- reciprocal trust
- an executive team with the willingness to receive and process suggestions from all levels of the business — especially ideas that may be different than expected
- potential for innovation and organizational agility
- opportunity for improved engagement levels and trust
- capacity for improved performance and effectiveness
- motivated employees

With obstructed bottom-up information flow, the same result occurs as when only top-down flow dominates: suboptimal decision-making because of the flow of inaccurate or insufficient information. When bottom-up flows are restricted, employees feel voiceless, trust is low, change is resisted, and strategic initiatives are generally misunderstood and therefore under-supported.

Lateral Communication Channels

Author Sree Rama Rao clarified lateral communication saying, "Lateral communication usually follows the pattern of work flow in an organization, occurring between members of work groups, between one work group and another, between members of different departments, and between line and staff employees. The main purpose of lateral communication is to provide a direct channel for organizational coordination and problem solving."[2] Some organizational communication strategies focus predominantly on vertical communication channels. These tend to be formal channels in which executives participate. Internal communication strategies should also seek to improve inter- and intradepartmental communication, so the organization can improve its responsiveness to internal challenges and by extension, its agility in the marketplace.

Optimizing Communication Channels

In some organizations, top-down, bottom-up, and lateral communication channels all operate simultaneously and optimally. Optimized channel operation doesn't necessarily mean communication is perfect. The ideal state is multidirectional, simultaneous information flow. Advanced internal communication strategies are facilitated by leaders who take ownership of information dissemination, making sure that if the channels malfunction, people can still receive the information they need.

To fortify the multidirectional flow of information, leaders should acknowledge that communication is not limited to transferring information; it requires preserving relationships. This is where self-mastery and the "we" disposition come into play.

The frequency of communication is another important consideration. Frequency can refer to the number of times different messages are transmitted or to the number of times the same message is communicated. Given the diversity of learning styles, attention spans, and filters, the same message usually needs to be communicated multiple times using different modes of transmission.

Although this doesn't apply to everyone, some people can hear information multiple times, yet each time they hear it, they insist it is the first time. Listening to a repeated message can be a challenge for some, but it is better for a leader to ensure a message is heard, retained, and understood by a majority than to open the door to various people risks because of low retention.

From a strategic vantage point, employees should receive information that is relevant to their daily duties and useful for helping them understand their changing contexts. Contextual change is continuous, so the frequency of communication should be sufficient to support ongoing prioritization, reduced time wastage, and overall responsiveness; in other words, balance.

Using Appropriate Communication Modes

Choosing your modes of communication is another critical part of the process. An email sent out as the initial and only announcement of a complex change is ineffective. Some organizations also try to consolidate relevant FAQs within that single email, but this doesn't dispel anxiety in the way that face-to-face communication can. Additionally, people don't always read emails; if they do, there may be a delay, or the tone might be misunderstood. The best way to communicate significant change is to send the same message through multiple channels, using face-to-face communication as the first line of contact.

As a reminder, communication modes include meetings, focus groups, newsletters, emails, video journals, social media, intranet, and even the grapevine. To choose the most appropriate mode (or modes) of communication, you should answer the following questions:

- Which communication modes are most effective in your workplace? Why?
- Who is your target audience and what are their preferred communication modes?
- Which modes will best facilitate flow and balance?
- Which actions can leaders take to enhance the communicative infrastructure and reinforce IFB?

Developing an internal communication strategy is central to improving the quality of your organization's interconnectivity. As part of the IFB planning process, determining the right modes is also an important skill for leaders to develop. Even though communication modes support interconnectivity, relationship quality determines if the messages will be trusted.

When strategizing messaging, segmenting your audiences is critical. Different messages should be carefully crafted and targeted at internal and external stakeholder groups. Differentiation is necessary, not to mislead, but to strengthen understanding. As a collateral point, keep in mind that selecting the appropriate messenger is just as important as crafting the message.

Meetings

Meetings represent only one mode of communication. I am highlighting them in this section because they can facilitate change and can be misused, causing considerable time wastage. Meetings should be engaging experiences, enabling real-time exchange of information by bringing multiple perspectives to one location (virtual or physical) to create solutions.

In some organizations, information is presented in meetings and either there is no comment, or people say only what they think decision-makers want to hear. No real thoughts are shared, no new ideas—just silence, agreement, or lots of meaningless corporate speak. Employees sometimes choose not to contribute their ideas because experience has taught them to conceal them.

The IFB Model can be used to improve the quality of meetings. Here's how: the chairperson starts by diagnosing and analyzing the quality of team interconnectivity. This entails understanding the team's engagement during meetings and identifying the quality of collaboration that occurs between meetings. The chairperson should also seek diverse views to create safe psychological space. Understanding relationships is not enough, though. The meeting chairperson should also determine the quality of work and information flows, and the execution of decisions between meetings.

If the meeting chairperson identifies a need for improved interaction through trust building, they should consult with each participant to seek their perspectives on how they can contribute to improving the quality of conversations. The intention behind having the chairperson start with one-on-one meetings is not to create or reinforce *dyadic* relationships, but instead to gather information that can be used to improve meeting quality.

But IFB is not a linear model, so the chairperson's focus should be on strengthening relationships concentrating simultaneously on the structure of meetings themselves, to identify opportunities to refine them for better flow. One way to add structure is by setting guidelines for communicating during meetings. In this way everyone who would like to contribute can, and feel safe doing so. The more people there are who can contribute meaningfully to a conversation, the more robust the solutions are likely to be.

Effective meeting chairpersons understand that to facilitate flow, the agenda provides a guide for the conversation but should be flexible enough to allow a change of direction if needed. Therefore, leaders who are working with the IFB framework need to synthesize new information and be flexible enough to course-correct during and after meetings.

Moving from Dyads to Multiparty Communication

Sometimes leaders establish relationships, so they can speak with one person at a time. Although onlookers may perceive this as a "divide and conquer" strategy, this may not be the intent. Rather, such a relationship constitutes a *dyad*. Not every leader can build a team in a way that involves simultaneous conversations with multiple team members simultaneously. Sometimes this happens because they are uncomfortable with being challenged. Instead, they conduct closed conversations with one team member and then approach another and another, incrementally changing the conversation as they speak with each person.

When this happens, the last person in a dyadic exchange with the leader can benefit most from the previous conversations. Additionally, leaders can put themselves at risk by excluding the previous persons from the full range of ideas shared in the separate conversations. This can happen for various reasons; sometimes it's because it's a common cultural practice to communicate in this way at other times, leaders lack the skills necessary to harness the energy of creative tension.

When leaders use dyadic conversations exclusively, team members can get the impression that there is no transparency, and this perception corrupts team-building attempts. These leaders may or may not make a conscious effort to omit information, but when dyadic conversations happen more often than team conversations, leaders can limit the ability of the team to grow and improve results.

When a leader is adept at office politics and relies heavily on dyadic conversations, each conversation will deliberately contain different details. If the leader's actions are intentionally designed to avoid transparency, marginalize, or sabotage team members, long-term trust building is very difficult.

So why is it important to build a relationship with the entire team, instead of managing relationships with one person at a time? One reason is that employees can become suspicious and distrustful when they speak with each other and realize their leader said something different to each of them.

I don't want to paint the picture that one-on-one conversations with your team members are not optimal. In fact, they are very necessary. However, while they may be essential, if they are used exclusively or predominantly, they can create imbalances within a team. When leaders become adept at determining which type of conversation is best and when it is appropriate, collective performance can come into balance with individual achievements.

Effective group communication is more complex than one-on-one communication. When it is functioning well, leaders are exchanging information with and integrating ideas from many people at once.

As a leader implementing the IFB Model, you will also need to hone your listening skills by getting better at detecting group nonverbal signals, emotional contagion, and other informational behavioral patterns. This is an especially useful skill when trust levels are low.

Nonpersonal Relationships within the Relationship Infrastructure

So far, we have explored interpersonal relationships and how they interact through communication, channels. The Relationship Infrastructure also includes nonpersonal structures, which we will explore in this section.

There are numerous types of structures within organizations. At the very top of the structural hierarchy is *corporate governance*. There are also organizational charts, job descriptions, delegated authorities, policies and procedures, risk assessments, and others. We will review each type separately, then integrate them into IFB theory to help you understand how they interrelate.

Corporate Governance

Corporate governance is the framework of rules and controls that boards use to operate. A sound governance structure records and holds the board and executives to baseline standards. Here are a few examples of the types of documents that can make up a governance framework:

- corporate governance guidelines/manual (including policies and procedures for making corporate decisions and guidelines for monitoring strategic actions)
- board committee charters
- code of conduct
- corporate and social responsibility philosophy

To facilitate smooth operation, boards delegate authorities to executives. Formal delegated authorities provide structure for decision-making. The board assigns approval authorities to the executive team and the document should highlight which authorities can be further delegated. This structuring document provides clarity about who is approved to assume risks on behalf of the organization.

Organizational Charts and Related Structural Tools

Shifting from the board to the operation, structure shows up in a variety of forms: organizational charts, job descriptions, performance appraisals, policies, and procedures, to name a few.

An organizational chart is a diagram that illustrates the configuration of roles within an organization, highlighting relationships from the perspectives of position ranking and workflows. The organizational chart establishes a framework for interconnectivity that facilitates communication, turnaround time, promotions, transfers, communication, and even decision-making. Clearly defined organizational charts also provide employees with enough information to plan their careers.

Ideally, organizational charts are informed by the strategic plan and are aligned with supporting job descriptions that articulate duties and workflows for every role. Some organizational charts indicate clear paths for most job families, others do not. If your organization defines its career paths based on its organizational chart, your chart may provide clear insights into various promotional and transfer opportunities. Performance appraisals should be used to link your organizational chart (roles) to your strategic goals and objectives. All these structures are connected and can support flow and balance if they are thoughtfully orchestrated.

Case Study: It's In The Past

Audrey works for an organization where her manager (Brandon) and the supervisor in her department are quite young. She has occupied the same role for six years and spent time completing certifications with the intent of positioning herself for a promotion. Audrey believes her career plateaued four years ago because back then, two of her peers were promoted while she remained at her existing pay grade.

Audrey believes that a promotion is the only next step for her career, but because she was held responsible for a costly incident four years ago, it doesn't seem like she will be considered for one. From her perspective, her career has stagnated despite her best efforts to turn the situation around.

Sometimes, when employees work for the same department or company for an extended period, *institutional memory* can negatively affect their careers, even if they have taken deliberate steps to improve their professional brand. In this case, Audrey can use the organizational structure to consider a lateral path into another department. Although it is possible that other departmental managers are aware of the mistake Audrey made four years ago, at least one of them may be willing to place greater value on her current achievements and give her a shot.

Career paths can be vertical, lateral, or a combination of both. When they are clearly defined, they can empower employees, providing options they can use to plot their career trajectories. Career paths may exist within a single company, but sometimes an employee has to leave an organization so they can continue on their chosen path.

Without defined paths, employees either leave a company or just wait around until someone else leaves and hope they will be considered for a promotion. If they wait long enough, they may be promoted eventually, not because they are the best person for the job, but because they are the best person available at the time. In the long term, this is not ideal for team growth and it does not accurately reflect the IFB principle of orienting your organization to be prepared for change as a constant.

By defining career paths and career development (systems, policies, etc.), organizations provide employees with alternate ways they can structure their development for themselves. Organizations benefit from empowering employees, because it can lead to building a more fully developed, engaged workforce strengthening the collective relationship between employees and their employers.

Types of Organizational Charts

There are different kinds of organizational charts, and each has unique characteristics. These attributes can provide insights into the kind of culture that operates within an organization. For instance, hierarchical charts tend to be associated with cultures of bureaucracy and control; flat organizations can support innovative cultures.

Some charts reflect a strong outward focus, like organizations that demonstrate commitment to *social responsibility*. Others are more inwardly centered. Given our continuously changing environments, organizational charts can evolve or devolve over time, due to planning (or the lack of it) or counterproductive organizational design practices like manipulation of the chart based on political agendas.

Your organizational chart should be based on strategic priorities in a way that allows the chart design to best facilitate performance. Strategically aligned organizational charts (even misaligned ones) connect people through their roles and related workflows. When integrating IFB design, strategic priorities should be embedded within this particular structure and so should trust considerations. The positions represented on the chart should correspond to the job descriptions and procedures associated with those roles. Here are some of the different kinds of organizational charts that companies use:

- Traditional hierarchies rely on a chain of command for connectivity. Within this type of structure, communication should follow a defined path but sometimes doesn't. Some hierarchies allow people to communicate freely with anyone along the chain of command while in others, entry-level employees are strictly forbidden to communicate formally with persons more than one level above them.

- Flat organizations can operate with more agility because there are fewer bureaucratic layers and restrictions; therefore (ideally), these structures can enable effective connectivity and communication across levels. Flat organizations can have hierarchical or matrix features.

- In matrix organizations employees can have at least two reporting relationships, one related to their functions and one to the product or service the organization offers. In these organizations, employees from multiple functional areas work together in teams. If the culture permits, this structure can facilitate improved communication thanks to less formal restrictions on who can communicate with whom.

- Divisional structures separate an organization into self-contained divisions formed to create products or for other strategic reasons (geographic location, for example). Depending on culture and communication practices, a divisional structure may operate in a silo. As with functional structures, it can be hierarchical or flat. Functional structures separate companies into functional areas such as accounting, marketing, sales and service, and so forth.

- A holocracy is a structure that decentralizes the management of teams and allows them to self-organize. Because management is decentralized, so is decision-making and power.

- A network organization is a hybrid structure that expands to tap into external resources. This type of organizational structure goes beyond internal stakeholders; it is one in which a group of independent companies or subsidiaries organize themselves and operate in a way that they can appear to be a single, larger entity.

As with other types of interconnectivity, obstacles to connection can reside within an organizational structure. Perhaps people who should be collaborating are embroiled in conflict, or the structure is poorly planned and workflows are not optimized. In some instances, what appears to be a blockage may not be, so leaders will need to take a deeper look at their organizational charts, regardless the configuration, to ensure it is designed according to IFB principles.

Some organizations have poorly defined (or undefined) organizational charts where overlapping duties lead to conflict and diminished trust. Impaired trust can potentially leave gaping holes in an organization's performance. Leaders can also generate low trust by appointing friends to roles based on loyalty and not merit or fit.

Certain leaders resist updating their organizational charts for decades, even though the combined dynamics of strategy and external pressures can generate the desperate need for a flexible, modern structure. When structures are stuck in the past, they become irrelevant to the business and an inhibitor to growth. Some organizations get around this by changing the structure informally, through delegation. This can happen when an owner of smaller, growing business delegates more and more work, overloading their top performers instead of revitalizing their organizational chart.

On the other end of the spectrum, I have encountered organizations that constantly change their organizational charts based on frequently shifting external pressures, internal politics, or an apparent whim. Constant, disconnected, or perceivably unethical changes to the organizational chart can generate profound distrust. This low trust level increases doubt in the quality of leadership. When the structure is constantly shifting, and trust levels are low, there is also a higher risk of losing good people, especially if they are overwhelmed and feeling undervalued because of incoherent changes that never seem to be successfully implemented.

Organizational charts should have more dimension than only being based on strategic considerations. If two people in a department cannot work well together but they both add value to the organization, this should also be taken into account if their skills are difficult to acquire. In an IFB organizational chart, it is essential that decision-makers are willing to consider interpersonal dynamics between employees during the design phase. If such factors are overlooked or underestimated, they can neutralize team effectiveness by creating a toxic culture that leads to reduced output and imbalances that affect the ability of a team to achieve or exceed its goals.

Policies and Procedures

Operationally, policies and procedures provide structures of accountability that also facilitate interconnectivity and flow. Policies establish ground rules (or guidelines) within an organization, providing the context for procedures. Procedures provide standards for execution of work and like policies, they can be formally documented or informally communicated via word-of-mouth. Procedural manuals should outline how a process should be executed, how it connects with related processes, and when each stage of that process should be completed. When followed, policies and procedures create predictability through standardization.

For procedures to be effective tools that facilitate interconnectivity and flow, employees participating in a process should be familiar with the steps from end to end, even if they are not taking part in every stage of the procedure. This helps them understand why they are doing what they are doing so when they are faced with unfamiliar circumstances, they are equipped with knowledge they need to problem-solve.

Here's what can happen when an employee only knows the segment of the workflow that is assigned to them:

A retail operation implemented new point-of-sale software that was very different than the previous system. For reasons unknown, all but one of the employees were trained on only the part of the process they were expected to perform. Quite naturally, the one person who learned the entire system was inundated with questions and saddled with correcting other people's errors. In this situation, decision-makers compromised flow because employees lacked the knowledge of the end to end process that would have allowed them to understand how each module interconnects, thus reducing bottlenecks.

Considering the nature of policies and procedures in the context of building an IFB organization, it is important to understand how employees will relate to them. For instance, in environments dominated by control, decision-makers can be meticulous about documenting standard operating procedures and may require employees to learn, regurgitate, and comply with an inordinate number of policies. In organizations that highlight innovation, too many policies and procedures can neutralize their creative advantage.

Some decision-makers have a habit of issuing policies in reaction to unexpected, isolated events that really require ingenuity and leadership. In their zeal for managing risks, they attempt to use policies—a structuring tool—to control circumstances that competent managers should resolve by engaging staff and using effective leadership skills. Too many policies, can restrict the ability of an organization to sustain balance and to be agile when unforeseen events require responsiveness.

Sometimes policies are so restrictive that various rates of flow decelerate. This can be caused by policies that introduce multiple layers of required approval, or by the lack of understanding of the full spectrum of implications of a new policy by those tasked with formally defining and recording them.

When policies are used to dictate how work gets done and people in leadership positions aren't given the discretion they need to make judgment calls, managers become a tool through which policies operate, instead of the reverse: policies being tools used by managers. Because the overuse of policies is both a cause and an effect of the absence of trust, this approach does not work in an IFB context.

Overly restrictive policies affect the collective emotion of a team, leading to frustration. Frustrated employees can in turn cause slowed work and other flows because frustration can manifest as burnout, passive aggressive behavior, or avoidance. Fear is another emotion conjured by strict policies and low tolerance for errors. Mistakes, procrastination, and cover-up can emerge when threats like "zero tolerance" are implied or expressed.

When gaining an understanding of the relationship between policies and procedures, it is important for leaders to acknowledge inconsistent, undocumented policies and procedures within their organizations that can override and contradict written ones. Depending on the context, they can be a potential risk when consistency is linked to the customer experience, branding, and other strategic priorities.

Strategy

Strategy is the outer layer of the Model of Interconnective Infrastructure. It connects the internal operation with external stakeholders such as customers, regulators, or vendors. Internally, a strategic action plan contains goals and objectives that connect people, departments, and workflows, establishing a path to achieve the vision of an organization.

Strategic plan execution requires the *coordination* of all layers of the Model of Interconnective Infrastructure and collaboration to get things done. As previously emphasized, effective strategic execution and successful change initiatives rely heavily on trust-based relationships and communication. Since communication practices can have a profound effect on the success of a plan, they are especially important. However, a business's ability to execute a plan is also shaped by structural considerations and operational (flow) facilitators such as available resources and competent employees.

Traditional and unconventional *performance management* processes should use tools that link strategy and organizational performance with individual performance. When operating optimally, the performance management process should deliver on priorities articulated in the strategic plan because individual goals should cascade from organizational goals. For this reason, the performance management process is an integral part of the interconnective infrastructure; it supports individual accountability to strategic goals.

Revisiting the Model of Interconnective Infrastructure

This section will help you integrate the ideas and concepts introduced in Chapters 2–4 strengthening your understanding of the applications of the Model of Interconnective Infrastructure. This list is a partial one, created to provide examples of nonpersonal and mixed (personal and nonpersonal) relationships that exist within organizations, so you can start to view relationships from an IFB perspective:

Relationships between Employees and Policies

Employees have a variety of relationships with policies and procedures; polices can be embraced, ignored, or even misunderstood. Sometimes employees exhibit a lack of curiosity which leads them to implement policies based on word of mouth. In other work environments, employees don't take policies and procedures seriously, simply because there are no consequences for non compliance.

Policies and procedures constitute a framework for accountability — interconnectivity between policies, procedures, and people is essential to building quality flow. Here are a few questions you can use to explore this type of relationship: Which policies contribute primarily to engagement and morale? What is the general sentiment of employees toward policies and procedures? Do employees have a better relationship with formal or informal policies? Why?

Relationships between Policies

As already highlighted, relationships exist between different policies. The following questions can help you assess these relationships: How do policies align with or contradict each other? How does the alignment or contradiction within and between policies affect the vision, mission, and values of our organization? What are the most influential informal (word-of-mouth) policies? What are the differences between these important informal policies and their formal (documented) counterparts? Which type of policies — formal or informal — carry the most weight? Why?

The Relationship between Goals and Actual Performance

In some organizations, there is no clear connection between goals and actual performance. Instead there is a stronger connection between performance and job descriptions and the job descriptions are not connected to strategic goals. This becomes evident when the collective performance curve indicates outstanding performance of the team, but the business goals are not being met or exceeded.

Questions you can use to examine the situation include: How aligned are our performance expectations with our strategic priorities? What evaluative system do we have in place to check the efficacy and relevance of our performance instruments? How achievable are our performance goals? How are persons being held accountable when they don't meet their goals? How much does office politics infiltrate the performance management process? How does our reward system tie into performance management?

The Relationship between Decisions and Outcomes

The quality of decision-making can predict outcomes. Low-grade decisions tend to be based on insufficient facts, assumptions, undisciplined emotion, cultural norms, and outdated mental models. Quality decisions are based on accurate information, leaders who can navigate their emotions, empathy, competence, scenario thinking, and other skills such as risk assessment and creativity. In an unpredictable, complex environment, well-considered decisions can lead to unwanted outcomes and weak decisions can lead to acceptable results. Nonetheless, it is still prudent to invest time and resources in making quality decisions so you can minimize the risks related to failed change initiatives.

A few questions that help determine the relationship between your decisions and their outcomes include: Which biases are driving decisions? How much research are we doing? How disciplined are we with fact-based decision-making? How are we ensuring that we are weighing more than two perspectives? How are our decisions affecting morale and engagement?

The Relationship between Strategic Planning and Execution

There are circumstances where strategic plans are of a low quality, or there is no plan. Sometimes plans can be well thought out and aligned with the vision, mission and values, but the execution team may or may not lack the skills required to implement it. In some cases, the execution team hesitates to adopt a plan because team members have not bought into it. If a strategic plan is not being executed, decision-makers should not only focus on operational and resource challenges, they should also consider the relationship of the implementation team with the plan to understand why it is not advancing as expected.

To take their leadership to the next level, decision-makers should become adept at understanding how the layers of the model of the interconnective infrastructure align with or contradict each other. For example, there are organizational leaders who espouse the values of trust, teamwork, and collaboration, but their performance management and reward systems incentivize individual accomplishments.

When reward systems contradict core values, the actions being rewarded will be reinforced. To reverse this, leaders need to be willing to take a balanced, considered approach toward understanding personal and non-personal relationship dynamics so they can support IFB transformation wherever possible.

CHAPTER 5

FLOW MOTION

If you study the rhythm of life on this planet, you
will find that everything moves in perfect symphony
with everything else.

—Suzy Kassem, American thinker, poet,
writer, and philosopher

Flow emerges when there is progressive movement through your interconnective infrastructure, whether these systems are human or otherwise. Flow can ensue when a strategic priority is executed sequentially by different people or when information moves through formal and informal channels.

Relationship quality directly affects flow and can show up on your strategic agenda as engagement. Your engagement level is not only tied to the quality of your relationships, it also affects flow.

This chapter investigates flow. I'll provide insights into configurations, types, steadiness, and drivers of flow as they occur in an organization committed to IFB principles. The chapter also defines a process you can use to establish flows within your organization by diagnosing your flow state, designing a new interconnective infrastructure, and enabling flow through the modified structure.

What Is Flow?

We have established that flow is a state of movement. It ranges from mechanical motion guided by structures to movement that is creative, unbounded, and unstructured. Within organizations, different types of flow can coexist including, but not limited to:

- workflows
- information flow
- succession (the flow of people through a career path)
- training and development (the flow of knowledge designed to enhance other work-related flows)
- cash flow
- the flow of ideas (innovation)
- emotions (which can operate like a virus, flowing from person to person with a lack of *self-awareness*)
- business growth and cycles
- customer flow (buying patterns based on the time of day, season, etc.)
- turnover and recruitment (representing the flow of people into and out of an organization)

In positive psychology, flow is described as a zone that people get lost in when doing something that deeply engages them. The definition of IFB flow incorporates creative states of flow like this as well as procedural-based and automated flows that adhere to operational standards.

Why Flow Is Important

Organizations are constantly in motion, whether decision-makers perceive these movements in all their configurations or not. Flow that exists within organizations mirrors the nature of flow in the human circulatory system. In this system, blood moves through an intricate network of veins and arteries, transporting oxygen and nutrients throughout the body.

This critical network then takes blood back to the heart. Likewise, the workplace is composed of a network of human relationships. These relationships have the shared purpose of facilitating different kinds of movement, keeping the corporate entity alive and healthy. Like the artery and vein network, relationships facilitate workflows, information, customer service, and other critical flows.

Given the pervasiveness of varieties of flow within organizations, it is prudent for decision-makers to recognize the intricacies of critical flows, understanding why they operate the way they do. Flow is important because it is intimately linked to organizational performance. As a result, the quality of flow directly affects an institution's ability to sustain or improve its performance levels.

Understanding Flow

Figure 5.1 highlights four perspectives of flow: the configuration of flow, flow facilitation, rates of flow and drivers of flow. The configuration of flow refers to the patterns of flow that exist within an organization. Configurations can be linear or nonlinear. Flow facilitation describes how different types of flow are enabled throughout an organization. It can be organic, closely managed, or optimized.

Decision-makers and managers approach flow depending on team goals and their perception of the need for organic or managed flow. Organic flow is shaped by interacting external and internal environmental factors that keep things in motion without deliberate interference. Managed flow requires involvement of people who work together to control flow. Optimized flow is immersive. Coworkers experience it when they trust each other, connect, and can get lost in a state of creativity together.

The rate of flow refers to the pace, or tempo of flow as it travels through an interconnective infrastructure. Together, the configuration of flow, flow facilitation, and rates of flow are directly affected by the drivers of flow. Flow drivers are the forces behind the movement. They propel it and contribute to balances and imbalances within an organization.

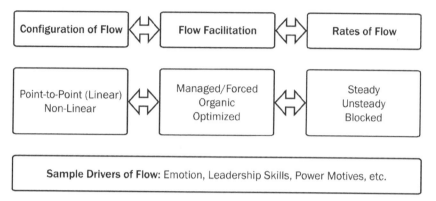

Figure 5.1   *The Flow State*

Configurations of Flow

In change-based organizations, flow can be an indicator of the capacity for change. Various characteristics of flow bring the potential for organizational responsiveness to light, they draw attention to trust levels or planning and execution skills, and they contribute to the profitability of an organization.

When flow happens, it can be linear, shifting from one point in time and space to another—much like how a product is assembled on a production line, then sent to a wholesale outlet, and then a store. Another type of linear flow happens when an employee is promoted up a hierarchy, not accepting lateral moves, aiming only for upward mobility.

An overlooked type of linear flow can exist when an established process is diverted onto a new path to achieve results. The improvised process sustains a linear progression but if it is reactive and inadequately connected, it may contain inherent weaknesses due to the quality of relationships and the competence levels of individuals involved in the alternate path. This means existing Band-Aid solutions like this need to be closely observed when diagnosing flows, so they can be brought into balance, over time.

Communication loops are an example of nonlinear flow. These loops can operate in a circular formation when information is communicated from the top of the organization, through the layers, to the front line. Then responses to that information are sent up through the layers of the hierarchy, back to the originators of the initial message. As long as there are open, healthy channels, the communication loop should support multiple types of flow.

Nonlinear flow can also transpire in meetings when participants shift into the zone and unexpected results happen. When a team shifts into the zone there is a fluid, unscripted process that emerges where ideas are shared, sometimes in a seemingly random way, and built upon using respectful, engaged, and empowered language. When in the zone, team members lose all sense of time, sometimes marveling at how fast time passed by while they were collaborating. These teams are engaged and can experience fun or intensity when in the zone.

Another example of nonlinear flow can emerge during negotiation processes when one party is resistant to a recommended solution, and then a sequence of seemingly unrelated events causes that person to change their mind. Some refer to this as synchronistic — simultaneous occurrences that appear to be disconnected yet meaningful, with no clear evidence of causal connection, yet with the power to shift outcomes.

How Flow Is Facilitated – Managed, Organic, and Optimized

Managed flow occurs in environments where planners and implementers intentionally orchestrate different combinations of flow. Managed flow is controlled; this happens when facilitators demonstrate little to no interest in flexibility, forcing flows to meet specifications. On the other end of the spectrum, managed flow can refer to the implementation of planned innovations to flow that solve existing problems or grow the organization's capacity for improved performance. Managed flow can occur in multiple circumstances:

- when implementing strategies
- during the execution of routine duties
- when there are multiple, granular structures affecting the work simultaneously (e.g., policies, procedures, and authorities)
- when employees are micromanaged

When flow is forced, business owners or executives dictate priorities and there is no room for discretion. Forced flow does not allow team members to provide meaningful input into solutions and to make matters increasingly tense, there is probably no tolerance for mistakes. Forced flow is linked to team disengagement because flow achieved in highly controlled environments can be driven by emotions like fear and frustration.

Sometimes executive decisions are out of touch with the realities on the front line. When executives make substandard decisions for this reason, the low performing change activities are exacerbated when the same decision-makers refuse to listen to suggestions from line staff, labelling them as resistors early in the change process.

Organic flow is not forced or dictated by decision-makers, but guided by the uncoordinated convergence of internal and external pressures. This type of flow happens naturally — decisions are made in the moment by affected individuals. Technically, organic flow can occur in any type of organization, but I have witnessed it more often in organizations with a lesser degree of structure.

An example of organic flow is what happens when an employee unexpectedly calls in sick and no one else possesses the skills needed to execute the absent employee's duties. Instead of the manager deciding who should complete the work, she collaborates with her team to decide how the work will be distributed in the short term. When the manager finds out that the absence will be prolonged, she checks in with her team again to determine if they are burnt out or if other latent challenges exist so she can take proactive action.

In this example, when flow was disrupted by an unexpected absence, the manager collaborated with the team to distribute the work because she had no cross-training plan in place that could provide better coverage for the unplanned absence. While the manager was able to distribute the work in the short term, she had no clear understanding of the impact of the additional work, distributing based on who could do the work instead of a more integrative approach that also included consideration of workload distribution and other factors.

While this analysis highlights potential risks associated with organic flow, this does not have to be the case; opportunities can also emerge. The absence can help the manager identify successors for various roles, ideas for developing the team more effectively and opportunities for the manager to seek development for herself.

The peak state of organic flow is optimized flow. Mihály Csíkszentmihályi, the author of *Flow: The Psychology of Optimal Experience*, defined what IFB terms "optimized flow" in an interview with *Wired* magazine: he said it is a state of "being completely involved in an activity for its own sake. The ego falls away. Time flies. Every action, movement, and thought follows inevitably from the previous one, like playing jazz. Your whole being is involved, and you're using your skills to the utmost."[3]

Optimized flow occurs both individually and within a team. As Mihály Csíkszentmihályi suggests, individuals can enter a heightened state of flow where creativity, problem solving, and productivity make extraordinary performance possible.

Teams can also achieve this state, but it is not an easy feat when trust is damaged. When optimized flow occurs within a cohesive team, members enter "the zone" together. Sometimes not all of them make the transition together, but enough of them achieve it to amplify the creative experience. In this collective flow state, these team members are not hindered by the boundaries of time and space. Instead, they are deeply absorbed in an intense, sometimes fun, shared activity. In fact, they may become so absorbed that they're surprised when the meeting concludes — *how could so much time have passed so quickly?*

Teams capable of optimized flow are more than a cohesive unit when they are in an optimized flow state; they operate as a single entity with the benefit of significantly expanded capacity. They can slip into nonlinear flow just as easily as linear patterns.

These teams are not perfect; they experience conflict, but they know how to channel it constructively. Trust is mutual, and they know each other's work styles. All this helps them collaborate effortlessly. Additionally, each team member is willing to speak up and possesses intermediate to advanced leadership qualities.

The following systems and resources support managed, organic, and optimized flow:

Talent When leaders tap into talent (versus competence), flow outcomes can be driven beyond previous limits. These leaders know it is not enough to establish a competent team. They know they need people on their teams whose talents are aligned with organizational goals.

When an employee or leader occupies a role that is aligned with their talent and vision, they are more likely to go above and beyond if the culture supports them in their growth and creativity. In some organizations, this is called the "right fit." Seeking the right fit keeps intrinsically motivated employees engaged.

Empowerment Unproductive power dynamics that are associated with fear can facilitate and even drive flow, but flow can mutate based on power plays and other influences. When power operates as empowerment, employees are talented, accountable, and allowed to grow and make decisions. They are all part of a shared power system. In some cases, this means they are authorized to make judgment calls and willing to make them.

Leader Quality Leaders can be a source of inspiration or discouragement. They can contribute to emotion by making (or not making) decisions and sharing ideas. Leadership skills and intentions also skew dynamics toward power or empowerment, and these dynamics directly affect the morale and capacity of teams.

Decision-making	Decisions affect all components of the IFB Model. They should be based on as many relevant facts as possible and made and communicated at the right time. Such decisions can create a sense of security or discomfort and still be facilitative. Decisions that drive flow can be forward-thinking or they can maintain the status quo. They can also impede flow in various ways. For instance, when decision paralysis exists, the lacuna creates bottlenecks, slowing workflows and threatening engagement.

Rates of Flow

Whether flow is moving in a loop or from one point in a straight line to another, different rates of flow can occur. These rates range from slow to fast, or even hyper-fast. Flows can exhibit rhythms that show up in short bursts followed by longer ones that correspond with cycles that are external to the organization. The rate and rhythm of flow may be steady, intermittent, or blocked. As you consider the different rates of flow articulated below, keep in mind that speed and tempo can apply to organic, managed, and optimized flows, depending on the drivers:

Steady Flow	Steady flow is continuous. It can manifest as flow with no breaks, with speed that doesn't change significantly. An example of this type of steady flow is when a customer service team is moving customers in and out of a customer service area in a steady stream.
	Leaders should consider the possibility that even though flow may be steady, output may still be suboptimal. Therefore, it is not enough to consider the rate of flow in isolation. As a decision-maker, you also need to understand the context of flow: the capacity of the team, availability of resources, absenteeism trends, etc.

The following anecdote demonstrates the need to consider the rate of flow in the context of other factors. Kate was the assigned leader of a project. Funds were disbursed to her to hire consultants for technical assistance with her project. As is customary, Kate provided the prospective consultants with the Terms of Reference for the project and once selected, the chosen consultant started the work.

For the duration of the project, the consultant provided Kate with regular updates. Admittedly, Kate didn't pay close attention to the outsourced project because she was immersed in other strategic activities that consumed her time. When the project concluded, the consultant delivered a final presentation that was completely unrelated to the Terms of Reference.

Kate's executives were surprised and disappointed; even with Kate's apparent involvement, the recommendations missed the mark by a wide margin. In this case, the flow of activities related to the project was steady, but the recommendations were irrelevant because Kate didn't ask the right questions during the updates.

Intermittent Flow Intermittent flow can show up in a variety of forms. It is punctuated, and these interruptions can occur in a pattern or randomly. Intermittent flow is evident when sales commissions are available for a finite period. When the commissions are high enough to motivate performance, salespeople make a concerted effort, but once the incentive is withdrawn, the surge of effort declines or ceases completely.

Intermittent flow does not completely cease, the bursts of energy can be equal in length or they can vary in rate and tempo. For example, in some organizations, when an important message is communicated from executives to managers, managers are expected to communicate the message to members of their respective teams at a coordinated time.

In reality, some of these managers deliver the message at the prescribed time. Others are delayed by unforeseen challenges. Still others may completely forget about making the announcement. If this type of intermittent flow persists, the grapevine will make up for the information gaps, becoming a primary vehicle for the transfer of information, filling in the gaps with rumors and opinions.

Intermittent flow can be beneficial when it is synchronized with cycles and seasons. The clothing industry does this by producing different types of apparel for each season. So winter clothing is sold at a certain time of the year, summer clothing at another time, and so on.

Blocked Flow The difference between blocked and intermittent flow is that blocked flow is completely obstructed. There is no movement and the potential for movement may or may not exist.

Each type of flow is appropriate or inappropriate in different circumstances. When it comes to blocked flow we typically assume it can only be problematic, but even blocked flow can be advantageous. One example of this is when a new product is scheduled to be introduced to its target market and there is a structural flaw that can affect brand integrity, and by extension, long-term profit margins. Decision-makers can decide to delay the launch until the fault is corrected.

There is no "best" rate of flow. Therefore, when incorporating flow considerations into your business model it should be a deliberate, thoughtful process, so the rates of various flows can be aligned with your strategic priorities. Each organization has different proficiencies for establishing interpersonal connections that enhance all aspects of flow. Here is an example:

Case Study: Functional Incompetence and the Dangers of Intermittent Flow

Functional incompetents can be consciously or unconsciously ineffective. On the surface, they may seem to be functioning. In fact, some go to great lengths to simulate the appearance of productivity using self-promotion, blame, charisma, power, and other strategies to hide their shortcomings.

Trisch is a manager who used her influence to get promoted. She tends to misrepresent the truth and is always positioning herself as a victim overcoming insurmountable odds, so she can lower everyone's expectations of her. Her intent behind playing the sympathy card is so her supervisor can overlook her superficial explanations and mendacity.

Like the Pied Piper, Trisch has lulled members of the executive team into thinking she is a top performer. She reinforces her "all-star" status by regularly highlighting the deficiencies of her team members — artfully ensuring her voice is the only one heard so she can plant the seeds of doubt, reinforcing negative perceptions of her colleagues among decision-makers. Trisch is skilled at keeping everyone at arm's length, never allowing connections to happen that will dispel the myths she's created.

Trisch's deep, dark secret is that she is functionally incompetent. She tries to create the impression that she is always at the top of her game, but her leadership skills nor results line up with the brand she articulates. In fact, she is profoundly incompetent, even positioning work produced by others as her own, never acknowledging the talent or contributions of her team members. Trisch is unaware that her team members are onto her games. They remain silent because they prefer to minimize the damage she has already done.

The people who work closest to Trisch know she is a manipulator who uses excuses, red herrings and victim language to deceive executives into not only to accepting her misrepresentations, but into valiantly defending her. As a result, members of Trisch's team perceive themselves as being powerless. Knowing they will not be listened to by executives, members of her team believe they have only two choices: put up with her behavior or resign. As long as they remain immobilized, Trisch reinforces the divide between members of her team and the executives by minimizing their access to each other.

Trisch blocks flow in multiple ways, and these blockages lead to intermittent flow that is unproductive for the team. She blocks the establishment of relationships and opportunities for promotions, and she creates bottlenecks that cannot be addressed because she always has a plausible excuse that executives buy into.

Trisch rarely has an original idea, so she represents other people's ideas as her own—but she is unable to execute them. By taking the credit for other peoples' ideas, Trisch hinders the development of her team members, inhibiting their potential for career growth.

As a decision-maker, it is important to identify dynamics like this so you can facilitate healthy relationships that support flow in ways that help your business to grow sustainably.

When flow is blocked by dysfunctional behaviors, decision-makers may need to consider some type of rehabilitative action. These behaviors not only lower trust in the manager, but by extension, they can damage trust in the entire organization. Distrust can manifest itself when decision-makers appear to be

- out of touch with team dysfunction and the effect it has on performance;
- closed to feedback or inaccessible;

- unfair in their actions (i.e., unable or unwilling to investigate opinions, excuses, badmouthing, and finger-pointing).

For authentic flow—not just the appearance of it—to exist, executives should attune to the entire team and remain open to diverse viewpoints. They cannot allow their biases to be manipulated in ways that further impair trust and cause them to complicit in political machinations, contributing to dysfunction.

Drivers of Flow

Drivers of flow are the forces behind flow that propel movement through each of the interconnective structures (relationships, communication, organizational structure, and strategy). There might be a dominant driver—such as fear—but multiple drivers propel flows.

Drivers of flow are important to define because they are the impetus behind flows and they affect a leadership team's ability to achieve and sustain balance. For instance, a fear-based work culture characterized by low tolerance for mistakes, high reliance on policies and processes, and punitive reactions toward employees, can produce strong or weak business performance. In controlled, fear-based cultures that feature strong results, morale may be low. If morale is low for a sustained period, and market conditions are inviting, these organizations will eventually lose top performers as they burn out.

In teams where innovation is an important cultural feature, trust, collaboration, and creativity can drive team performance (flow), but leaders also need to consider the quality of their interconnective infrastructures and other factors like the decision-making skills of leaders, team competence, communication practices, and operational systems. The list below outlines the variety of drivers of flow:

Emotion   In organizations that feature a climate of anxiety and low trust, anxiety and fear can drive performance, sometimes contributing to outstanding results. The ever-present threat of losing their jobs puts employees in a perpetual state of high alert because they are in survival mode.

For the IFB Model to operate as intended, trust and connection are non-negotiable. When trust is a cultural theme, team members experience positive emotions that drive performance in synergistic ways. Instead of survival mode propelling performance, inspired emotions drive results.

Vision   Establishing a vision that people understand and embrace can drive flow. This is especially apparent when there is no unifying vision, and the lack of one leads to confusion, conflicting agendas, demotivation — or even worse, untapped potential.

Values   Values operate at both individual and team levels. For the IFB Model to operate at its best, leaders should ensure that employees accept their core values — starting with the Pillar of Trust. Therefore, appointing leaders who model the core values and hire recruits who are naturally aligned with those values is key.

Values drive employees and leaders at a deep level. When they share values, they can connect with people who have similar motives. It is important to state here that sharing values does not necessarily mean people have the same views. Honoring and encouraging diversity is an important component of the IFB Model.

Ideas   When the IFB Model is operating optimally, idea generation should be the norm. It is a long-term model, that can support leaders who are generating ideas over the long term. It is not enough for leaders and employees to generate ideas, though. An equally effective system of planning and implementation ought to be in place to action these ideas, so they can drive flow.

The drivers of flow provide insight into why flow is happening (or not) and what is sustaining or impairing it. Examination of your drivers can indicate the risks to the sustainability of each type of flow. One reason for this is that sometimes flow drivers can conflict with each other and lead to blocked flow. For instance, a leadership team decides to implement changes, but the proposed changes don't make sense to frontline staff. To make matters worse, top performers perceive the changes as having negative implications for them.

Flow and Interpersonal Relationships

When designing flow, achieving an optimized flow state requires synchronizing simultaneous flows founded on strategic priorities. Optimizing workflows requires relationships that are high on the trust spectrum. In the presence of trust, competence, and other connective characteristics, team engagement and capacity growth are possible. In the absence of trust, flow may exist, or even exceed expectations, but primary drivers not based on trust can introduce risks.

Inclusive practices also facilitate flow. Leaders of teams where inclusion is an inherent practice are in an ideal position to harness diversity. For instance, when high-performing teams with advanced communication skills as well as a record of inclusion encounter divergent views, they know how to synthesize this information without slipping into intractable conflict.

Leadership effectiveness is critical when facilitating flow because competent leaders model desired behaviors and envision the team and its workflows from multiple perspectives. They understand the importance of troubleshooting workflows and the interpersonal relationships behind them so they can take proactive steps to transform team norms that don't reflect core IFB and other constructive values.

The decision-making skills of leaders directly affect flow. Some leaders are unable to make decisions for a variety of reasons. Others are empowered to make decisions and trained to carefully weigh the pros and cons of each alternative, so they can minimize delays and capitalize on opportunities.

Facilitating flow through interpersonal networks requires leaders who can design flow in ways that can deliver the best possible results. Here are a few examples of flows that are supported by the quality of interpersonal relationships:

- communication
- change initiatives
- workflows
- ideas

When flows are operating at their peak, as defined by the strategic plan, they support the entire team rather than a select few. Multidirectional flows are important to every organization; they should be sustainable and healthy from interpersonal, intradepartmental, and interdepartmental perspectives.

The Nonpersonal Aspects of Flow

The nonpersonal and interpersonal aspects of the organizational interconnective infrastructure are interdependent, so flow is the result of their interaction. More specifically, policies require people to adhere to, interpret, and execute them; strategies need people who possess the necessary skills to implement them; and perhaps most obvious, communication cannot happen without people on both ends — it's a two-way street.

Leaders use policies to form the cultural norms of the organization and underpin the execution of strategy. They also drive the quality of communication, which affects both routine activity and strategic projects. Even though communication, structure, and strategies are nonpersonal, people are the force behind their operation.

Flow and Communication Channels

The quality of information flowing through communication channels is contingent upon the trust levels between the persons communicating. Leaders and employees can use a variety of tools to communicate with each other and sometimes the choice of tools can enhance trust or lead to distrust. It is important, therefore, to choose your communication tools wisely. We provided lists of communication modes in Chapter 4. Here is a list of additional tools that can be used to enhance or facilitate flow:

- video journals
- seminars
- memos
- town hall meetings

Ideas, information, emotion, and opinions are all transmitted through communication modalities. Drivers of information flow include the occurrence of an extraordinary event, the value an organization places on an effective internal communication process, the predisposition of leaders, and emotion. The absence of a robust, formal internal communication structure can activate a shift to an informal communication structure, such as the grapevine.

When messages are standardized and coordinated through formal communication channels, leaders have added control over the accuracy and tone of their messages. Formal channels sometimes preferred because the grapevine can be undisciplined and sensational, transmitting emotion in an undisciplined way.

How Emotion Affects the Flow of Information

Trust influences the accuracy and quality of information — especially if sharing information makes the person sharing it vulnerable. Realistically, there are cultures in which attempts to grow trust will be intensely resisted. In cases like this, trust will probably not undergird connectivity in a way that supports collaborative action, but shared goals may.

Because of the link between trust and safety, the level of trust influences which messages get communicated, the accuracy of these messages, who receives them, and who does not. Even when overall trust is at a healthy level within a team, different levels of trust exist between various team members.

Emotion can guarantee a message is sent, but it can also distort it or prevent it from being communicated at all. Emotion affects the mode of communication; it can also cause information to be communicated more efficiently or more slowly. Conversely, the emotion of fear can also cause information to move faster than usual. For example, fear can lead to withholding information, affecting the quality of workflows.

The content of a message can trigger emotion within its sender and if the sender is emotionally unaware, those receiving the message can be positively or negatively affected if they are unable to self-navigate. The meaning of a message can have the same effect. Given the potential potency of emotions, as a leader you should pay attention to them — through the words you use, your tone, the content of your message, and your body language when communicating with the expectation of facilitating flow. Your team members are more likely to believe your nonverbal communication than the content of your message; it is therefore important to be disciplined about monitoring your internal reactions and channel your emotions productively.

Leaders elicit a variety of responses from their team members, so selecting a trusted messenger is critical to flow, especially when the message is unpopular and flow is critical. If the messenger is trusted and respected, the message stands a much better chance of being trusted and accepted. However, in some organizations, even though individuals within a department may be trusted, the organization can have a weak internal brand and information originating from leaders it may be viewed as suspect.

In addition to identifying the right messenger, decision-makers should also consider the following morale-related topics:

- how the decision can affect the climate
- the best time to communicate the information
- The right messaging for different audiences
- how the information can be coordinated for simultaneous dissemination
- how to ensure uniformity and clarity of the messages

Leaders are not the only ones to affect the quality of flow. The entire team should be willing and able to demonstrate self-mastery and other qualities that help to grow trust.

Flow and Organizational Structure

As you are aware, your organizational chart defines your structure, contributes to shaping your culture, and indicates the kind of leadership that is necessary. Whether your chart is flat, hierarchical, or adheres to some other configuration, it provides a platform for the movement of people into and out of different roles within the organization.

Within organizational structures, flow exists as promotions, transfers, demotions, and terminations. An organizational chart with anomalous roles that appear unnecessary or illogical may indicate that something innovative or manipulative is going on, or that the chart was not adequately defined. Unproductive manipulation typically happens in organizations that continually make small changes to the structure for political reasons, not adequately considering how those changes will affect flows.

Improving the flow of people through an organizational chart involves succession planning and talent development. Decision-makers can create beneficial flow when they base promotions, transfers, succession plans, and learning opportunities on competent planning and fair decision-making practices.

Workflows are supported by organizational charts and are executed as part of daily responsibilities. The quality of workflows is affected by policies and procedures, the availability of resources, the collective competence of the team, learning opportunities, and the effectiveness of technology.

Policies and procedures provide guidelines for workflows and related decision-making. Ideally, policies should be designed with some flexibility built into them. They should not be overly granular, nor should they be too ambiguous. The point of equipoise between rigidity and flexibility will differ from one organization to another.

Succession planning supports the movement of employees through an organizational chart. It involves developing employees to assume different roles. Planning for succession and talent development prepares organizations for movement of people in the event of anticipated or unexpected vacancies.

Succession planning and talent development operate in tandem with recruitment and retention—together they coalesce into flows that operate in a loop where there is a steady stream of employees entering an organization and while others leave.

Sometimes a succession plan does not generate prepared successors in time for a vacancy to be filled. This means leaders need the right decision-making skills to strike a right balance between internally developed employees and external acquisitions. The combination should be defined by the cultural vision and strategic goals of an organization.

Inadequate talent development practices can be problematic: they can cause decision-makers to place underprepared internal candidates in roles prematurely, blocking succession opportunities for high potential team members who are further down the ladder. Inadequate practices can also result in bringing in external hires who restrict opportunities for others. From a strictly pragmatic perspective, if you are not developing your talent at a rate that is compatible with changes in your external environment, competitive forces can squeeze your organization right out of the market.

Although job descriptions define employees' duties, each one is part of a larger group of tools that provide structure for work and other flows. Job descriptions are more effective when they are written in a way that connects relevant work and other flows. In this way, unnecessary impediments to flow—such as omitted essential duties or job overlap that can lead to conflict—can be avoided.

When considering whether performance management tools are drivers or facilitators of flow, I prefer to categorize them as facilitators. This is because they provide the framework for flow, whereas drivers tend to be internal motivators. Despite this, others may consider them to be drivers because they define performance expectations that are linked to rewards.

While performance evaluations, 360-degree multi-rater assessments, delegated authorities, and other performance enhancing tools are intended to facilitate flow, unreasonable goals can engender apprehension, which can result in unnecessary mistakes or lapses that negatively affect flow in the medium to long term. Fear can also drive highly functioning employees and strong results, but it is difficult to support optimized flow, because fear suppresses creativity and sometimes disrupts (true) synergies.

Flow and Resources

Resources directly affect the efficacy of the IFB Model. In addition to people, they include an organization's cash, materials, and assets. When resources are in short supply, work can be suspended or bottlenecked. An unplanned stoppage or delay in important workflows can present serious challenges to an organization's strategy.

Technology is a resource that serves to both drive and facilitate flow, even though investing in technology (hardware and software) doesn't guarantee performance. Technology drives flow by automating it, and facilitates flow by permitting input, enabling processing, and providing output. If the technology acquired is not the right solution, or if users are not adequately trained, flow can be genuinely compromised.

Money as a Resource

I deliberately excluded revenue, profitability, and investment as drivers of flow. This is because money is an effect, not a cause. In multiple organizations, the prevailing practice is to create a budget annually, forecast regularly, honor accounts payable, and make investments all in an effort to create the effect of making more money.

Unconscious money mantras like "Don't spend what you don't have" or "Save for a rainy day" reflect some leaders' relationships with money. Positive ones like "I will always have the money I need" and "Money makes the world better" stimulate an entirely different range of emotions. As long as thoughts of scarcity, stockpiling, fear, or greed influence decisions about organizational expenditure and investments, they can hinder flow.

Similarly, decision-makers with positive money mantras will attract the money they need as a resource to purchase other resources. So it is not the money that attracts or repels, it is the thoughts and emotions behind your financial decisions that drive flow.

Flow and Strategy

While strategy is part of the interconnective structure, it is also a flow driver because it defines what gets done, the urgency of the work, and whether money or other resources will be allocated to an activity.

Strategy is based on the vision, mission, core values, and purpose of your organization. Therefore, the essence of these strategic considerations should be incorporated into everyday decisions, work, and interactions. Strategy is one of the potentially unifying platforms that supports the flow of results in the present and future. It dictates where attention should be placed because it organizes workflows according to goals and priorities. Strategy is also the framework for the formulation of shared goals, which can help bring employees and departments together, especially when is trust is damaged.

Strategic plans are usually driven by multiple flow drivers: belief in and adherence to the organization's vision, mission, and values; clear definition of deliverables; engagement; and a leadership team's capacity to connect meaningfully with their colleagues.

Removing Obstacles to Flow

Whether you are completely redesigning flow or removing obstacles from an existing system, a well-thought-out blueprint of your flow substructure is essential. Flow charts or process maps can supplement procedures, strategic plan implementations, and problem-solving activities. When it comes to IFB, they can be used to identify and remove obstacles to flow — like malfunctioning technology, inadequate training, or ineffective leadership.

Obstacles to flow can emerge at any point during a process, which means leaders need to monitor connectivity regularly — especially in circumstances in which weak interconnectivity knowingly exists. In Chapter 3, we explored the nature of relationship architecture. We learned that interpersonal relationship patterns directly affect flow, especially when the relationship architecture is weak.

When considering removing obstacles to flow, a quote by Albert Einstein came to mind: "No problem can be solved from the same level of consciousness that created it."[4] In other words, when the people who made an inferior decision attempt to solve the resultant complications without introducing new perceptions of the challenge and addressing their emotional ties to their failing idea, they may attempt to correct an unsuitable idea that will remain inappropriate, no matter how much they try to improve it.

Flow and interconnectivity operate interdependently so leaders need to be able to perceive them in an integrated way. The following list identifies interpersonal dynamics that can be blind spots that can hinder flow:

- autocratic managers fuel low trust levels and can cause delays in output when employees are forced to refer every decision
- overanalyzing that delays decision-making
- fear of confrontation, resulting in decreased productivity because no one is willing to rock the boat
- ineffective planning and execution that lead to failed change implementations and potentially compromised results
- incompetent managers and coworkers who fuel low engagement levels
- the lack of a shared vision that can lead to delays, mistakes, and lack of coordination — all of which can block flow
- ineffective communication (uncoordinated timing, underperforming communication channels, etc.)
- low trust that negatively affects engagement

- when there are silos, communication can be hindered due to divisive norms embedded within each team

When executives can't clearly perceive an obstacle, a holding pattern can result. One example of this is when decision-makers can't fully visualize or understand the vision for flow and unconsciously revert to actions that are familiar and safe. They take past, sometimes irrelevant, modes of thinking and integrate the new into the familiar. Despite decision-makers' best efforts, their inability to perceive unconscious habits while executing change can lead to little or no change in flows, blocking the potential for flow enhancement.

Case Study: Recognizing and Removing the Obstacles

Lilly and Ann recently met their new department manager, David. The previous manager, Marie, is retired and has a personal friendship with Lilly that developed during their work in the same department eight years ago.

David is younger than Marie and new to the organization, so he doesn't have an established network of organizational relationships. Ann views Marie's departure as an opportunity to advance her career. She joined the company three years ago and believes she would be further along in her career if she had not been subjected to Marie's limiting biases.

Within David's first week of joining the team, he scheduled a meeting with the members of his team to discuss their roles and career aspirations. However, Ann had an alternative plan in mind. When the two met, Ann seized the opportunity to complain about Marie and the perceived favoritism she exhibited toward Lilly. In the interest of understanding team dynamics, David allowed Ann to express herself. As it so happened, other employees also seemed to share this opinion.

When David met with Lilly, he asked her about the rumors in a way that suggested to Lilly that he believed they were true.

Lilly was disappointed that David seemed to have made up his mind about her. To make matters worse, she wasn't entirely sure who complained about her, so she became suspicious and stopped engaging the team as she had in the past. It was hard for Lilly to trust anyone now that she was aware of how they really felt about her.

Because Lilly felt attacked, she withdrew from the members of her team. This had far reaching effects because Lilly was a top producer, so her withdrawal affected overall results, creating delays due to bottlenecks and impaired communication. Overall team results declined because Lilly stopped collaborating as she had in the past, she no longer wanted to be part of a team that betrayed her.

Lilly's changes in behavior presented a significant flow challenge because what her coworkers failed to tell David was that Lilly consistently outperformed the rest of the team. They also neglected to mention that she always assisted her coworkers through peer coaching and providing clarification about policies and procedures.

In this case, the rate of flow decelerated because David appeared to jump to conclusions about Lilly without establishing the facts for himself. As David was new to the team, he should have been cautious about drawing conclusions too soon. Now trust issues exist within multiple relationships because he unintentionally alienated his best performer.

To correct this, David can obtain the missing information, apologize to Lilly for his premature reaction, commit to different behaviors in future, and stick to them. Then he should demonstrate behaviors that bring balance to the team and ensure each member feels valued.

Shifting Systems of Power

When power and political dynamics are present within organizations, they can be helpful or create obstacles to flows, depending on how they are used. Power can become a significant obstacle to flow when it is used unproductively; in fact, some power dynamics can sacrifice the welfare of the team to strengthen personal agendas.

Within organizations, people exhibit unique patterns of interaction that define systems of power and influence. When leaders decide to shift their cultures away from unproductive power structures, they should first understand why those dynamics exist. Early identification of root causes can lead to better informed IFB design and planning.

As noted in our exploration of interpersonal relationships, leaders cannot dictate how relationships should operate. Attempting to force interaction is just another abuse of power. Therefore, when a major cultural shift is necessary, leaders should invite their team members to participate in developing cultural models and plans that refashion unproductive patterns of power into empowered ones.

CHAPTER 6

INTEGRATING INTERCONNECTIVITY AND FLOW

*Leadership is unlocking the people's potential
to become better.*

— Bill Bradley, professional athlete and politician

This chapter reinforces the notion that interconnectivity and flow happen consecutively and simultaneously. You will be provided with tools you can use to analyze interconnectivity and flow in an integrative way. They can provide rich insights into opportunities and risks related to interconnectivity and flow within your organization. As you read this chapter also keep in mind the reality that even though there are inseparable linkages between interconnectivity and flow, all three components of the model — interconnectivity, flow, and balance — operate as a unified ecosystem.

Despite constant motion, space exists within the IFB Model. For example, the space between interconnectivity and flow exists as potential, and adept leaders can detect potential within relationships and take proactive steps to close the gaps between their current state and future possibilities.

From an organizational perspective, silos establish space within and between departments. This space represents potential for enhanced productivity that can be achieved using conflict resolution skills, adaptive leadership, training, and effective communication practices. Leaders should be able to detect these opportunities, so they can maximize them. The following questions can facilitate this exploration:

- Where is the potential or space?
- Why does it exist?
- How can we stimulate engagement between two siloed teams?

Chapter 6 introduces the Interconnectivity and Flow Tool, a resource that provides decision-makers with insights into the relationships between interconnection and flow. They can use this information to investigate causation. The Interconnectivity and Flow Tool is versatile because it can be used to delve into internal and external connectivity and flow combinations. Chapter 16 expands on this tool, providing guidelines for using it to develop and implement plans for IFB.

Why Integrating Interconnectivity and Flow Is Important

Viewing an organization from the combined perspective of inter-connectivity and flow can help with troubleshooting, problem solving, strategizing, and numerous other exercises. It also reduces the need to rely on anecdotal information by providing a more objective framework for insight and assessment.

Individual emotion is directly linked with personal and team flow states. When a person is in the zone, they are in a creative, productive, and unfettered state. The integrated Interconnectivity and Flow Tool can be used to enhance this.

In environments dominated by control, people can be motivated extrinsically by job security concerns or the related fear of being marginalized for nonconformance. If control is a dominant characteristic of your culture, team members are most likely limited to a narrow definition of flow that involves getting the job done within rigid parameters established by policies and procedures. In circumstances like this, the Interconnectivity and Flow Tool can be used to clarify control dynamics, highlighting existing and potential obstructions that need to be removed so leaders can open the capacity of their teams.

The Interconnectivity and Flow Tool

The Interconnectivity and Flow Tool illustrates six combinations of interconnectivity and flow that can exist within an organization. One combination of interconnectivity and flow may prevail, or there might be multiple configurations—a different one in each department. Leaders who don't envision or understand the dynamics of interconnectivity and flow in their organizations run the risk of making substandard decisions. When this happens, these leaders can be blindsided by unexpected outcomes.

For instance, a sales director launched an incentive program designed to enhance the results of her team. She was excited about the opportunity for employees to earn additional income, but once the program was launched, there was very little interest in the incentive.

In this example, the director offered an incentive to the sales team to help the business meet and exceed established targets. Incentives worked in the past, so it seemed like a surefire way to stimulate results. A month after the launch, executives were at a loss to explain why the enhanced commission opportunity produce the anticipated results.

After investigating the circumstances, decision-makers discovered that they had overlooked the fact that the sales director was recently appointed and the relationship between her and her team was impaired because of her divide and conquer approach to leadership.

The sustained tensions led to low trust levels so team members who used to work together amicably were no longer willing to collaborate. If the executives had recognized this earlier in the process, they could have realized the team was divided and disengaged; in response, they could have taken steps to rebuild trust, so the incentives could have the desired effect.

Figure 6.1 is a framework for mapping the state of interconnectivity and flow for interpersonal relationships. It is a prioritizing tool that can be used along with the Relationship-Strengthening Potential Tool already introduced. It highlights combinations of interconnectivity and flow that can exist within an organization.

Leaders interested in applying the IFB Model should remember that no combination is better or worse than another. They are each appropriate in some circumstances and less so in others. As with other aspects of the IFB Model, the suitability of the combinations depends on the vision, mission, and strategic goals of your organization.

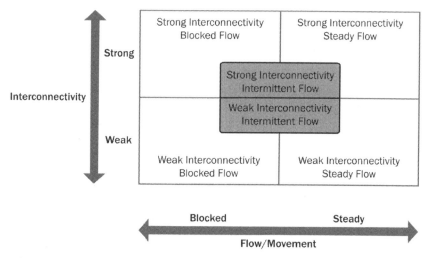

Figure 6.1   *The Interconnectivity and Flow Tool*

Two dimensions of interconnectivity are reflected in the tool: strong and weak. The types of flow represented are steady, intermittent, and blocked. The difference between blocked and intermittent flow is that blocked flow is completely obstructed. You will recall that steady flow occurs when movement is continuous, and the rate of flow doesn't change much. Steady flow can shift into optimized flow from time to time. Intermittent flow is movement that happens in equal or unequal intervals. Steady flow can change pace, or it can shift to intermittent flow.

The Interconnectivity and Flow Tool is flexible enough to highlight both optimal and underperforming connections. If an employee relates well with their team members, but is not performing up to standard, decision-makers can determine whether the person's performance can be improved. You shouldn't allow bias to cause you to miscalculate any employee's value to the team. This is a disservice to both the employee and the organization.

Figure 6.1 identifies six combinations of interconnectivity and flow that can help decision-makers better understand their current state and craft an appropriate plan. They are further described below.

Weak Interconnectivity, Blocked Flow

When this configuration exists, connectivity is weak or nonexistent and there is no flow at all. This may happen by design or because of impaired relationships and low trust. Sometimes trust levels are so low that people refuse to speak with each other. Depending on how long trust has been impaired, the relationships may not be salvageable.

I encountered this circumstance when consulting with a company operating in a mature market that was not making a profit after being in business for decades. The executive team lacked cohesion and as a result the entire company operated in silos. In fact, the executives actively undermined each other and sought to protect themselves at all costs. The company did not restore its financial standing until after the senior team was able to address their deep trust issues and started to collaborate.

The Relationship-Strengthening Potential Tool can be used as the basis for a conversation about the importance of trust, engaging the executives in the work relationship so they can buy into doing what they can to connect in ways that will better facilitate flow.

Strong Interconnectivity, Blocked Flow

Blocked flow results from planned stoppages or uncontrollable external factors like unexpected changes in demand, technical difficulties or resource scarcity. When strong interconnectivity and blocked flow coexist, relationships can be healthy or otherwise. When they are healthy, factors within or beyond the control of the team may contribute to the blockages.

As a diagnostic precautionary note, sometimes employees within a team or network seem to be strongly connected but are not. This sometimes happens when connections are politically motivated and those alliances shift when power dynamics change.

When considering what to do about strong interconnectivity and blocked flow, it is important to distinguish between healthy and unhealthy cohesive connections. When the strength of connectivity within an interpersonal network is assumed to be productive when it is not, the best change plans can fail.

While strong interconnectivity appears to offer the potential for improved future flows, it is no guarantee. Therefore, a deeper dive into the purpose and interactive norms of relationships can help you determine the relationship strengthening potential, better informing your planning process. The map of your relationship architecture can provide insight into this.

Weak Interconnectivity, Intermittent Flow

Intermittent flow can accompany weak interconnectivity. These fragile relationships can result from a variety of contributing of factors, namely:

- ineffective leadership
- highly political work environments
- unforgiving dispositions
- new team members
- difficult personalities

Whether only one of these factors or a combination of them exists, they can lead to weak interconnectivity and intermittent flow. For example, Jake and Sarah are members of an executive team. They only communicate with each other when they attend the same meetings. Trust eroded between them because they were both told they are strong contenders for the role of CEO.

Sarah discourages members of her team from communicating with Jake's department unless she is aware of it. While Jake didn't make the same request of his staff, they noticed the changes in communication and followed suit. As a result, important work was not being completed satisfactorily and critical deadlines were sometimes missed.

As with other combinations of interconnectivity and flow, decision-makers should consider the goals of the organization and then determine which relationships are most critical to team performance. If a relationship characterized by weak interconnectivity is contributing to intermittent flow and that flow needs to be changed, decision-makers can determine if potential exists for persons in the weakened relationship to improve their interactions. If not, staffing or the organizational chart and related process flows may need to be revisited.

Strong Interconnectivity, Intermittent Flow

Even though relationships may be durable when there is strong interconnectivity, intermittent flow can occur for various reasons:

- The team is inadequately trained.
- Market trends are shifting.
- Decision-makers are not sufficiently open to making changes.
- Intermittent flow is the plan.

One circumstance in which strong interconnectivity and intermittent flow may coexist is in unionized environments where the relationship between management and the union is strained. In settings like this, relationships among union members and within the management team can be strong even if the two groups are at odds.

Non-unionized senior leaders should view complex situations from the perspective of what is best for the entire organization. Union representatives may be more concerned about the best interest of their members. When conflict emerges between these stakeholder groups, the damaged relationships can trigger intermittent flow in the form a series of strikes or slowdowns.

Strong interconnectivity and intermittent flow can also happen within an underperforming team characterized by enduring relationships. In this situation, competence challenges, resource issues, and disengagement can all contribute to intermittent flow. When considering a solution, leaders should determine if intermittent flow is acceptable before they consider corrective action.

Weak Interconnectivity, Steady Flow

We have already established that steady flow can happen despite compromised connections. The example we will build on is when steady occurs when anxiety is driving it. In circumstances like this, employees in survival mode will do whatever it takes to meet their goals.

Sometimes their apprehension leads to intermittent or blocked flow because fear can cause errors. In spite of this possibility, disconnected teams that perform under duress can generate high-performing results. Leaders can identify weak interconnectivity by listening to how members of the team communicate with each other. Comments like, "I'm not here to make friends" suggest individualism, not an interest in connectivity.

Employees who work in environments that value structure and stability experience weak connectivity yet achieve steady results. In such cases, granular policies and procedures create an ever-present need for conformity, because the consequences of noncompliance are an effective deterrent.

Sometimes weak interconnectivity has nothing to do with controls. Competition can generate conflict and compromise relationships. As a result, relationships with coworkers can be sacrificed unless a given relationship is essential to a personal success agenda. Despite the risks, competitive environments can drive high-performing results because one or two individuals can vastly outperform the rest of the team, exceeding established team goals without collaborating.

When decision-makers identify weak interconnectivity and steady flow they need to determine whether there is potential for improving work relationships. If there is, they should envision how enhancements can expand the capacity of the team (keeping in mind the team will need to participate in and support any proposed changes).

Strong Interconnectivity, Steady Flow

Strong interconnectivity and steady flow can lead to high performance when trust, effective communication, and shared goals exist
within and between teams. When these circumstances coexist, no
individual's work is more important than anyone else's, and everyone respects each other. Though conflict may exist, it is effectively
managed and leads to healthy outcomes. Under these conditions,
innovation and even optimized flow are possible if the team can shift
into the zone and operate there for a period.

When steady flow doesn't meet a company's performance expectations, the root causes need to be uncovered and addressed. When
a steady rate is too slow to meet established goals, decision-makers
should evaluate the reasons why and take steps to correct it. While
gathering information it is important to keep in mind a slow, steady
rate of flow doesn't have to mean the team is underperforming—it
can mean the product or service is labor-intensive. For example, an
haute couture gown with thousands of hand-sewn crystals takes a
great deal of time to create and this is acceptable. In contrast, if a
fast-food restaurant is serving at a slow rate, this signals a litany of
complaints.

Plotting Your People on the Interconnectivity and Flow Tool

During the diagnostic phase of the IFB change process, leaders can
use the Interconnectivity and Flow Tool (Figure 6.1) to plot multiple
(dyadic) interpersonal relationships to determine which ones are
facilitating or impeding flow, and which ones require strengthening (or not). By plotting relationships on the tool, leaders will have
a visual depiction of the relationship dynamics that reveals opportunities and risks—some already known, some hidden. The Interconnectivity and Flow Tool can uncover opportunities to strengthen
relationships, so changes can be made to prioritized relationships
after using this tool to analyze the ecosystem.

We have already established that leaders can also use the
Interconnectivity and Flow Tool to plot relationships between

departments. By using the tool to assess systems from a bird's-eye view, decision-makers can examine who is connected and seek to uncover the nature and quality of those connections.

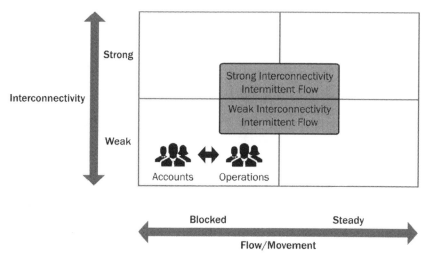

Figure 6.2   *How to Use the Interconnectivity and Flow Tool*

In Figure 6.2, two departments are represented. The finance department is a high-performing unit. The accounts payable team, operating within this department, typically processes vendor invoices by the prescribed deadlines — with the exception of requests made by the operations manager.

As it happens, the operations manager once worked in the internal audit department and was particularly steadfast in refusing to change an audit note assigned to the accounts payable team. Two members of the accounts payable team strongly contested the audit note, but their arguments fell on deaf ears.

Five years after the audit, the members of the accounts payable team are still bitter about this blemish on their otherwise perfect records. As a result, they are slow to respond to the operations manager's requests for vendor payments, causing poor vendor relations, and increased operational risks. When the operations manager complains, the accounts payable team always has a plausible excuse for their delayed responses.

In Figure 6.2, the relationship between departments is plotted in the weak interconnectivity and blocked flow quadrant. Based on the strategic goals of the executive team, the operations department needs to improve its performance. The relationship between finance and operations was identified as one of the causes of underperformance so decision-makers should determine if there is potential for improving the relationship between the accounts payable team and operations manager. Leaders should also consider the relationships between the operations department and vendors, assessing risks and planning how they might potentially mitigate those risks.

After you plot relationships on the Interconnectivity and Flow Tool, you can decide which individual, interdepartmental relationships can facilitate improved performance if strengthened. Once you define your priority relationships, you can proceed with stimulating transformation.

Designing Flow in Relation to the Interconnective Infrastructure

The remainder of this chapter provides ideas you can use to design flow that moves through the interconnective infrastructure in accordance with your strategic plans. Before starting this process, you should define your vision of flow, clearly articulating it using positive statements. So instead of saying, "We want to eradicate policies that impede flow," you should position the statement as, "We want to establish policies that facilitate flow." This wording is important because it sets a positive tone, more effectively facilitating the flow of ideas.

Figure 6.3 illustrates how trust, interconnectivity, flow, and balance overlay each other and function in an integrated way. The Pillar of Trust is at the heart of the entire IFB Model, so by extension, trust affects the quality of relationships, and the quality of relationships affects flow leading to balance or imbalance.

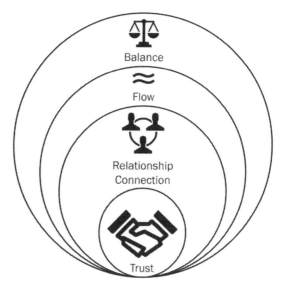

Figure 6.3 *The IFB Model: Another Vantage Point*

Relationships and Flow Design

During the flow design process, leaders can use the information gathered from the Relationship Map and the Relationship-Strengthening Potential and Interconnectivity and Flow Tools. When applying these tools during the design process, leaders can use diagnostic information to craft ways to optimize connections and related flows.

Leaders Enabling Flow through Relationships

Leaders who wish to empower others take the time to understand the fluctuating states of relationships and the effectiveness of flows. Such leaders know that trust and respect are the foundation for healthy flow, so they are diligent about identifying obstacles to collaboration and transforming systems that are not aligned with it. Because different types of flow happen both simultaneously and consecutively, flow in one context can affect flow in another.

Case Study: Interdepartmental Flows and Relationships

The back-office team depends on the customer service department for its daily work; it sets deadlines for the customer service department so work can be processed in time for delivery the next day. When the customer service department is late, workflows are interrupted, causing the back-office team to wait until the customer service department forwards the completed work.

Back-office employees become frustrated when the work from the customer service team is routinely late. They resent always having to work after hours while the members of the customer service department go home on time. They don't mind being delayed occasionally, but they do mind frequent late nights. As animosity grows, morale deteriorates. It makes matters worse when attempts to control overtime costs cause the back-office manager to defer processing to the next day, adding the work overflow to the regular workload.

In this case study, the relationship between the two teams is weak and workflows between departments are not operating according to set deadlines. Members of the back-office team feel they are being penalized for something that is not their fault, while the team causing the delays is being rewarded by leaving work on time and receiving better bonuses.

To resolve this challenge, leaders need to view flow from a strategic perspective, reviewing customer traffic, work flows, and other patterns to understand the reasons for delays. Flow also needs to be analyzed from the perspective of relationship quality, because focusing exclusively on process challenges will not necessarily strengthen relationships in ways that can sustain desired results.

In the context of a merger or acquisition, employees in each organization have unique ways of relating to each other. To understand organizational compatibility from people and cultural-risk perspectives, leaders can use the IFB relationship mapping tool kit to define how individuals and teams interact within each organization.

The tools also help decision-makers understand how these organizational patterns of interaction are compatible or oppositional. In this way they can better determine what needs to be done to minimize people risks related to a merger.

Designing Flow through Communication Channels

Information should be communicated in a way that ensures the message being sent is received when and how intended. Therefore, the ability of a team to articulate clear, well-timed, trusted messages is essential to flow.

Depending on the content of a message and the climate of the organization, a trusted leader may be the best person to deliver a message. However, even though a trusted messenger may be ideal, if the message compromises trust in the messenger, the leader delivering the message can end up with a damaged reputation and risks not being trusted in the future.

Opening communication channels is an important part of the design process. An internal communication audit provides insight into what needs to be done to improve communication. The following questions can help you consider the quality and effectiveness of your attempts to communicate:

- Which communication modes are you using?
- Which ones are effective? Which are not? Why/why not?
- Which communication modes are not being used and should be considered?
- Which messages need to be communicated and how often?
- How effective are the messages? What is the best way to assess their effectiveness?

The ability to open channels of communication and enable flow is an essential IFB leadership skill. Another critical leadership competency is identifying which relationships can facilitate improved information flows and which ones cannot.

Meetings are one type of communication mode that should be evaluated. Opening channels of communication requires reviewing the effectiveness of interactions during meetings. Decision-makers should review who should attend, who attends, what the agenda should be, the effectiveness of the chairperson, and how the meetings can be improved so they are most efficient.

Decision-makers should pay attention to communication modes and channels, so they can observe patterns of flow. These IFB leaders are aware that the accuracy and timeliness of information moving through channels affects a variety of flows. Therefore, they know that quality communication not only needs to be accurate and well timed, it also should be transparent, thoughtful, considerate of diverse views, and fair.

When contemplating communication channel design, be sure your design identifies targeted groups and individuals (both internally and externally) and pairs them with compatible modes of communication. This increases the likelihood of dissemination and review of information being shared. For instance, some teams consisting of a majority of millennials use popular online applications to connect with each other. Because this is one of their preferred communication modes, they are more inclined to engage.

When you decide to match communication modes to the preferences of your team, consider the demographics and which communication tools will best stimulate their engagement. You should also think about what you can do to mitigate the risks related to ineffective transmission of your message (delays, resistance, etc.) and build contingencies into your flow plan to address the potential for communication failure.

Designing Flow in Relation to the Organizational Structure
Organizational structures can enable or constrict flow, either inten-tionally or inadvertently. Because of this, effective flow design requires careful consideration of relationships—as previously

indicated — as well as an understanding of the mechanics of the types of flow these relationships enable.

Board Governance and Flow

Board members facilitate flow by supporting executives with their strategic planning efforts or by getting involved (sometimes inappropriately) in the operation. Board overreach can lead to conflicting priorities or inadequacies related to delegated authorities; it can also underscore deficiencies in the code of conduct or underperformance of the executive team.

When designing flow, decision-makers should take care to illuminate board practices during the diagnostic phase so a baseline understanding of board-facilitated flows and obstructions can be established. Board governance documents, interviews with upper-level managers and executive directors, and an examination of the minutes can also support the diagnostic process.

Designing Organizational Charts

The next structure to consider is the organizational chart. The configuration of your organizational chart can enable flow based on how you structure your departments and related job descriptions. When designing your organizational chart, one school of thought is that the design should be based on the strategic needs of the organization. While this purist approach may be preferred by some organizational design specialists, a more holistic approach should be the standard when applying IFB principles.

Well-rounded IFB design methodology involves integrating social dynamic considerations into the chart design. This is because work flows often involve human interaction; therefore, wherever there are damaged relationships, there is the potential for these relationships to interfere with the capacity of team members to operate according to the chart design.

Additionally, if participants in the organizational chart design process have mixed agendas, the office politicians around the table can persuade others to make changes to charts, that do not serve team goals. For example, when politics infiltrates the design and planning phases, reporting lines may be altered, or workers can be transferred or promoted based on power plays. Therefore, it is important for decision-makers to pay strict attention to unproductive informal dynamics, so they can design organizational charts that serve the greater good.

Succession and Flow

You can facilitate flow through your organizational chart by developing a robust succession plan. With a succession blueprint supported by a talent-development plan, top performers can be positioned for internal promotions when an appropriate role becomes available. Even transferring employees laterally into positions that are a better fit can create desired flows, sometimes affecting multiple departments.

Some organizations employ weak talent acquisition practices, recruiting employees based on passive sourcing strategies. These organizations tend to spend insufficient time actively seeking potential employees, to find the best possible fit. Instead, they opt to limit their efforts to an existing pool of applicants. While flow can be possible when new hires are not the best fit, team performance is better served when new employees are the right match for their respective roles and cultures.

Based on observation, the more conscientious leaders are focused on developing talent, the more likely it is that they can engage their teams and retain their best people. Without effective succession and talent-development plans, vacancies can be filled with underdeveloped internal candidates, or external candidates who may not be compatible with the organization.

Career paths define potential routes employees can take to achieve their work-related goals. These paths should be aligned with current and future organizational charts and provide employees with sufficient alternatives for their development. As noted, movement along career paths can be lateral, to gain breadth of experience, or vertical, to assume additional responsibilities. Not all career paths are linear. An example of a nonlinear career path is a spiral one, which has elements of both lateral and vertical movement.

Career paths can be leadership-focused, or they can establish structure for expert paths that develop employees' technical competencies. This means experts can develop a combination of technical skills specific to their strengths as well as the needs of the team. When employees possess the required competencies and drive, and those skills are aligned with their talents, they are more likely to take ownership of their careers and performance. When employees assume ownership, their engagement supports strengthened patterns of flow.

Another structural tool that's important to include in the design and planning of succession flow is job descriptions. If ambiguous duties, or overlapping ones create conflict they can be clarified or separated, not only to resolve conflict, but to also optimize workflows facilitated by the relationships.

Policies, Procedures, and Flow

Two critical components of organizational structure are policies and procedures. Before planning the integration of IFB in an organization, a review of the policies and procedures and how they support or obstruct flow can provide designers with the information they need to determine if existing guidelines are counterproductive to envisioned IFB outcomes. As a precautionary note, policies and procedures should not be examined in isolation. As with other structures, reviewers should also pay attention to the cultural context and the capabilities of employees implementing changes.

When decision-makers adopt a practice of creating policies every time an extraordinary situation occurs, managers are not given the space to develop their problem-solving acumen. When this happens, these decision-makers undermine the collective ability of the management team to lead and make decisions. To better support flow, decision-makers should determine where the organization should exist on the spectrum of innovation and control. With this information in hand they can revisit the policies and procedures to identify which ones need to be created, changed, or eliminated to achieve their goals.

When reviewing your structure in preparation for IFB design and implementation, remember that formal and informal policies and procedures can exist concurrently. Sometimes informal policies and processes are more prevalent than documented ones; this often results from not taking time to commit them to writing. Informal policies are especially important to formalize if they override or contradict formal ones.

The presence of both formal and informal practices can result in dominant nonstandard processes and general confusion. While irregular practices may get work done, they aren't always the best way to go. This is because when nonstandard practices prevail and something goes wrong, it can take much longer to resolve errors. Employees attempting to correct these errors may not be familiar with the nonstandard practice, so they are learning while they are deconstructing the failed process.

Case Study: Technology Inc.

Technology Inc. recently replaced a software solution that was no longer meeting the needs of the business. Based on the sales pitch, the company expected the functionality of the new technology to give it a competitive advantage.

Once Technology Inc. purchased the software, multiple issues derailed the implementation process causing delays and significant cost overruns. Employees recognized the inadequacy of the software almost immediately and because their feedback was being ignored, they stopped using the new technology.

To make matters worse, the responsible executive refused to acknowledge the new technology was not performing as expected. Her resistance to the feedback from the customer service team led to a stalemate because employees continued to insist that the technology was negatively affecting their ability to meet established customer service standards.

After being ignored, the customer service team took matters into their own hands and informally adopted a manual system they used whenever the technology malfunctioned. They reverted to processing entries this way because (from their perspective) the manual process worked where the new one didn't. By word of mouth, the manual process was informally instituted slowing down service.

Instead of rejecting feedback, the executive responsible for the project needs to be open to the input of those tasked to implement the new technology so the company can attempt to establish the intended quality of flow that should have been facilitated by the new technology.

The standardization of policies and procedures is especially important when a business is in growth or expansion mode and branding is a high priority. It is also critical when two organizations are merging and alignment of their policies and procedures is critical to the success of their integrative efforts.

It is realistic that given daily pressures, employees can become reliant on asking questions rather than reading policy manuals. In organizations where this is the prevailing practice, if policies and procedures are documented but not adhered to, operational risks can result. When leaders within these organizations rely on a convention of oral communication of policy and procedural information, flow can be negatively affected by erroneous interpretations and execution.

Another counterproductive policy-related scenario can occur when policies are in place and being followed, but the policies have not evolved with the business. This happens when no one is assigned responsibility for ensuring that policies continue to be relevant. This neglect or oversight creates a dynamic where out-of-date policies can constrain the business.

Your vision for policies and procedures should clearly illustrate how policies will affect your organization, what types of situations warrant policies and procedures, and which scenarios allow leadership discretion.

Case Study: Fast Growing Inc.

Fast Growing Inc. is experiencing unprecedented growth. It accumulated $50 million in assets in the last two years, and leaders rely on policies and procedures to improve their likelihood of success. Over the years, Fast Growing Inc. ended up with six different sources of policies and procedures. Guidelines were recorded in manuals, emails, best practices documents, and flow charts. They also distributed their standards via word of mouth.

With so many sources of policies and procedures, the contradictions were confounding for employees. On the other hand, some team members perceived this as an opportunity and used the multiple sources of policies and procedures to their advantage, electing to adhere to the versions that best support their agendas.

As organizations grow, it is incumbent on decision-makers to ensure that satisfactory structures are established. Structures like policies and procedures should be reviewed periodically to ensure they are not unintentionally limiting organizations when growth goals are a priority.

While some policies and procedures are more flexible than others, it is important that they facilitate work flows effectively, ensure quality standards are upheld, and are clearly communicated. Outdated, irrelevant ones should be removed regularly to minimize risks.

Integrating Flow and Strategy into Your Design

Members of a team should all be familiar with the vision, mission, and values of their organization. For flow to be driven by shared goals, these three components of strategy require buy-in by the majority at a depth where each component is aligned with everyone's mental and emotional models, thereby becoming an integral part of their workplace DNA.

When decision-makers align the strategic goals of the organization with the performance goals of employees, optimized flow is possible.

More specifically, strategic HR goals are connected to operational goals, operational goals are connected to sales goals, and sales goals (and others) should be integrated into individual performance management tools—the entire process should be connected. If the team is cohesive, and coworkers buy into established goals, optimized flow can happen.

Creating a design for your strategic plan means ensuring the elements of your plan are appropriately defined and connected, so they can facilitate flow. Designing strategy using IFB principles requires ensuring the strategic plan adheres to IFB principles. This is not a typical strategic consideration, but it can help organizations identify potential obstacles and opportunities that can be addressed during the planning, implementation, and balancing phases.

As with other design processes, IFB strategic design happens before and during the planning process. It involves applying the IFB Model to the basic elements of strategy previously emphasized: the vision, mission, core values, and goals. This strengthens the plan and enhances its potential for successful execution. Answering the following questions can help leaders make decisions that culminate in strategic IFB design parameters that inform the planning process:

- How can we ensure there is a clear relationship between our vision and goals?
- Where should we place our emphasis in the short term, so we can strengthen our probability of long-term success?
- How will flows introduced by the strategic plan affect or be affected by flows related to daily transactions?
- What is the relationship between our talent development goals and strategic priorities?
- What are the barriers to successful execution of our plan? (Consider the interconnective infrastructure and balance.)
- How ready is our organization for change?

This is not intended to be a complete list, so feel free to add questions to support the conversion of your strategic plan, ensuring that it operates in accordance with your IFB framework.

In an optimized state of flow, individuals and teams experience suspension of time because they are so absorbed in their creative work. Attaining this state requires very healthy relationships based in trust and competence.

In organizations where flow is adequate, teams can still yield high-performing results. This can be more than sufficient; it is conceivable that an optimized flow state may create imbalances in some circumstances. As you continue to explore, remember that balance has a unique configuration in every organization. What works for one will not necessarily work for another.

CHAPTER 7

THE ART OF BALANCE

Life is a balance between what we can control and what we cannot. I am learning to live between effort and surrender.

—Danielle Orner, writer and actor

Flow and balance are as intricately linked as interconnectivity and flow. For instance, leaders can take steps to enhance information flows, facilitating the movement of messages through their communication infrastructure. By enabling information flow, leaders provide team members with the knowledge they need, when they need it, with the goal of easing tensions.

When relationship quality is weak, this can cause message distortions and imbalances. When relationships are healthy, they have the potential to facilitate communication more accurately. IFB leaders know that interpersonal relationship quality directly affects the communication infrastructure, and structures influence flows and balance.

Bottlenecks are another example the effects of each component of the IFB Model on the others. They impede flow, creating imbalances within teams and organizations, especially when sustained over the long term. Productivity deceleration caused by these logjams leads to lower profits, which also manifests itself in reduced work hours for some—and reduced hours can trigger low engagement levels. In sustained unbalanced situations like this, relationships suffer because team members become frustrated by bottlenecks that affect their performance.

Even intentionally blocked flow needs to be facilitated so that balance can be maintained. For instance, strategic decision-makers choose to discontinue an existing product and introduce another, the operations team may need to balance the rates of production of both products so the slowdown of the existing product is synchronized with the initiation and acceleration of the new one.

Coordination with the goal of ensuring internal organizational balance requires managing people networks, developing individuals and teams, facilitating production processes, and other activities. External balancing includes strengthening vendor relationships and conducting market studies to ensure products continue to be aligned with the tastes and preferences of consumers.

Orchestrating a state of balance during and after an IFB implementation process requires leaders who can be deliberate about implementing all three components of the IFB Model. As previously mentioned, interconnectivity resides within networks of relationships where some connections are stable while others shift. Flow exists as perpetual movement through multiple human networks that operate simultaneously. Balance is not a destination or event; it is continuous, proactive, reactive or spontaneous. Achieving balance requires leaders who can detect tensions in an organization and determine where the greatest risks lie so they can initiate appropriate balancing actions.

Though planning and execution are necessary for balancing various conditions at work, balancing is an art that requires instinct, awareness of the tensions embedded within interconnectivity and flow, and openness to exploration through trial and error. With external environments more frequently characterized by volatility, uncertainty, complexity, and ambiguity, encountering the unexpected is now the norm so adaptive skills have become increasingly valuable.

Leaders in IFB organizations require competencies they can use to perceive the presence of imbalances. Some balancing skills are innate, while others can be learned. Acquiring and sharpening these abilities is critical, as they aid leaders with correctly determining whether something is truly out of balance—as opposed to merely giving the appearance of being out of balance.

Here is one example of how leaders can bring an organization into balance. A regulatory agency needed to modernize to better meet the needs of the industry it regulates. There were a number of changes in the industry, but the agency was slow to introduce laws. Internally, agency decision-makers needed to update technology and restructure their organization, so they could be better equipped to enact the required laws.

Given persistent internal and external tensions, there was overwhelming pressure to align the agency with the evolving needs of its stakeholders. In response, agency leaders eventually made internal changes with the goal of catching up with the industry. But while the gap existed between evolving industry practices and the agency's relevance, there were deep differences of opinion about unregulated activities, and these divergent views caused tensions to grow.

Before the gap was eventually addressed by the regulatory agency, decision-makers spent time and money researching best practices, preparing new legislation, restructuring departments, and developing staff. After the changes were successfully implemented, agency leaders believed the organization was finally in balance, both internally and externally.

However, they took so long to catch up, the industry had already shifted again. Right timing and scenario thinking—a flexible strategic methodology that allows leaders to generate multiple scenarios—are important balancing skills that the senior regulators needed to get ahead of, or keep up with, changes in their external environment.

The regulators needed to constantly keep abreast of trends and use that information to forecast future shifts so it could keep up with (and influence) the industry. This means that balancing organizations is a constant and critical element of strategic and transactional conversations and activities.

Internal balancing requires leaders who can clearly perceive their organizations' intrinsic needs. They should ensure people risks are minimized through development, engagement strategies, and other initiatives. They also need advanced decision-making skills that will help them determine the right time to start, stop, and continue people, and other activities to ensure their organizations maintain balance. Balancing does not necessarily require compromise, sometimes it requires ingenuity.

Defining Balance

Tensions exist in organizations in multiple configurations: profitability vs. growth; long-term vs. short-term orientation, and high-performing vs. low-performing are three examples of such tensions. Each tension exists on a spectrum and multiple spectra can form a snapshot of the tensions that coexist within an organization.

Sometimes, as you address the tension on a single spectrum, you may create imbalances in others so you need to understand how they interact with each other. Therefore, as you define balance for your organization, you and your team can decide which tensions should be priorities, what balance should look like for each of those dimensions, and how you plan to bring them into balance.

Balance, in the IFB context, is not a utopian state in which everyone is carefree and there are no tensions. More realistically, work environments are dynamic and unpredictable, and varying degrees of tension coexist within each organizational ecosystem whether they consider themselves to be in balance or not.

Within organizations, balance functions as it does within the human body. Imbalances can develop within the body while it continues to function (sometimes optimally). Some of these imbalances take time to manifest, while others are immediately apparent. Our body's capacity to heal itself, depends on internal and external factors. Internal factors include the state of our immune system, the type of illness, and our attitude toward it. External factors include the effectiveness of medication the quality of our diet, and patient care.

Balance operates similarly within organizations. Both balance and imbalance coexist internally and externally — sometimes apparent, other times unseen. Therefore, leaders need to be skilled at detecting high-risk interconnective and flow imbalances so they can correct them proactively. Like the human body, performance is possible even when imbalances are present, so an organization can be profitable or successful in an out-of-balance state. However, there can be high opportunity costs associated with this that may not be immediately apparent.

Each organization has unique strengths and weaknesses that continually contribute to internal tensions. This is exacerbated by external factors. If leaders attempt to address every perceivable imbalance this would be futile. Instead, decision-makers can work toward creating and sustaining balance in critical areas of their organizations.

Without advanced balancing skills that engage the team, leaders may attempt to forcefully achieve balance using poorly coordinated, or reactive (unbalanced) actions, as opposed to coordinated responses connected to the vision for IFB, people considerations, and the strategic direction. Coercive action only serves to perpetuate imbalances.

As a reminder, balance can be considered at any stage of the IFB process — it doesn't have to be the third step. It can be planned and implemented regardless of which part of the model is being activated. The same is true for interconnectivity and flow. Each component of the IFB Model is connected to and overlaid by the others, operating simultaneously.

Figure 7.1 provides a visual representation of the balancing process that occurs within the IFB Model. IFB balance involves identifying, defining and prioritizing dimensions that should be in balance, using this information to plan and implement interconnective and flow changes, and then, adapting the design to address projected and unexpected curve balls.

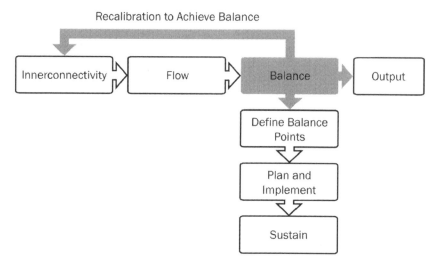

Figure 7.1   *Balance in the Context of the IFB Model*

The Importance of Balance

The path to achieving balance in one organization can be completely different in another—even among organizations in the same industry. For instance, two retail banks are achieving record profits. One uses a model that depends on improving operational efficiencies and increasing margins, while the other focuses on a single niche market to drive revenue and using aggressive sales tactics. Both achieve their respective definitions of balance, albeit through different business models.

As I will continue to emphasize, organizations can experience profitability whether they are in or out of balance. However, multiple studies show that it is trust, paired with healthy interpersonal interaction, that makes growth and innovation possible and sustainable. Interpersonal interactions fueled by trust and respect are necessary for the type of innovation that can drive business growth beyond profitability levels that are possible when the business culture is toxic.

So when taking balancing action, decision-makers should carefully observe how employees relate to each other and how those relationships contribute to or detract from balance. As part of their planning process, leaders should consider how the more influential relationships can be harnessed to achieve balance in the priority areas of the business.

Balance can happen in several ways: organizationally, it can be orchestrated from the top-down, it can start with an individual, or it can transpire because of concurrent personal and team balancing efforts. Personal, intrinsic balance occurs when there is alignment between an employee's personal values and goals and their actions. Once individuals display inner balance, they should orchestrate balance between their internal vales and the values of their employers.

Decision-makers who are competent at achieving intrinsic balance are better equipped to recognize external imbalances, determine underlying causes, make tough decisions, and initiate and execute balancing action plans. Although this book focuses on leaders, these skills are necessary to varying degrees, at all levels throughout organizations. The more people hone their balancing skills, the better the organization will become at flexibility, innovation, problem solving, people development, and growth.

Case Study: Coming Back into Balance

Sometimes a decision can temporarily create further imbalances, despite the intent to rectify existing or potential challenges. At other times, they do bring about anticipated results, restoring or maintaining balance.

Rita was an executive who worked for a company for more than two decades and was proud to be an integral part of their success. A year ago, her company merged with another organization, and Rita's leadership style was no longer relevant or appreciated. Over the years, Rita developed a style that was predominantly autocratic, but employees from the new organization were accustomed to a more adaptive leadership style. After the two companies merged, Rita's team expanded and employee morale dipped, creating imbalances within the departmental culture that affected customer service and business development.

After the company provided Rita with several opportunities to improve her leadership skills, it became apparent that she had no intention of making changes to how she led. This continued to create imbalances until Rita and her employer mutually agreed to part ways.

Rita's refusal to adapt her leadership style triggered imbalances within her team because the new employees made up 60 percent of her department and they could not relate to Rita's micromanaging style. Rita's successor was a junior executive who came from the other company. He was selected because of his proven ability to demonstrate the desired leadership skills. After Rita's departure, the new executive brought the department into balance. This required building and developing the Pillar of Trust.

Balance and Imbalance

Both balance and imbalance are inherent within interconnectivity and flow. Balance can turn into imbalance, and imbalance to balance. Both can be necessary, optional, or even unwanted, so one state is no better than the other. The appropriate state depends on the strategic goals established by organizational leaders. For example, decision-makers can achieve a healthy state of balance and then decide that while this is fine for the short term, maintaining the status quo will undermine the business in the long term.

When considering balance and imbalance, leaders need to be able to discern when a state of balance is no longer relevant or appropriate. They should also recognize when the current state of balance is approaching the full extent of its usefulness, so they can adapt, especially when there is significant risk. Decision-makers who are adept at maintaining balance do not under- or overestimate factors capable of throwing their operations into disequilibrium.

When decision-makers take their eyes off important balance goals, they risk slipping into an unproductive, out-of-balance state. In some instances, imbalances can lead to balance because risky, out-of-balance conditions can draw the attention of decision-makers who have the power to take corrective action. Sometimes imbalances can be deliberately orchestrated — like reducing supply to stimulate demand for a product or service.

Leaders in an IFB organization should be empowered to take collaborative action so they can reinstate balance when necessary. This may require rethinking delegated authorities and other structural tools. As you consider internal balance, remember that true balance cannot exist in a vacuum. Balance within your organization should be orchestrated in a way that establishes balance between your organization and its external environment.

When bringing your organization into balance, multiple core values require consideration. One of these is integrity, because it is central to the IFB concept of balance. When leaders value this attribute, they should identify where they fall on the continuum. This can be measured using a climate assessment or uncovered using qualitative data collection methods.

Once they establish the current state, organizational leaders may decide to work toward achieving balance. In transactional organizations this may mean they decide to shift from a predominantly transactional emphasis to an innovative one. Decision-makers might come to this conclusion when they realize they need both transactional and creative activities to survive. Before planning, they will need to decide how much emphasis they will place on both practices and how much they are willing to invest in resources because this type of change may require new staff, modified communication flows, and a more flexible strategy.

Leaders who decide to shift their activities from transactional to innovative might opt to place more emphasis on innovation until they achieve the desired balance state. To accomplish this, they can hire new staff, identify and develop employees with innovative proclivities, and assign leadership roles to early innovators so they can become champions for change. If the desired state requires a measured, incremental shift to innovation, the intent is not to get everyone to become innovative; rather, it is to create the proposed mix of innovative and transactional activities.

Types of Balance

Like flow, balance can be organic or managed. Organic balance flourishes when equilibrium unfolds naturally, without a plan. This can occur when dynamics within relationships naturally offset imbalances. An example of this is when two colleagues regularly go to lunch together until one abruptly leaves the organization. The lunches offered the colleagues an opportunity to provide each other with confidential support. Because of the abrupt departure, the remaining employee started to go to lunch with another coworker. If the new lunch partner does not treat their casual conversations as confidential, the result can create other imbalances.

Leaders who manage balance proactively understand the nuances of their culture and its generally accepted norms. They know when action is needed and when it is not. They know diversity can be healthy even though it may create periodic imbalances. They also know which imbalances will have a greater impact on the team. Such leaders approach balance as an art by taking balancing action when it matters.

Managed balance can also happen as a reaction. I witnessed this when a change in an industry forced an organization to adopt a reactive sales strategy to remain competitive. The company had an opportunity to respond earlier, but decision-makers underestimated the impact of the change because of their ability to diagnose the situation. To stay in the game and maintain their revenue-generation goals, decision-makers were forced to adopt a reactive, somewhat unclear strategy.

To manage balance, you need to pay attention to the quality of relationships and flow drivers so you can understand what is emerging as people interact. This will also help you understand whether balance is actual or apparent.

It is also important to consider the possibility that the lack of clear evidence of conflict does not necessarily mean you are in a state of balance. I have encountered decision-makers who have assured me that there was no conflict within their organizations when significant people-related tensions were present. In some instances, they were eventually blindsided as the conflict emerged from its latent state. When leaders are willing to resolve conflict, emergence can be a gift. When it festers under the surface for a long period, it can have far-reaching, unproductive effects.

If fear is present within an organization because of power struggles, leaders with political motives may aim to keep the climate in a state of imbalance because their personal agendas are a priority. For instance, sometimes power-hungry leaders create further imbalances by using threatening language. This leads to disengagement for nonpolitical team members if they are being forced to take undesired actions. It can also undermine the motivation of coworkers who aspire to power and politics, or it may inspire them to act similarly when they end up in a position of power. Whatever the case, power struggles preserve unhealthy imbalances.

Unproductive political work environments are risky; they can have far-reaching effects on organizational balance. This is because they can perpetuate people-related risks involving leadership, performance, retention, and succession — among others.

Even operational risks are affected by people considerations. In some teams led by autocratic leaders, employees may conceal evidence of operational risks. In such circumstances, when autocratic leaders find out and attempt to create balance by imposing a substandard solution, the outcome will likely be the opposite of what they are trying to achieve.

Types of Imbalances

When imbalances exist within a culture for an extended period, it can be difficult for leaders to shift important organizational dimensions into balance. Similarly, when certain balanced states become the hallmark of your organization's success, these states can make it challenging to make radical shifts because they've become part of your brand.

Causes of Imbalance

The complexity or number of changes in conditions that lead to imbalances doesn't matter. A single change in your conditions can lead to an imbalance as convoluted as multiple, successive, or simultaneous changes. Regardless the complexity, it is important to understand what makes an imbalance simple or complex so it can be resolved at the origin.

When seeking to uncover the origins of imbalances, decision-makers ought to be disciplined about identifying root causes. For instance, a nonprofit organization recently experienced a change in its executive director. Because of the differences in leadership styles, team members who used to speak up and share their ideas, stopped participating in meetings when the new executive director joined the team. It may be too soon to tell if there is a long-term imbalance but there is a change and it would be more productive to investigate – and not assume – the cause so the team can be brought into balance proactively.

Fewer ideas means team performance is potentially compromised. In this example, while it was clear that coworkers were not participating as they had before, it was difficult to get anyone to admit the executive director's leadership style was the cause. How can team members safely express their concerns to the person they perceive to be the perpetrator?

Alternatively, engaging the board with their concerns would also compromise the potential for building healthy work relationships. Unless the Board makes it their business to attune to workplace dynamics, the team will have to wait for relationships evolve – if they do – to address the leadership gaps.

It is not easy to improve engagement when the cause can be traced to an executive and historically, the executive was not held accountable. However, if the leadership team already has some type of engagement diagnostic in place, it can be used to provide insights that can help decision-makers determine why it declined.

Office politics is another well-known cause of organizational imbalances. Unproductive political dynamics tip the balance of power within an organization, especially when there are competitions for power at multiple levels. In highly political circumstances, the powerful minority consider themselves the primary possessors of power and influence, and the majority is subjected to the dynamics they create.

When enduring political intrigue yields shifting alliances, organizational goals can devolve into secondary priorities. Constantly shifting alliances make it difficult for team trust to be cultivated and for IFB principles to take hold.

When political players are overly focused on personal political agendas, their power can become an obstacle to team balance and performance. Unproductive power tends to be worn as a badge of honor and status, so when personal agendas override team goals, the privileged minority spend more time protecting their power base, carefully monitoring their networks, and constantly reinforcing relationships than doing what it takes to build their teams.

Highly political cultures can develop layers of power dynamics that not only contribute to imbalances, but also make it difficult to distinguish their true causes. This is because when unproductive political activities have penetrated a culture, clarity can be obscured by practices like corruption and deceit. These practices can lead to division and acrimony.

Emotions—such as fear, anger, and frustration—often emerge when office politicians are competing for power. People who choose not to engage the games remain on the periphery, hoping to avoid becoming casualties of war. When power-focused politicians are constantly in competitive mode, they can become consumed by the need to protect themselves and the people in their power networks who protect them.

This is all compounded when power ambitions damage relationships between people vying for status and the benefits that come with it. Relationships impaired by power are open to fear or anger. Fear of losing the power they have, and anger towards people who try to undermine them. When fear and anger are behind flow, imbalances emerge; some are covert, others obvious, and many are difficult to reconcile.

When a power player resigns from an organization, if the cultural practices that supported the power dynamics groomed a successor, the power dynamics will remain the same. Power dynamics organize into familiar patterns, even if the new appointee comes from another organization and is compatible with the existing system.

Cultures can exist within cultures in an organization, and each subculture can be similar to or different from the overarching culture. When subcultures are different from the overarching culture, this can sometimes be attributed to the nature of the work or skills required. In some cases, subcultures can even affect the dominant culture. Whatever the case, it is important to keep an eye on the diversity of cultures within your organization so you can detect existing and potential imbalances.

We have established that cultures with a disproportionate emphasis on structure and controls can thrive, meeting or even exceeding targets. You may ask yourself, "How can an imbalance exist if goals are being met or exceeded?" The answer is that some organizations prefer an emphasis on controls, and when controls are overly restrictive and your workforce longs for creative expression, voice, and the feeling of being valued, imbalances can be latent, revealing themselves as low engagement.

When leaders protect profitability at all costs and are unable or unwilling to perceive the side effects of imbalances caused by such single-mindedness, they may be forced to react when unforeseen imbalances lead to unanticipated outcomes. Leaders who set out to achieve organizational balance should first identify and remove the obstacles to perceiving imbalances. They include (but are not limited to):

- bias (positive and negative)
- generally accepted habits
- groupthink

- suspicion
- entitlement

Restoring balance is largely dependent on effectively facilitating human interactions. As with other components of the IFB Model, balancing can involve leaders emulating a productive value system, finding alternative placements for employees who are not the right fit, or recruiting new employees.

Balancing activities can also include training, but keep in mind the considerations that training comes with a learning curve and it should not be applied in isolation. Training should be accompanied by operational and other relevant plans, especially when imbalances are complex ones where cause-and-effect associations are unclear.

When leaders decide to initiate balancing action, they should acknowledge that sustaining balance or correcting imbalances calls for an investment of time, talent, and funds. If the total required investment is prohibitive, leaders can pursue IFB-related changes in stages, taking incremental steps toward a future balanced state. At each stage, leaders will need to evaluate the effects of their balancing efforts to ensure organizational equilibrium is sustained or achieved, whichever is appropriate.

The IFB Model of Balance

In complexity theory, an unclear cause-and-effect relationship exists when challenges are nonlinear and constantly evolving, yielding contradicting qualities. When a culture is imbalanced due to complex circumstances, leaders face unpredictability and difficulties requiring them to continuously sense and interpret information while attempting to bring their environments into balance.

Figure 7.2 provides a framework for the IFB Model of Balance. As with the IFB Model, it also operates in a loop. Even though this model emphasizes continuous balancing, remember that both interconnectivity and flow are integral to achieving it. The IFB Model of Balance is designed to support leaders in shifting their institutions to change-based organization status, so they can address change as an ongoing phenomenon rather than a one-shot initiative.

Diagnosis is the first step in the balancing process; it defines the current state. It can be facilitated as a scoping exercise. Scoping is an activity that provides decision-makers with information they need to determine the extent of change required. Data-gathering tools used during this process include surveys, focus group sessions, observation, and interviews.

In the IFB context, diagnosis is not an event—it is a process. Information gathered from diagnostic (scoping) processes is useful for designing the desired state. It helps decision-makers determine whether to modify existing systems or to replace them entirely.

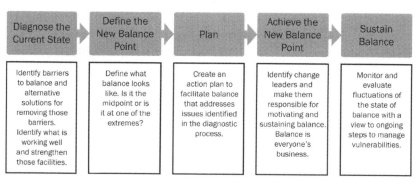

Figure 7.2   *The IFB Model of Balance*

The second step in Figure 7.2 is to define the new balance point. This involves considering the strategic direction of your organization, envisioning your ideal balance point (identifying where it should be on a spectrum), and designing a path to get there. Defining a new balance point can be pursued after change leaders analyze data collected during the diagnostic phase and envision desired future states.

Once leaders define balance points for high-priority dimensions of their organizations, they should review them all to ensure the new design doesn't create dynamics that contradict or neutralize each other. Then they can plan and implement the IFB balancing process. When it comes to balancing, the implementation stage requires execution, observation, and adjustment. Once the desired state of balance is achieved, leaders can then take the necessary steps to sustain it. This phase requires ongoing monitoring of the environment and taking actions necessary for bringing critical dimensions into balance.

As you consider Figure 7.2, you should contemplate the possibility that unforeseen circumstances can strengthen balance or introduce imbalances. They are inevitable within any organizational ecosystem, so consideration of multiple scenarios during the planning stage can minimize risks related to unplanned eventualities. As you have likely experienced, it is not possible to predict every possible scenario, so attunement, adaptability, and agility are also essential for reducing the potential effects of unexpected occurrences.

Diagnosing the Current State of Balance

We have established that on any given day, people within an organization can experience multiple tensions. Some of these pressures are obvious, others require deeper investigation. The critical ones should be prioritized because creating an exhaustive list can be confusing or worse, daunting.

Decision-makers can use the mission, vision, core values, and strategic goals to define priority dimensions, whether they are in or out of balance. Once priorities are defined and key dimensions selected, leaders can facilitate exercises to diagnose their current state of balance and if appropriate, they can analyze the trends and other factors that contribute to this state.

Previous examples of scoping (diagnostic) activities include interviews, surveys, and focus groups. The list of scoping activities also includes observation of daily processes and review of available data. When implementing the IFB Model, your scoping exercise(s) should identify and analyze the critical organizational dimensions that are linked to your strategic direction.

For example, when employee engagement is a strategic priority and a company's engagement survey results indicate only 26 percent of their workforce is engaged, they should not only use their scoping exercises to investigate causality, they should also seek to understand the spin-off tensions created by disengagement. In this way their strategic plan can also take derivative tensions into consideration.

When it comes to the IFB Model of Balance, priority tensions should be monitored continually so leaders can identify beneficial and unproductive patterns and then act on this information proactively. Preemptive adjustments depend on a variety of considerations like: costs, competing priorities, and readiness for change on the part of leaders and employees. Therefore, some of these changes have to be planned.

When leaders and their teams attempt to cover up tensions during diagnostic exercises, it makes it difficult to determine if there is true balance. False Balance Appearing Real (FBAR) is a condition in which team members appear to be operating in a balanced state, but it is merely a façade. Sometimes those involved in the diagnostic process can read between the lines and perceive this anomaly, but sometimes it is not so easy.

Realistically, leaders can attempt IFB implementations in organizations that have a track record of low engagement and trust. This can be a challenge because the scoping process should elicit accurate information. Some decision-makers attempt to overcome this by asking questions that focus on the work and process rather than the people. When trust is low this approach may help, but there are no guarantees. In some organizations, it would be better to first take the time to build trust before attempting to implement the IFB Model. This will of course take longer, but it will potentially yield more successful outcomes.

Using Balance Scales to Define Your Current State

Once the diagnostic process is complete, leaders can determine which dimensions are critical and require monitoring. Prioritization of your critical tensions requires addressing these questions:

- What should the desired state of balance look like? (You should consider the priority dimensions individually and collectively.)

- What will leaders do differently once the organization is in balance?
- What are the skills your leadership team will need to achieve and maintain balance?
- Which resources do we need to achieve and sustain balance?
- Which dimensions need to come into or remain in balance (according to strategic and IFB priorities)?
- Which dimensions will we allow to remain out of balance and for how long?
- If critical dimensions are in balance and they drift into disequilibrium, will the imbalance throw other important dimensions out of balance?

Figure 7.3 provides an example of how priority organizational tensions can be plotted on a scale to represent the current state. In Figure 7.3, the leaders responsible for scoping established the current state of balance and plotted it on the scale of innovation and control. This exercise helped them realize that while they were improving in the priority area of innovation, controls were being neglected, thus exposing the organization to potential risks.

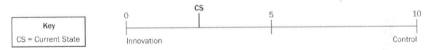

Figure 7.3   *Sample Innovation/Control Scale – The Current State*

In Figure 7.3, the scale represents the balance point (current state) of the dimensions—innovation and control. This same tool can also be used to support the definition of potential (future) balance states. Continuing with this example, the vision of the organization is to shift toward the midpoint on the continuum, so control and innovation can coexist with just enough emphasis on control, ensuring it does not adversely affect their goals for innovation.

Defining Future Balance Points (Establishing a Vision for Balance)

A balance point is a marked position on a scale that represents the current or desired state of tension between two polarities. So if a dimension is characterized as trust versus distrust, a point on the scale between these polarities can represent the current or desired state.

Even though some shift less often than others, balance points aren't static. They capture a state at a specific point in time. In Figure 7.3, the balance point represents the current state and is identified as "CS." Establishing the current state allows the design team to envision and design a desired balance point based on the strategic direction of their business.

There is no prescriptive list of organizational tensions (dimensions) that should be analyzed to determine whether your organization is in balance. Each leadership team should develop its own customized

Interpersonal Relationship Dimensions	Communication Dimensions
• Integrity vs. dishonesty • "We" vs. "I" disposition • Work vs. life balance • Engagement vs. disengagement • Inclusion vs. exclusion	• Coaching vs. criticism • Harmony vs. conflict • Multidirectional vs. unidirectional flow • Free to speak up vs. unsafe to speak up • Effective vs. ineffective messaging
Structural Dimensions	**Strategic Dimensions**
• Reward vs. punishment • Innovation vs. control • Leaders vs. managers • Competence vs. incompetence	• Strategic vs. transactional • Strengths vs. weaknesses • Opportunities vs. risks • Actual values vs. espoused values • Shared goals vs. personal agenda

Table 7.1 Examples of Balance Dimensions (Based on the IFB Interconnective Infrastructure)

list of priority tensions, informed by tools like its strategic plan, IFB priorities, enterprise risk assessments, audit results, core values, cultural priorities, and engagement survey results.

Table 7.1 exhibits organizational dimensions categorized according to the components of the Interconnective Infrastructure. These and other related dimensions may be important to leaders who are responsible for balancing organizations. As with other lists in this book, the lists below are not intended to be exhaustive. They are cited to stimulate your thinking.

Once you map the current state of various tensions, you can plot the desired state for the same dimensions shortly thereafter or wait until you complete the prioritization process during the design phase and then only plot the ones that take precedence.

Design and Plan

When change leaders complete the diagnostic and visioning exercises they will have created multiple scales identifying where balances and imbalances currently exist. After prioritizing tensions, leaders should remain open to the possibility that not even all the important imbalances warrant attention or adjustment. Why is this so? Changing one priority tension can concurrently shift one or more of the others in planned directions. Keeping this in mind, leaders can then focus on the dimensions that bring the most beneficial strategic results, ones they can leverage to create a favorable domino effect in the short to long term.

Prioritizing Goals Using the Balance Wheel

To prioritize the dimensions of organizations that require balancing, the executive team can facilitate an exercise that determines how satisfied they are with the state of each dimension. Viewing multiple critical dimensions at once supports deeper reflection on where balance and imbalances exist, their causes, and how these dimensions can be leveraged to establish, or recalibrate balance to improve the long-term viability of the organization.

Figure 7.4   *The IFB Balance Wheel Example*

Figure 7.4 is an example of how decision-makers rated their satisfaction with the dimensions plotted on the scales during the diagnostic exercise. Their satisfaction with each dimension is rated on a scale of 1 to 10. The ratings for each of the tensions are:

- operations (supports the strategic goals of the business vs. does not support) 8/10

- internal communication practices (effective vs. ineffective) 3/10

- innovation (meets the needs of the business vs. does Not Meet) 9/10

- adequate Structure (vs. inadequate structure) 9/10

- trust (vs. distrust) 3/10
- client care quality (high vs. low) 5/10
- profitability (exceeds expectations vs. does not meet) 7/1
- engagement (vs. disengagement) 3/10

This list of tensions is intentionally different from the list in Table 7.1 to show you the range of possibilities for balancing considerations. This list represents a mix of strategic and IFB tensions. You can create as many balance wheels as you need to make the best decisions possible. The point of this exercise is to help you prioritize. It brings clarity because it provides a big picture perspective that can help you uncover and address unexpected relationships.

The company in this example relies on controls to achieve its strategic goals. Generally, engagement levels are low, and this is echoed by the trust satisfaction score. This company drives profitability by enforcing compliance with policies and procedures. The research and development department remains innovative because it maintains a different culture from the rest of the organization. This satisfaction rating may also reflect the possibility that leaders of a company with profits driven by tight controls have a different definition of innovation than decision-makers in innovative organizations.

Product innovation is rated 9/10 because research and development are core strengths of the company. However, the teams are siloed and because of weak communication practices and low trust levels between R&D and the rest of the company there is a weak connection between the innovation and operations teams.

In other words, innovations are not being operationalized as planned, yet the company is sustaining profitability thanks to its granular policies and micromanagement of managers. This indicates there is an opportunity to grow the company even more.

The dimensions of the organization in Figure 7.4 represent a combination of goals derived from the strategic plan and the IFB Model. To distill your important dimensions into a diagram like this, define them in the diagnostic exercise, categorize them (if necessary), and then assign an overall satisfaction rating from 1 to 10 to each dimension. If you have more than eight dimensions to be prioritized, you can create additional organizational *balance wheels*. Once the wheels are populated with data, executives can answer the following questions to analyze them:

- As you study the wheel from a macro perspective, what does the shading suggest to you about balance?
- What should the priority dimensions be? Why?
- How can you leverage the priority dimensions in ways that can build compromised ones?
- Which dimensions of your organization are the most important to keep in balance? Which are the least? Why?
- Which dimensions require strengthening? Why?
- Which dimensions don't require immediate attention? Which ones can wait?

After answering these questions, you can create future balance wheels that reflect different scenarios. Your analytical process should take multiple dimensions into consideration. Therefore, when planning your balancing activities, you should recognize the interconnectivity of all dimensions, regardless their perceived criticality. The future options should all meet the following IFB criteria:

- Where there is low trust, the option should build trustworthy behaviors within leaders initially, and then throughout the employee population.
- The options should facilitate flows that are in alignment with strategic goals.
- The options should all include people development if new or evolved skills are necessary.

- The balance state options should have a built-in system of accountability that holds leaders accountable for putting measures in place to support their strategic definitions of success.
- The options should build or sustain employee engagement.

Sometimes decision-makers overcorrect and attempt to achieve balance by shifting from one extreme to another. For example, this can happen when leaders decide to shift from being closed to transparency. If they attempt to make an immediate shift without addressing impaired trust and other inherent cultural challenges, the instantaneous flip may only generate heightened suspicion and, in some cases, anger. Executing decisions like this requires leaders who understand that mental and emotional models also need to shift for buy-in to occur.

Timing is another important component of design. Plans can fail for multiple reasons: unrealistic timelines, premature execution, unexpected delays, unaddressed emotions, overestimated competence, miscalculations of readiness, or bureaucracy. Timing is especially important to consider because multiple resources are required for change and several projects can be underway at the same time. Timing and balance are closely intertwined and should be carefully considered.

Plan to Achieve New Balance Goals

It is important to emphasize once again that when planning to execute balancing activities, decision-makers should keep the Pillar of Trust, interconnectivity, and flow in mind. They should also keep their strategic plan at the forefront of their balancing process — it has strengthening potential.

During and after the balancing process, priority tensions should be monitored to ensure they are really in balance and not merely an illusion of balance. In fact, facilitating changes based on IFB design methodology means the diagnostic, design, planning, and execution loop should happen regularly so imbalances can be addressed proactively. The following case study is a practical application of the IFB Model of Balance:

Case Study: A Tale of Two Candidates

Ray, a department manager, recently handed in his letter of resignation. His employer has a decision to make because two assistant managers are qualified to fill Ray's position. Greg, one of the candidates, has advanced technical skills and a proven track record for achieving individual results, but his interpersonal skills are sorely lacking. The other candidate, Luke, demonstrates evolved emotional intelligence skills, average results, and enjoys sharing relevant information with his coworkers.

The selection committee decided to appoint Greg to the manager's position because of his drive and track record. When he assumed the new role, executives found that Greg's autocratic leadership style was not only failing to develop the team, a once-engaged team now seemed to be disgruntled. In response to declining team spirit, Greg took matters into his own hands and attempted to do much of the team's work himself.

The previous manager, Ray, left the department in a balanced state: trust, productivity, resources, people development, profitability, and so on. He paid close attention to his coworkers so when imbalances emerged, he took immediate action. Ray knew his team was not perfect, but despite their differences, they collaborated, communicated respectfully, and demonstrated inclusive behaviors because Ray modeled these skills.

The selection committee didn't take the time to understand what was really driving performance, so when they appointed Greg to the vacant position, they disrupted the equilibrium of the team. Greg valued results, productivity, and following directives above all else and as a result, the department rapidly slipped into a state of imbalance.

Retrospectively, the executive team decided to invest in developing Greg, so they documented a development plan to address his leadership gaps. They also provided Greg with success measures that would determine the effectiveness of his development plan. Finally, Greg's supervisor told him he would check in with him periodically to determine if the desired balancing efforts were being achieved.

This scenario illustrates balance in need of restoration. The new tensions are different than the previous ones because Greg and Ray have different strengths. What the executives can do is identify the current imbalances, decide if they can be addressed based on Greg's strengths, then work with Greg to support him in achieving self-balance and team balance, capitalizing on his unique mix of skills.

Before the executive team appointed Greg, the first step should have been to conduct a diagnostic exercise to better understand the dynamics within the department. Focus group discussions or interviews could have helped to deepen the executives' understanding of what was driving the team's strong results.

If the diagnostic exercise indicated that Ray's leadership style was a primary driver of the team's high performance, decision-makers may have been more amenable to appointing Luke to the position, with the understanding that even though his results were not as strong as Greg's, his leadership style could have more than compensated for his performance deficiencies. If Luke had been chosen, the balancing action plan would have been a very different one.

Diversity and Balance

When decision-makers are interested in making diversity and inclusion important parts of their cultures, they should recognize the latent potential that exists within differences. They know that when coworkers think alike, little to no creative tension is possible. This kind of thinking is counterproductive to IFB principles. In circumstances like this, decisions go through a homogenous collective filter, so people responsible for final decisions miss the opportunity to consider sufficient alternatives before moving forward. In the presence of active groupthink, leaders are likely unaware of the imbalances that may exist; if they are aware, they might diminish their value.

Groupthink maintains the status quo and depending on how long it has been going on, the team may be significantly out of balance. Groupthink creates blind spots, so when it prevails, leaders may overlook higher-quality solutions.

When diversity leads to conflict, it can trigger imbalances if no productive steps are taken to overcome it. When differences lead to innovation—or even optimized flow—this is a beneficial outcome that can lead to sustainability.

For the most beneficial version of balance to occur, inclusive practices should be encouraged and divergent points of view embraced. Determining whether the configuration of diversity within your organization is reflective of your external environment or not should be dependent on your strategic priorities.

When decisions are complex, some leaders solicit multiple views by having one-on-one meetings with team members. Until leaders share or encourage multiple perspectives in a single meeting, they will have neither the benefit of a full spectrum of ideas nor the opportunity to integrate them into a solution that can gain the acceptance of the majority.

The creative tension that emerges from encouraging a variety of perspectives is only possible when leaders and their team members feel safe expressing and remaining open to a variety of views. Freedom of expression happens when trust exists, it enables open communication and minimizes unbeneficial power games that contribute to disequilibrium.

Balanced Decision-Making

Balance within an organization is largely affected by the decisions that are made and how they are made. Decision-making norms can disrupt engagement, form bottlenecks, lead to profitability or support the strategic direction of your organization. In some instances, decision-making is centralized and employees are obligated to act on directives. In others, decisions are made collectively, allowing multiple contributors, building commitment.

Sometimes decisions are made based on irrelevant historic data and the biases related to that information. When biases are in play, decision-makers can fail to perceive the existing environment clearly and miscalculate, especially when group-think is active.

If decision-makers are unable to adequately weigh the key factors that contribute to their organizational imbalances, they may not be able to address them adequately. High-quality decisions require facts and an understanding of how decisions affect the team and other critical stakeholders. Therefore, to avoid ongoing imbalances, leaders should obtain accurate information, if possible, then analyze it using critical thinking methods so decisions can be better informed.

Failed decisions made to rectify imbalances may be revisited using the IFB Model. If you tried a solution that did not work, you can consider when and why it was implemented and how it failed before completely dismissing it as an option. There may be an imbalance embedded within the decision that is related to timing.

Balance is the central element in facing an unpredictable external environment. When leaders sharpen their balancing skills with practice, they are in a better position to seamlessly integrate it into their daily activities. The IFB Model assumes change, both planned and unplanned, will be constant. Therefore, developing balancing skills, especially in times of increasing unpredictability, is no longer a luxury — it is essential.

Part II:

Establishing Your Pillar of Trust

Part II explores the heart of the IFB Model: The Pillar of Trust. This is an important component of the IFB framework because it affects the entire model. Without the Pillar of Trust, the IFB Model will still function, but instead of trust as its foundation, leaders achieve balance using other paths, such as an emphasis on controls and transactions or office politics. Both systems can exhibit a state of False Balance Appearing Real (FBAR).

Part II describes each element of the Pillar of Trust separately, even though they operate in an integrated way. Integrity is the foundation of the pillar; it is an important personal attribute that leaders rely on to build and sustain their own trustworthiness, as well as the trust willingness of their teams.

The second element of the pillar is self-mastery. This refers to a person's ability to effectively interact with others. When it comes to self-mastery, there is a wide range of options: neurolinguistic programming, mindset shifting, religion-based strategies, and positive thinking are only a few. For this IFB exploration, self-mastery refers to emotional intelligence.

The third component is the "we" disposition; this element of the pillar references your team's ability to trust, care about, and collaborate with each other. The "we" disposition is the outward-facing, connective aspect of the Pillar of Trust and with it, leaders and employees can build resilient relationships and healthy extended networks.

CHAPTER 8

TRUST: THE GLUE THAT BINDS RELATIONSHIPS

Trust is the glue of life. It's the most essential ingredient in effective communication. It's the foundational principle that holds all relationships.

—Stephen Covey, educator and author

Paul Zak, researcher and author of *Trust Factor: The Science of Creating High-Performing Companies*, found that trust is a relational emotion that's linked to the production of oxytocin—a hormone that plays a role in social interactions and bonding. This hormone regulates interpersonal connectivity, telling us when to engage or give, and when to hesitate. Researchers believe oxytoxcin facilitates the human connective process. Among other descriptors, researchers call it the trust hormone because without it, deep connection is not possible.

So we see that trust is not only a social experience or feeling, there is biological research that establishes oxytocin as an instrument of trust. When I decided to make trust the foundation of the IFB Model, I took into consideration the fact that oxytocin facilitates connectivity by causing people to regulate their behaviors. Because self-regulation—i.e., self-mastery—is one of the critical behaviors that underlies the Pillar of Trust, other compatible values can be added to the framework, but the values of integrity, self-mastery, and a "we" disposition are permanent features.

The Pillar of Trust is key to cultivating a trust-based culture where people spend less time monitoring each other with suspicion and more time collaborating. Building trust to this level is not easy, especially when there is deep distrust. Therefore, before you consider strengthening the Pillar of Trust within your team, you should determine which team members will be genuinely receptive to trust building and work with them first. You will need champions to help you with this cause.

Cultures can progress through an evolutionary path that mirrors the way human beings progress through a life cycle. However, trust will not grow just because a decision-maker coordinates training or coaching for selected individuals—it requires deeper commitment and a more holistic, thoughtful solution.

For instance, if your business is in growth mode and cultural norms are overly political, team members may identify trust building as contradictory to their personal agendas and resist it. If this is the case, it would be futile for leaders to attempt to build trust by organizing training without also addressing profound, interpersonal rifts.

Your cultural transformation plan should address root causes that contribute to unproductive systems of behavior, so you can methodically support your team with moving through its unique growth process. Because trust building is a fragile process when your team is in a state of low trust, leaders should prevent troublemakers from corrupting or delaying development plans meant for leaders and their teams.

This chapter provides a bird's-eye view of the Pillar of Trust and sets the stage for a deeper dive into each element of the pillar in the rest of Part II. It also provides insights into what the Pillar of Trust is, why it is important, and how you can use it in advantageous ways.

Introducing the Pillar of Trust

A pillar is an upright support to a structure. For our purposes, a pillar is a vertically orientated relationship relying on integrity-based values that start with individuals and emanate outward to others. Depending on the organization, some pillars can support complex cultures, while others crumble when challenged by corruption and other unproductive underlying forces.

As you continue to consider the Pillar of Trust, keep in mind that the construction of a durable Pillar of Trust doesn't guarantee all relationships will be healthy or resilient, but it can mean enough of them are, and team members are making conscientious efforts to keep them that way.

In Figure 8.1, the Pillar of Trust underpins the entire IFB Model. When implemented effectively, it forms part of an organization's blueprint for acceptable behaviors, so it can be used for developing team members and guiding conversations at all stages of implementation of the IFB Model. When leaders embody the tenets of the Pillar of Trust, employees can sense that they care about them and know their contributions to the organization are not only welcome but valued.

The IFB Model views organizations as ecosystems that are constantly in motion. Therefore, goals for developing your Pillar of Trust need to be established with the expectation that your organization should be constantly changing.

When structuring the IFB Model, ensuring that the Pillar of Trust is given adequate attention is vital to the successful design and implementation of the entire framework. If the characteristics

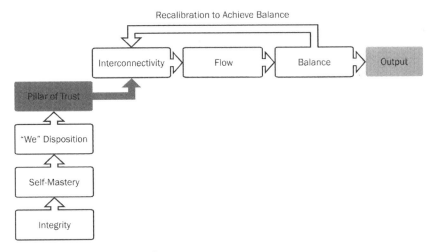

Figure 8.1   The Pillar of Trust

of integrity, self-mastery, and the "we" disposition are not already embedded within your culture, transformation of the leadership team should be your highest priority. This process may involve developing existing leaders, recruiting new ones, or a combination of both.

To reemphasize: leaders should establish the Pillar of Trust within their teams, both individually and collectively. When the pillar is operating as intended, it can also enhance how the organization interfaces with the community it serves, positively affecting brand, customer service quality, even regulator relationships.

Why the Pillar of Trust Is Important

Modern trust statistics paint a sobering picture. Paul Zak's research[5] indicates that employees at high-trust companies

- demonstrate 50 percent higher productivity;
- experience 40 percent less burnout;
- have 106 percent more energy at work;
- experience 74 percent less stress; and
- report 29 percent higher life satisfaction.

If these statistics are representative of the superpowers of trust, then why does the 2018 Edelman Barometer of Trust report indicate the world is navigating a crisis of trust, with declining trust levels directed at NGOs, businesses, governments, and the media? There are multiple reasons for the erosion of trust. Perhaps one of the overarching reasons is that the truth has become increasingly difficult to identify or recognize—even when it is right in front of us.

According to the Edelman report, 2018 is the year of the battle for truth, so the appetite for truth and trust is growing. With an expanding desire for trust emerging from the trust crisis, it follows that our ability and willingness to connect authentically with each other is also being challenged.

When trust is firmly rooted in organizations, coworkers are more likely to care about and connect with each other; this leads to improved engagement and heightened performance. Even if team conflict emerges, when the Pillar of Trust is healthy, coworkers can sustain mutual respect and high performance.

According to a global workplace survey—the "Organizational Vitality Report 2017"[6] facilitated by Six Seconds—leaders tend to overestimate the existence of trust, believing it's 21 percent higher than frontline employees perceive. This perception gap means leaders may be less inclined to adequately address trust-related team challenges, because they are unable to accurately identify the urgency of the current state. So what contributes to this distorted view? Multiple cultural features can play a role: office politics, reward systems, performance measurements, and relationship quality are only a few.

Distinguishing Between Trust and Loyalty

Trust is situational, so a single employee may trust others depending on the quality of relationships they maintain. At the highest level, stakeholders can trust each other unconditionally, thanks to a mutual, extended track record of reciprocal trustworthiness and willingness. These relationships are authentic, and some vulnerability relating to work considerations is possible. At the next level of trust on a descending scale, we find that while coworkers are familiar with how team members think, they don't know their hearts; they are not willing to allow themselves to be vulnerable.

At the third level on a decreasing scale of trust, we see that relationships are superficial. In these relationships, stakeholders may or may not perceive potential for trusting each other. If they don't, shared goals can be used to achieve cohesion. Then there is the level of trust between known and unknown entities who don't trust each other. These relationships may be reconcilable and emotionally charged. The fifth level of trust is one of intense distrust that also exists between known and unknown stakeholders. In these cases, there are no perceivable opportunities for developing a bond of trust.

Trust is possible when team members can be unwavering in their reliance on the interdependence and integrity of people, processes, and resources. In the presence of trust, team members can feel safe, and safety is a license for various freedoms. As with any license, you can choose to use it or not.

Loyalty can be a by-product of trust or unproductive interpersonal dynamics. It emerges when people are devoted to a cause, country, group, or leader, and like trust, their devotion can be value-based or blind. Loyalty and trust are connected but different. Loyalty is about allegiance. Trust, on the other hand, happens when you feel you can rely on the integrity of a person, process, or thing.

When leaders are in the process of establishing an IFB organization and building trust is a high priority, loyalty can develop as a by-product of the initiative. This can be beneficial since loyalty can deepen connections, but on the flip side, when trust is nonexistent and loyalty is expected, people can feel out of sync with their personal values and preferences. Remaining in this state long enough can trigger team disengagement.

For instance, leaders who insist that their coworkers are either with or against them are attempting to coerce team members into choosing a side so they can identify who is loyal to them. Choosing a side to demonstrate loyalty means there are divisive dynamics at work, and division leads to imbalances.

Loyalty also emerges when coworkers care about each other or when a person feels a sense of obligation, or even guilt. Blind loyalty materializes when a team member is devoted to a person or cause, despite the damage they cause themselves or those within their orbit. When coworkers are blindly loyal, they can be willing to override their internal value systems to execute directives or even anticipated expectations.

Blindly loyal coworkers are extrinsically motivated. They learn to justify inappropriate requests because their sense of allegiance outweighs their commitment to their own ideas and values. When building the Pillar of Trust, decision-makers should strive to uncover these misplaced loyalties as best as possible, because loyalty that is externally motivated can be troublesome when there are unproductive power dynamics.

Social stratification within work environments can be divisive, causing separation based on loyalties: marginalizing those who refuse to play according to political rules, while bestowing power upon coworkers who demonstrate allegiance. When team members are preoccupied with attaining or maintaining their status, they can fixate on strengthening their personal networks of loyal followers at the expense of team building, thereby destabilizing the organizational ecosystem. Perpetuating (divisive) loyalties is the antithesis of cultivating the collaborative, connective behaviors that should result from effective implementation of the IFB Model.

Leaders who value a healthy mix of trust and loyalty can generate support without having to create codependent dynamics or exploit people's vulnerabilities. Decision-makers who choose a balanced route are dedicated to building healthy relationships within their respective networks, taking time to further refine them when gray areas surface. They know that when trust is present strengthened relationship cohesion has higher potential for successful outcomes.

The Goals of the Pillar of Trust

The three core values of integrity, self-mastery, and a "we" disposition are minimum requirements for the Pillar of Trust so decision-makers are free to supplement these values with additional ones that don't undermine trust. This is possible because the Pillar of Trust is an integrative framework, allowing the uniqueness of the culture to materialize while preserving trust. Here is a list of goals associated with implementing the Pillar of Trust:

- Talent development, engagement, and retention are important opportunities for application of the Pillar of Trust.

- To fortify the quality of relationships and networks that operate both within organizations and externally. With a foundation of trust, healthy relationships and networks are better equipped to support overarching cultural change through improved performance, organizational agility, and sustainable growth.

- To help balance the tension between the goals of sustaining of a business and improving short-term performance.
- In addition to developing core competencies that are aligned with the pillar, enriching trust depends on rooting out behaviors that undermine it. This is because when distrust is pervasive, external stakeholders can detect it.

Using the Pillar of Trust to Correct Goal Imbalances

As I pointed out in the chapter about balance, teams can achieve successful outcomes while their organizations continue to exhibit imbalances. Here is an example of how this can happen: when success is narrowly defined as shareholder wealth creation through profitability, all plans exist to achieve these two goals. It becomes a single-minded focus. As a result, work gets done and targets may be stretched and exceeded, but at the expense of employee engagement and operational risks. It is reasonable for leaders to decide that trade-offs may be necessary in the short term, but when it becomes the norm, they can generate imbalances that jeopardize long-term sustainability.

Employees burn out when they operate from mental models underpinned by fear, obligation, or survival rather than passion and purpose. When burnout becomes the prevailing theme, it is a sign of imbalance — which can be accompanied by low morale and engagement.

Ideally, success should be defined in a way that connects the accomplishments of an organization with the achievements of its people and the success of the community it serves. A narrow definition of success based on one-dimensional goals like profitability causes decision-makers to use people as a means to an end, and this approach is inherently corrosive.

Once the Pillar of Trust is established, employees should not be given the impression that they are being used; instead, they should be invited to participate in a mutually beneficial journey. This can happen when leaders focus on strengthening relationships and networks that drive performance and balance.

Establishing the Pillar of Trust: An Organizational Development Plan

Whether a change initiative is an immediate priority or not, reinforcing the Pillar of Trust within individuals and teams can benefit organizations. Participation in building the Pillar of Trust is not restricted to leaders; rather, it should be built by everyone who decides to adopt it. The more your team members take ownership of building the Pillar of Trust from both perspectives, the more likely your transformational plans will be successful.

Establishing the Pillar of Trust requires an organizational development plan that targets the IFB knowledge and skill gaps of the leadership team. For best results, the plan shouldn't stop there, it ought to extend to your entire team. Here are a few considerations for organizing your plan:

- *Envisioning*: The vision of an IFB organization is an image of its future state. In fact, it should be a projection of multiple possible states of balance, and potential paths to them. When envisioning the Pillar of Trust, decision-makers should also picture the skills they will need to lead within the IFB paradigm. Too many leaders leave themselves out of the development equation, affecting the potential for transformational success.

- *Developing Leaders from the Inside-Out*: The IFB Model focuses on developing individual leaders, and their teams. Individualized development plans should be created for decision-makers, as each leader possesses a different mix of competencies. The plans should be focused on strengths, leveraging the existent competencies of individuals and teams.

  Formal and informal leaders can successfully coexist. Formal leaders within IFB organizations can recognize informal leaders as viable channels for achieving balance and concentrate on developing these leaders as IFB co-facilitators. If it is appropriate within your organization, formal leaders should try to blur the lines of separation between themselves and their informal counterparts, because trusted, informal leaders can be more effective at influencing colleagues to establish and sustain team cohesion.

For individuals, trust building can be contingent on what they perceive the character of others to be, as well as their personal values, goals, and willingness to trust others. When leaders are intent on transforming an environment characterized by limited trust or distrust to one inspired by it, they can start by creating and maintaining *safe space*. They can establish psychological safe space when team members care about each other, demonstrate transparency, tell the truth, and communicate respectfully. A majority of—if not all—employees need to buy into building safe space before it can materialize.

- *Developing Employees*: Implementing the IFB Model requires multiple competencies. In addition to the skills related to the Pillar of Trust, employees should also possess communication, technical, problem-solving, and other skills. The IFB Model operates as a value-based framework when the Pillar of Trust is functioning as intended, so depending on your organization's strategic priorities, resources, and other considerations, your sequencing of and investment in developmental activities may vary.

  Individual and team IFB development plans should close the skill gaps for competencies related to the Pillar of Trust as well as the rest of the IFB Model. Although flexibility exists in the IFB developmental planning process, here are a few developmental guidelines that apply:

  ○ You should make IFB developmental opportunities available to all staff.

○ Use the developmental path that delivers the best possible results.

○ Different levels of mastery are required for each IFB competency, depending on roles. Be sure you differentiate the learning opportunities as needed.

○ IFB development should be continuous because evolving employees are required to continually grow an organization.

○ Your IFB development plan is central to balancing your organization so IFB competency levels should be tracked and upgraded based on your balancing priorities.

When building trust, it is ideal for each team member to do their inner, transformative work and modify how they interact with coworkers as they progress. However, it is not realistic to expect everyone to buy into trusting others, especially if trust is not a natural predisposition of the team. Therefore, when trust is damaged, while development plans may support some improvement, other strategic actions like establishing shared goals may be more likely to gain traction.

- *Succession*: Succession is an IFB priority because it can facilitate organizational sustainability and growth. When succession and retention plans are effectively executed, they can help to keep an organization in balance because top performers who are promoted from within, when adequately developed, should understand the nuances of their cultures and how to harness them. Succession planning is also useful for protecting against flatter learning curves.

- *Defining Success Measures*: When implementing the Pillar of Trust to support the IFB Model, decision-makers should understand there will always be different experiences of and capacities for trust among coworkers. The intent is not to have trust manifest in the same way for everyone, but to move the organization beyond a collective trust threshold that distinguishes between a trusting environment and a distrusting one. This threshold should be defined by your organization when envisioning trust.

Using Mindfulness to Build Trust

Leaders can establish and maintain trust by ensuring communication always reflects mindful, interpersonal considerations, as represented by the following questions:

- How will the decision affect people individually and collectively?
- What's the best time to communicate?
- How can you allow the voices of your team members to be heard?
- How can you ensure consistency and clarity of your message? (For instance, is the same message being communicated by all leaders? Are your words and actions aligned? Are your actions aligned over time?)
- How can you demonstrate compassion through your words and actions?
- How can you communicate with courage and respect?
- How can you self-regulate? (Among other things, self-regulation includes the ability to discern divergent behaviors in the moment and manage yourself and your external circumstances seamlessly.)
- How can you demonstrate transparency? (Transparency is important because coworkers require the right information, at the right time, delivered in the right way, to execute their duties. Transparency also requires good judgment to determine the difference between what is confidential or private and what can be shared.)

Applying Trust to Performance Management

Trust is not always considered in conventional performance management cycles. This may be due to the design of assessments or because assessors undervalue trust. Other reasons could be that supervisors are uncomfortable with or overwhelmed by the process — because of how it makes them and their coworkers feel, or because of the volume of assessments to complete.

The absence of trust can also exist because the conventional performance management process can become politicized, causing rater bias, no matter how objective the tool may appear. In circumstances like these, low-performing employees feel judged and voiceless; and when they attempt to express themselves, one listens.

Models of employee development operate best from a foundation of trust and healthy relationships. For example, when appropriately executed as a developmental tool, coaching can deepen trust-based relationships, improve performance, and engage employees.

Because of this potential, some organizations only use a coaching model to improve future team performance instead of adopting traditional performance management tools that rate past performance. Coaching reinforces connectivity because well-executed coaching fortifies working relationships and focuses the team on achieving future goals, not exploring historic actions that they have no power to change.

The Pillar of Trust and Change–Based Organizations

A culture grounded in trust can foster innovation, problem solving, and even fun. If trust isn't already present or it exists in some departments and not others, establishing your Pillar of Trust can be a starting point for introducing and integrating value-based connectivity. When trust is present, there is more energy, less stress, higher productivity, and less burn-out. All these qualities are central to building high-performing, change-based organizations that treat change as a constant.

CHAPTER 9

INTEGRITY: THE FOUNDATION

*One of the truest tests of integrity is the blunt refusal
to be compromised.*

—Chinua Achebe, professor, poet, and novelist

The cornerstone is the first stone laid in the foundation of a building. The cornerstone of the Pillar of Trust is integrity. It is one of the primary reasons deep trust can exist among coworkers. For the entire IFB Model to operate as intended, integrity must exist at both the individual and team levels; if integrity levels are low, trust is not supporting flow — something else is.

Integrity cannot be imposed, it needs to be embraced. Some researchers believe it can't be taught because integrity is an elemental part of a person's character. Dr. Jason Jones, researcher and consultant,[7] found that not only can character be taught, but underperforming teams can become high performing when they focus on building character traits.

Teams typically consist of people with very different perspectives of integrity. Some leaders put extreme policies and procedures in place to attempt to impose integrity, but all this does is cause low-integrity employees to find creative ways to circumvent the rules.

Integrity should emanate from a person's core values and there are limitless definitions and prioritizations of integrity. Leaders should start by understanding their own perspectives of integrity and avoid judging others who do not share their value systems or definitions.

In fact, you should assume there will always be different interpretations of integrity among the members of your team. Despite this, you can set the stage for them to align with shared goals if the ae willing to buy into them. IFB Leaders can also support team transformation by modeling desired behaviors that support integrity-based interactions so they can slowly shift their cultures.

If decision-makers encounter low-integrity employees who are working to undermine attempts to build their teams, they should provide them with realistic opportunities to demonstrate productive interactions. If this doesn't work, they can consider whether these people will likely modify their behaviors in another role, and if the employee is unresponsive, they can then put termination on the table.

This chapter provides you with a variety of images of what integrity looks like when it's operating effectively in an IFB (or any other) environment. As with other character-related traits, it will take time to assess employees and provide them with coaching they need to align with intrinsic, integrity-based values.

What Is Integrity?

Integrity refers to a person's will to do the right thing, for the right reasons, even if others are not aware of their decision. There are two types of integrity: moralistic and structural. Moralistic integrity is associated with honesty, truth, and transparency. It relates to one's identity or character and forms at an early age.

When leaders possess moralistic integrity, they are honest with themselves and their coworkers. It also means their words, work, and actions are aligned with their intrinsic value systems. When internal and external congruence exists, these states are more likely to be predictable and expected; constructive behaviors can help coworkers feel safe.

Structural integrity involves ensuring that the integrity of your operation is sound. For instance, the organizational chart should be aligned with strategy. This type of integrity is important when establishing the Pillar of Trust because your ecosystem should perform as intended. Therefore, when leaders perceive integrity flaws within their structures, they should identify the causes and implement corrective plans.

In summary, integrity applies to the entire IFB Model, both moralistically and structurally, and is a foundational constituent of the Pillar of Trust. Integrity is a strengthening agent because when work relationships are characterized by it, team members can be honest and expect truth in return, instead of ingratiating, neutral, or even duplicitous responses.

Why Integrity Is Important

Integrity contributes to healthy work cultures supporting both individual and team growth. When leaders are trustworthy and capable of helping team members to move in the direction of who they are meant to be, the people around them may be more likely to accept them. By being authentic, respectful, and compassionate, leaders model trustworthy behaviors team members can emulate so they can close performance gaps.

Like other features of the Pillar of Trust, integrity supports engagement, and as you are likely aware, researchers have established crucial linkages between engagement and performance. The potential benefits of strengthening integrity within your culture are:

- It reduces stress.
- It opens the door for mutual transparency between leaders and employees.
- People want to work with/for—and do business with—people they trust.
- If leaders don't demonstrate integrity and lack power, there's a risk that others can dictate what is acceptable.

When leaders infuse their leadership skills with integrity, they are in a better position to free their cultures from unproductive undercurrents. However, they are not guaranteed success when they decide to demonstrate trustworthy behaviors. When leaders decide to grow trust at entry levels and higher, it takes time; they have to overcome suspicion during the restorative process.

The higher purpose of the Pillar of Trust is to facilitate liberated cultures through healthy relationships and networks. A liberated culture is one that's free from the confines of perpetual, toxic interactions. In IFB organizations, leaders are capable of attuning to and resolving imbalances that emerge due to these harmful permutations.

The requirements for maintaining an engaged team are constantly evolving with people joining and leaving teams. Despite shifts over time, integrity should remain a reliable constant. This is because a liberated culture, freed by integrity and other components of the Pillar of Trust, supports organizational agility — this is critical when your internal and external environments are unstable.

Integrity and Your Interconnective Infrastructure

Another reason why integrity is so important is that it is essential to the healthy operation of organizations, no matter where they are in their growth cycles. In fact, I would go a step further and say integrity is the cornerstone of the entire interconnective infrastructure because it supports

- intrinsic balancing of individuals, so they can self-regulate and remain true to productive values;
- balancing interpersonal relationships and networks, facilitating respectful interactions and trust;
- balancing your organization and its external environment, ensuring your organization remains relevant and trusted; and
- balancing over time. Leaders of balanced organizations are better able to be innovative and responsive to their environments.

Here's how integrity interrelates with the four components of the interconnective infrastructure:

Individual Integrity. Individual integrity is related to your honesty, your ability to demonstrate confidentiality, and your alignment with your values and purpose. When you know your "why," you are in a better starting place for identifying a role that's the right fit. Otherwise you can end up in a situation where your work doesn't awaken your engagement and satisfaction.

When leaders are out of sync with their personal integrity, others can detect it. When exposed, suspicion and frustration permeate interactions, compromising the ability of the teams to operate at their best. When leaders demonstrate integrity (and possess trust-building skills), they can facilitate connection, healthy communication, effective structures, and high performance.

Integrity and Communication. We tend to think when coworkers communicate with integrity, this means they are telling the truth, are fair, and transparent. While this may be true, integrity-based communication includes and goes beyond individual considerations. The entire communications network should operate in integrity. This means trusted messengers should clearly communicate information, and channels should be open and operational, letting information to flow in multiple directions without inappropriate restrictions. It also means leaders know when to initiate communication, especially when messages are uncomfortable.

Integrity and Your Operational Structure. As it relates to your operation, structural integrity, refers to the capacity of your structure to hold an organization together under various operational pressures without allowing it to disintegrate, either wholly or in part. As a reminder, operational structures include governance, organizational charts, policies, and procedures. All these structures should be aligned with their intended purpose, strategy, and each other—otherwise they can lead to unwanted tensions. For example, an organizational chart has structural integrity when it's aligned with your organization's strategic priorities instead of complicated personal agendas. When your organizational chart contains positions that were created to reward underperforming favorites, the integrity of the entire structure is compromised. Inadequate, micromanaged, or nonexistent policies can also contribute to low integrity structures.

Integrity and Strategy. Strategic integrity is present when an executive team's actions are aligned with their vision, mission, and strategic goals. Misalignments can also arise in organizations that are more transactional than strategic. This happens when decision-makers micromanage activities to the point where they lose sight of overarching priorities. Imbalances related to strategic integrity can also occur when a strategic plan exists, but the organization is weak on execution.

Deficiencies in strategic integrity surface when your strategic plan isn't relevant to trends in the community, industry, and among internal stakeholders. Another strategic integrity flaw can materialize when your organization has an undocumented plan that's constantly shifting. This is exacerbated when constantly changing plans are communicated selectively. In cases like this, teams responsible for executing these plans are in a perpetual state of frustration and confusion because they have to perpetually adapt to new priorities without accomplishing the previously articulated ones.

The Importance of Building Leader Integrity

Within organizations, the presence or absence of integrity is not only evident in what people say and do, but also in what people fail to say or do. Low integrity shows up when leaders neglect to properly give the right people credit for their work, allowing others to think they performed a task. It works both ways. The absence of integrity within a system of communication is also clear when employees are advised of a decision they know will not work but won't express their opinions because of the perceived price of speaking up; they are prepared to just wait and watch the chips fall. Without trust and safe psychological space, this fear-based behavior can be the norm.

As a leader, there's no guarantee that once you and your team create a trusting, integrity-based environment it will remain stable, especially when a valuable team member resigns and a new person joins. Conversely, when you hire a new leader with the expectation that they can build trust, there is no guarantee that your expectation will be fulfilled. When there is no initial buy-in to fundamental change, at least three things can happen:

- The new leader may be successful at establishing trust over time.

- The new leader may become disillusioned and leave or give up trying if low trust continues to affect the team's ability to perform.

- The new leader may conform to low-integrity behaviors.

Case Study: The Cost of Low Integrity

Gary is the new manager of a department. He works for a company that emphasizes policies, procedures, and compliance. Leaders at this company make an example of anyone who doesn't adhere to the rules, which they do to ensure everyone observes them. During his interview and orientation, Gary was sold a bill of goods. He thought he secured a position with a company that was devoted to innovation.

When Gary joined the team as a new manager, he was excited about the potential of his role. He wanted to engage the team in ways that would capitalize on their creativity. However, in the first meeting it became clear to Gary that most of his team members felt they would be wasting time doing any brainstorming. They resisted exercise saying that they had done it before and it never led to real change.

In Gary's coaching sessions with his boss, expressed his frustration. His boss was making all the decisions, overriding Gary's suggestions. Even low-risk decisions had to go through his reporting executive. Gary had virtually no delegated authority. As a result, not only was he trapped in a transactional role, he experienced decision bottlenecks that decelerated the productivity of the department.

Gary started to experience the sinking feeling that he had been misled. He became increasingly disengaged for variety of reasons—one of which was that the latitude he experienced with his former employer did not exist in his new role. He felt confined by the micromanaging style of his reporting executive. In fact, one day Gary worked up the courage to ask about his decision-making authority, but his reporting executive abruptly changed the subject. After his first month in the role, Gary grew increasingly distressed. No matter how he tried, he could not engage his reporting executive in an authentic conversation.

Gary had been a top performer for his previous employer. His new employer was not letting him do what he was capable of, so Gary's frustration started to affect members of his team. After two months with the new organization he was still unable to build an integrity-based relationship with his boss, so Gary decided this was not an environment in which he could grow; he resigned and was fortunate enough to be rehired by his previous employer in a more senior role.

When new employees feel duped by their employers, it is difficult to build trust, and when disillusioned recruits are managers, your organization can experience compromised team performance and increased risks. New hires can be misled intentionally or inadvertently by recruiters. This sometimes happens when recruiters hire based on a list of aspirational core values that don't reflect the actual values that exist within the organization.

Remember when diagnosing integrity, you should consider if you and members of your team trust each other. If not, you should determine whether your integrity—or lack of it—is a contributing factor. When your team members perceive themselves as being in low-trust, low-integrity work environments, they will not always reveal their skepticism. This is because their lower-order needs of survival, safety, and security are higher priorities. So, when diagnosing your current states of trust and integrity, you need an objective, confidential means for measurement.

The following list includes qualities and skills frequently linked with integrity. Some of the items are moralistic and based on character, while others are structural and can be guided by policies and leader modeling:

Honesty and Ethical Behavior   When leaders tell the truth and reward ethical behavior, they set examples for their direct and indirect reports to follow. Telling the truth should always be balanced because straight talk can be unproductive when it is used without empathy and thoughtful use of language. Therefore, when defining your core value of integrity, understand that telling the truth is not enough, leaders should also care about the well-being of others.

In environments where truth-telling is taboo because of cover-ups and power plays, people who are honest can become pariahs and they experience (sometimes extreme) marginalization. Reversing political dynamics that affect communication is difficult when executive team members are the primary political players.

Employees view leaders and coworkers who say one thing and do another as dishonest or dishonest. People perceived in this way may be aware of it, but perhaps not because those around them tiptoe around the issues to avoid becoming the target of the behavior. Even when the perpetrators are amiable, deceitful behavior is perceived as being low integrity and is not trusted.

Apology and Acknowledgment   Healthy relationships are essential to the overall performance of the team and if they are damaged, the parties involved should acknowledge the part they played in doing damage and apologize if appropriate. If you aren't initiating an apology but rather have been approached with one, in the spirit of rebuilding the team you can consider accepting it, whether you are also culpable or not.

If you initiate an apology and you feel you also deserve one but you haven't received one in return, just let it go. Your apology should be offered without the expectation of a reciprocal act. Everyone processes responsibility for their actions differently; some people can't perceive the part they play in their own drama. Apologies must be real if they are to be effective.

Transparency　　Transparency exists when leaders and employees are open, allowing appropriate information to flow, internally and externally. Transparent leaders maintain healthy channels of communication and understand the importance of circulating the right information, so they customize it to suit their audiences. They know how to share in a balanced way: not oversharing or holding onto it.

Transparency works best when team members trust each other. So, leaders in transparent organizations place just as much emphasis on reinforcing trust as they put on information dissemination. They know team members need to nurture healthy relationships—not only with their immediate leader; rather, they need to trust "leadership" as a whole. Otherwise, attempts at transparency—no matter how authentic—are only met with suspicion or contempt.

Leaders set the stage for others to be transparent by modeling desirable behaviors, making it safe and appropriate for others to follow suit. When leaders exhibit defensive, critical, or punitive tones and actions they make it difficult for employees to be transparent. If employees feel unsafe, transparency will live on as an unachieved goal.

Confidentiality   Leaders and members of their teams should be confidential when it comes to handling private information that can damage coworkers, clients, vendors, and other stakeholders. The only private information that doesn't warrant confidentiality are those related to harassment. Confidentiality is directly related to trust. When leaders don't treat private employee information confidentially, they're compromised, and this can obstruct trust and by extension interconnectivity, flow, and balance.

Grapevines exist within organizations and some of them offer users a vehicle for exploring the personal and professional lives of coworkers, attacking leaders, advancing political agendas, influencing, and so on. In some organizations the grapevine seeks the truth, while in others it can be sensational.

Grapevines can be particularly risky for some leaders because the currency is information. To participate in them means you have to exchange information, because if you don't enrich the grapevine, you will be excluded, thrown inconsequential scraps, or deliberately misled. On the other end of the spectrum, when you divulge confidential information that is injurious to others, you can strengthen unhealthy loyalties, preserving deep distrust.

Intrinsic Motivation   When you demonstrate personal integrity, you are guided — even driven — by an internal compass. You have the courage to stay true to your beliefs because you aren't willing to sacrifice yourself by surrendering to extrinsic pressures.

IFB leaders demonstrate intrinsic motivation by making unpopular decisions when necessary. They don't leave it there. These leaders engage coworkers, managing the emotional fallout through the effective use of meetings, coaching conversations, and empathy. Intrinsically motivated leaders can stand behind their decisions, while at the same time allowing others to communicate their views—even though the unpopular decision may be non-negotiable.

Aligning with Your "Why"

Knowing your reason for being—your purpose, your "why"—allows you to align with it. The trouble is there are people in the workforce who don't know their "why." Some are seeking it and others are oblivious. It is important to know your "why" so you can align with it and establish integrity within yourself.

Consistency

When it comes to consistency, you should be careful that there isn't so much of it that it organizes into groupthink, permeating your organization and stifling diversity. Balanced consistency ensures decision-making systems are predictably fair and honest. It doesn't mean your solutions lack out-of-the-box ideas, it means your core values shouldn't shift under pressure. If integrity is your goal, try to determine if your perception of your integrity aligns with the perception others have of you, so you can adjust if necessary. You should seek to unearth your colleagues' actual views, not because you're extrinsically motivated, but because you are intrinsically motivated to understand if your actions are translating into your intentions. It is equally important to keep in mind the possibility that you may receive feedback that is uncomfortable, even hurtful. When this happens, it is essential for you to keep your emotions in check.

Building Team Integrity

As we continue to examine team integrity, it is worthwhile to highlight the possibility that having only one person on a team who lacks integrity can destabilize the entire team in different ways.

Case Study: Leading with Integrity

Judy is the CEO of a small manufacturing firm that is experiencing performance shortfalls and she is uncomfortable about confronting her executive team about the problem. Before the declining revenue trend, Judy communicated openly about most things. This is the first time the company experienced a sustained decline in revenue and instead of discussing the challenges, Judy avoids this all-important conversation. The more Judy sidesteps the new reality, the more her stress levels mount, and her previously empowering commentary now reflects tones of sarcasm, blame, and impatience.

Senior team members are frustrated with Judy because she seems to be a different person. They are not comfortable with her new behaviors. They know their results are not what they used to be, and they wish Judy would just address the elephant in the room. Because of her changed behaviors, once healthy trust is now impaired. To make matters worse, Judy no longer seems to be confidential, complaining about members of her senior team in the presence of frontline staff. When asked about the changes by the board, she seems unwilling or unable to acknowledge the part she played in creating their new reality. In other words, Judy's actions lack integrity.

Building trust by demonstrating integrity means Judy needs to hold herself and members of her senior team accountable for their performance. She needs to communicate with them on a regular basis, so they can resolve their challenges together. Judy should also be willing to make tough decisions, shift to a solution-focused mindset, and stop venting about her senior team.

Transparency and Confidentiality

Transparency and confidentiality are both on the list of competencies that support integrity-based interactions presented earlier in this chapter. Both are important for trust building—even though they appear to be contradictory. Transparency exists when there's an appropriate level of openness among coworkers. When leaders and employees are transparent with each other, there are no hidden agendas and relevant, authentic information can flow at the right time through appropriate channels.

Confidentiality involves nondisclosure of private information; that is, private or classified information that might damage someone, personally or professionally. Both are necessary for strengthening the Pillar of Trust, so leaders should define the tension between the two dimensions and reconfigure boundaries to maintain healthy balance. Some decision-makers attempt to achieve this by establishing informal or formal policies that define what constitutes confidentiality and transparency.

In various organizations, employees believe transparency means placing all information in the public domain—even private information, when it can cause negative biases to form that can affect a person's career in the long term. This boundaryless definition of transparency can be detrimental and sometimes emerges because of low trust and tends to lead to entitlement.

When team members feel information is being hidden from them, emotions start to surface. In cultures that value speaking up, team members may demand transparency. As trust erodes, these employees can start to express anger and frustration because they believe that information is being withheld or spun. What typically happens under these circumstances is when employees are offered honest and open information, they continue to be suspicious of its authenticity and they express skepticism and criticize—a veritable catch-22.

If leaders share confidential information inappropriately, trust among members of their teams will naturally fall, especially if they violated clear boundaries set between themselves and their teams.

One type of violation can occur when leaders use confidential information to threaten employees. Other leaders assure employees of confidentiality to get them to speak freely and then intentionally divulge the information they agreed not to share. They justify this type of action thinking it is okay to share with certain people because of their roles, but these leaders were not transparent about their intentions with the person they persuaded to trust them.

When leaders find the right balance between transparency and confidentiality, their team members will know which decisions were made and why. This empowers everyone to make better informed decisions while maintaining or growing trust.

Facilitating Freedom of Expression

Psychological safety is an important outcome of implementing the Pillar of Trust. Employees who work together should feel free to express themselves, whether they have differing points of view or not. Team members who feel safe expressing themselves are more likely to remain authentic during a conversation unless there is a further dynamic caused by low self-esteem. When team integrity is present, freedom of expression can occur naturally, especially when the message is difficult. When leaders neglect team integrity, power dynamics can affect the efficacy of conversations.

Employees who are highly political can feel psychologically unsafe around straight-shooting bosses, and vice versa. This is because spin and political games can be exposed by leaders who are unwilling to lower their integrity to engage low-integrity behavior and their skill arsenal is limited to straight-shooting. When political players feel unsafe, they can do a lot of damage to the entire team because they will protect their agendas at all costs. Hence, savvy leaders can use other tools like powerful questioning through coaching to address political dynamics and build trust.

Safe space is maintained through tone and behavior. When coworkers are committed to team building, are conscious of their tones, and capable of managing how they say what they say, they can contribute to the maintenance of a safe space. There are various tones that support team building. A tone of curiosity is inviting and nonjudgmental. A wise tone can be developmental, a friendly tone inclusive. Team-building tones communicate support, authenticity, and genuine caring. They can be tough without being judgmental. When critical or uncaring tones are used by leaders or anyone else on a team, space that was previously safe and balanced can be destabilized.

Self-mastery is possible when the right balance exists between team and personal agendas. Self-mastery benefits the persons demonstrating it and those on the receiving end. No doubt leaders who demonstrate self-mastery will make mistakes from time to time, but when they are trusted, they are more likely to be forgiven. Leaders who operate in low-trust environments who are unaware of how they contribute to it, can experience great difficulty in building a trusting environment. These leaders need to be observant because if persons perceive trust building as a forced exercise, their colleagues will shift to survival mode and give the appearance of harmony when conflict lurks within the team's shadow.

Case Study: Standing by Your Convictions

Jim was a vice president in a large multinational firm. He asked Fran to process a transaction she knew was unethical. Fran was also aware that Jim was the type of person who would disavow any knowledge of the transaction should it be exposed. Jim tried using an assertive tone with Fran at first; but when Fran refused to comply, using an equally firm tone, he became aggressive.

The next day, Jim confronted Fran again, raising his voice to intimidate her into doing his bidding. When this didn't work, he called her after hours for the next two days using abusive tones and threats. Despite her discomfort, Fran was determined to stand by her convictions. She maintained her resolve and refused to process the transaction.

In this case, Jim attempted to use tone as an intimidation tactic. This type of behavior not only damaged Jim's relationship with

Fran, it also affected others who observed or heard about Jim's toxic behavior. They knew they could not trust him as a leader because of his bullying tactics and low integrity.

When bosses are perceived as bullies, team members shift into survival mode to protect their dominant safety and security needs. Trust dynamics mutate in this type of circumstance. Sometimes team members cover for each other to avoid attack, sometimes they only cover for themselves if the culture is characterized by blame.

Throughout this book, I have reinforced the notion that engagement levels affect the ability of your team to produce results. You should also recognize the reality that bully bosses can remain under the radar because there is no perceived safe space within an organization. You may not detect the bully because no-one is willing to report it and your experience with a bully may be very different than the experiences of others.

Sometimes bullies are the open secret that remains unnamed, or perhaps decision-makers are aware of the problem and being bullied as well. In the IFB diagnostic process, it is important for decision-makers to use tools that can uncover their proclivities. They should be willing to accept this information and take remedial action—even if the bully is a top performer or close friend.

When the blinders are on, decision-makers make excuses for bully bosses—defining their behaviors as "difficult," or necessary for results. To address this blind spot, decision-makers should be open to measuring their own integrity, self-mastery, and "we" dispositions so they can become aware of their willingness to clearly perceive bullying tactics for what they are and take corrective action.

CHAPTER 10

SELF–MASTERY

*If your emotional abilities aren't in hand, if you don't have
self-awareness, if you are not able to manage your distressing
emotions, if you can't have empathy and have effective
relationships, then no matter how smart you are,
you can't get very far.*

— Daniel Goleman, Emotional Intelligence

The journey from novitiate to mastery is a lengthy one. A novice is new to a skill, not yet demonstrating refinement or proficiency. A master is someone who has used a skill for ten thousand to twenty-five thousand hours. They invest in continually upgrading and expanding the skills they have mastered.

Self-mastery is potentially an extensive topic; it can include physical, mental, emotional and behavioral mastery and it refers to a person's capacity to stay on course, especially when life throws them curve balls. Self-mastery and perfectionism are two different concepts. People who achieve self-mastery are not perfect, but they have high standards and can access the skills they need to navigate emotionally charged circumstances.

Like the IFB Model, the Pillar of Trust is an open-source framework that is flexible enough to interface with and include other models of self-mastery and leader actualization. Because of the proven value of emotional intelligence in relation to organizational performance and balance, this chapter proposes it as the self-mastery competency of choice when investing in teams so they can become self-aware and self-regulated. Emotional intelligence is therefore proposed as the foundational self-mastery skill, but others may be added over time.

Applying the skills outlined in this chapter will help decision-makers and frontline employees successfully manage their emotions at work, but developing healthy mental models is an equally useful practice. According to researcher and author Peter Senge, "Mental models are deeply ingrained assumptions, generalizations, or even pictures of images that influence how we understand the world and how we take action."[8] These models can potentially influence emotions, behavior, and decisions — so it is an example of an additional self-mastery skill you can introduce to complement emotional intelligence.

What Is Emotional Self-Mastery?

Emotional intelligence is about being smart with your feelings. Emotional self-mastery occurs when leaders and employees can navigate their internal world and regulate their actions — particularly during stressful times — without being derailed. This is especially critical for leaders because when they demonstrate emotional self-mastery, it opens the door to team trust, engagement, and interconnectivity.

We should make a clear distinction between repetition and mastery here. Repetition of a skill doesn't guarantee mastery; repetition is merely the act of using a skill frequently. If you don't push the boundaries of the application of that skill (by avoiding venturing out of your comfort zone), true mastery will elude you.

When leaders master emotional intelligence skills, they are better equipped to navigate conflicts, ambiguities, and crises. The Six Seconds organization created a practice model based on emotional intelligence that transforms theory into practice.

According to their model, there are eight emotional intelligence competencies: emotional literacy, recognizing patterns, *consequential thinking*, optimism, intrinsic motivation, navigating emotion, empathy, and noble goals.[9] Mastering these skills takes time, commitment, patience with yourself, and practice because our emotional reactions are biologically hardwired in our neural pathways and it takes time to rewire them.

Why Self-Mastery?

Leaders are constantly faced with multiple decisions, and emotions have the power to enhance or degrade these decisions. Ross is an executive who reacts emotionally to stressful information. His reactions range from passive-aggressive behavior, to undisciplined outbursts. When Ross makes decisions while he is out of balance, his overactive emotional biases supercharge his decisions and lead to unjustified heavy-handedness or emotional fallout, followed by diminished trust levels.

When leaders demonstrate self-mastery and hold members of their teams to a similar standard, they encourage and inspire creativity and innovation. These are useful cultural attributes, especially when their environments are unpredictable, complex, and ambiguous.

Self and socially aware leaders who are committed to building Pillars of Trust, don't only know and regulate themselves, they understand the corporate landscape and are able to identify and navigate political land mines. They know how to play the game without sacrificing their integrity. They may even possess the skills they need to successfully influence others into healthier, empowered interactions.

Emotional intelligence also arms leaders who are both self-aware and socially aware with the capacity to view their teams from both micro and macro perspectives. They are conscious of their team's strengths and limitations and are disciplined about developing their own. They cultivate the various attributes that are the hallmark of emotional self-mastery. These leaders are

- conscious of the needs of and differences among employees who report to them directly and indirectly (they view members of the team holistically, so their perceptions are not unfairly tainted by the mistakes coworkers made in the past);

- aware of interconnectivity, flow, and balance, and how to achieve and sustain them through self-mastery;
- committed to integrity, fairness, inclusivity, and collaboration;
- able to consider various scenarios and their consequences before deciding;
- attuned to the team, understanding shifts in climate and able to take immediate steps to maintain balance;
- aware that certain people don't work well together and that it is counterproductive to put them in a potentially volatile work arrangement without mitigating risks;
- capable of rising above the confines of institutional memory and making objective, balanced decisions;
- aware of how they are perceived by their direct and indirect reports (they avoid working toward being popular or liked, and instead work toward being fair, respected, and respectful);
- able to allow others to express divergent views without fear of retribution;
- able to care about people without exhibiting signs of codependence;
- trustworthy; and
- appropriately transparent.

Emotional self-mastery is critical to IFB organizational success. Case studies and research that demonstrate the power of emotional intelligence show that it can enhance sales results and customer loyalty, improve operational efficiencies, and support the selection of top talent. From an employee perspective, it can strengthen retention and support engagement.

Emotional Intelligence: The Gateway to Self-Mastery

By developing self-mastery, we can recognize and navigate our own emotions, and strengthen our capacities to identify and influence the emotions of the people in our environments. At the foundational level, our emotional intelligence is anchored in self-knowledge, and knowing ourselves is contingent on our proficiencies related to recognizing and naming our emotions and the patterns that arise because of them.

With this information, leaders can recognize the triggers that cause their reactions and by being aware of what produces an emotional charge for them, they can develop skills that help them weigh the consequences, reframe the discussion, or display optimism. Together, these competencies reduce the probability of an unbridled reaction.

Most (if not all) models of emotional intelligence are derivatives of Peter Salovey and John Mayer's seminal research. For this exploration, we are using the Six Seconds KCG (know yourself, choose yourself, and give yourself) model of emotional intelligence.[10] Six Seconds is a global nonprofit organization with a clear vision of spreading the word about emotional intelligence or "EQ." I am deeply familiar with this model because of my partnership with the organization.

Without emotional intelligence, leaders are not attuned to the moods of their teams and unproductive emotional contagion can infect team interactions. Emotional contagion develops when an emotion within one person operates as a virus, transferring from one person to another. When the patterns of behavior triggered by emotional viruses are displayed by others, depending on the team's level of emotional self-mastery, these patterns can prolong the contagion. Together, integrity and self-mastery open the door to better self-management in the face of unproductive contagion so healthy interconnectivity and flow can lead to sustained balance.

Know Yourself

Knowing yourself involves understanding your strengths, weaknesses, thoughts, beliefs, values, emotions, and behavioral patterns. When individuals within a team are unaware of how they affect their environments, they can be triggered to react emotionally. A trigger is an event that causes an internal reaction. In the absence of emotional intelligence, a trigger can escalate an already volatile situation into pandemonium because of reciprocated, unregulated reactions.

Emotionally competent persons can also be triggered and because they are self-aware, they navigate their own emotions more gracefully and deliberately in the moment, while acknowledging their emotion. Afterward, they use constructive methods of discharging any residual unproductive feelings so they don't kindle contagion.

In your leadership role, it is important for you to practice introspection to identify your emotions and related patterns because displays of undisciplined emotion get in the way of building your internal Pillar of Trust and, by extension, the team's Pillar of Trust.

Sometimes it's difficult for leaders and team members to overcome their triggers because they are blind spots. One possible reason for this is that their neural pathways may be hardwired to initiate reactions (without thought) when they perceive provocation. A considered response requires conscious rewiring of unproductive pathways so new ones can be established. Here are a few ways leaders and employees can overcome their triggers and improve their emotional self-mastery:

- developmental interventions that include EQ self-assess-ments, mentoring, coaching, or training
- formation of an accountability system that sets the stage for leaders and team members to take responsibility for self-aware behaviors
- psychological support (which may be necessary for resolving deeper, personal issues)

Emotional self-awareness — knowing yourself — is a foundational skill that is a prerequisite for being aware of the emotions and behavioral patterns of those who work with and around you. The following reflective questions can start you on the path or deepen your self-awareness:

- Which emotion(s) am I experiencing?
- What triggered them?
- What are my emotions trying to tell me? (What is behind them?)
- How is my display of emotion aligned with my values and beliefs?
- How is the way that I process my emotions beneficial or injurious to me?
- How are my emotions injurious or beneficial to others?
- How do the emotions of others affect me?
- Which emotional patterns do I display most frequently at work?
- Who is affected by my unregulated emotions? How?
- How do my emotions destabilize or strengthen people's trust in me?

These questions support self-reflection and can expand to include the views of team members. Introspection is useful for the next step in building your emotional intelligence: choosing yourself.

Choose Yourself

Choosing yourself doesn't mean you are self-absorbed or you only exist to drive your personal agenda; it means that you choose to navigate your emotions, so you can engage others in healthy interaction. When you choose yourself, you can down-regulate your emotions, so you won't lose control and become a catalyst for unproductive workplace dynamics.

If you are part of an organization where leaders are not skilled at choosing themselves, trust levels are probably low. Choosing yourself requires mastery of four competencies that help you to consciously moderate your emotions. They are: consequential thinking, navigating your emotions, intrinsic motivation, and optimism.

Consequential Thinking

Consequential thinking is a skill that causes leaders to consider the consequences of their actions before responding. This competence can be divided into multiple sub-competencies. One is the ability to visualize multiple possible alternatives and their outcomes. Another is critical thinking, or the ability to analyze the potential outcomes.

Each of the KCG competencies work in tandem with others, and consequential thinking is no exception. Consequential thinking works effectively when leaders and employees can navigate their own emotions. If leaders allow their emotions to unwittingly influence their thinking and decisions, it can be hard for them to visualize diverse scenarios. Especially if their emotions lock them into single-mindedness, causing them to ignore other points of view.

Consequential thinking is a useful self-management tool, but as with other EQ skills, it is difficult to master in emotionally charged situations. Especially because leaders have only seconds to respond in tense or volatile circumstances, and shallow consideration of the consequences of an action can have disastrous effects on trust.

Navigating Emotion

Emotional self-regulation is the process of managing your emotions, allowing you and others to remain empowered within conversations by mutually contributing to maintaining safe space. Down-regulation of emotion requires leaders to use strategies to reduce their emotion before, during, and after conversations. On the other end of the spectrum, up-regulation is necessary when leaders need to show they care about team members.

Some circumstances will give you time to graciously step away from a situation and center yourself. Others require you to reduce your stress levels in the heat of the moment. *Mindfulness* and *reframing* are two skills you can develop to navigate your emotions in both situations.

Engaging in
Mindfulness

Mindful leaders can hold their awareness in the present and live in the moment. They don't preoccupy themselves with the past or future because these preoccupations can be intense sources of distraction. Being mindful doesn't mean leaders don't experience emotion; rather, mindful people are aware of their emotions and don't allow them to cause inappropriate patterns of behavior to emerge.

Mindfulness is an internal resource. It helps you attune to yourself and others, so you can engage your coworkers in ways that support collaboration. Mindful leaders exhibit behaviors that can facilitate the psychological safety of their coworkers because they are committed to building and preserving the Pillar of Trust for the team. Here are ways leaders and coworkers can engage each other mindfully:

- acting deliberately to develop relationships (for instance, a mindful coworker will not jump to conclusions about another coworker. Mindful employees will empathize with others, observe boundaries, and seek to understand the true causes behavior and take compassionate action where appropriate.)

- listening intently, respectfully, and actively

- asking powerful questions to understand a situation

- being considerate of others (considering their time, talents, preferences, etc.)

- empathizing and connecting meaningfully, in ways that reinforce trust

- taking a step back to center and clear your thinking

By being mindful of and effectively managing themselves, leaders can better position themselves to be mindful of others. Otherwise, their unregulated thoughts and emotions can cause them to be inconsiderate of others and compromise trust.

Reframing   Another tool leaders can use to shift their emotional states to productive ones is reframing. Reframing involves cultivating your ability to perceive and experience events, ideas, and emotions from completely different perspectives — ones that lower the emotional charge, shifting leaders from disempowered, reactive states to empowered ones.

Reframing is an especially useful self-navigation tool when it comes to self-mastery. Because of its transformative capacity, reframing can shift leaders into a growth mindset, so they can experience new insights and motivate productive behaviors.

Table 10.1 is a tool leaders can use to reframe challenging situations by transforming their perspectives and, by extension, their emotional states. This tool is especially useful when cultural norms no longer serve the organization and new ones need to emerge.

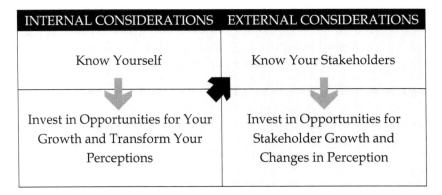

INTERNAL CONSIDERATIONS	EXTERNAL CONSIDERATIONS
Know Yourself	Know Your Stakeholders
Invest in Opportunities for Your Growth and Transform Your Perceptions	Invest in Opportunities for Stakeholder Growth and Changes in Perception

Table 10.1   A Reframing Tool

Reframing should start as an internal process, allowing leaders to view challenges in new ways, so they can envision better solutions. To perceive challenges from different perspectives, new leaders can be added to a team, or existing ones can be developed, starting with diagnostic tools that identify their aptitudes, personality traits, and motivations. Using this information during coaching sessions can help them achieve break throughs that eliminate antiquated, limiting perspectives.

Whether a situation is emotionally charged or not, reframing requires leaders to reflect on their challenges and observe them through new eyes. This skill is critical for decision-makers in an ever-changing external environment that puts pressure on leaders to adapt.

As we move across the reframing tool to external considerations in the top-right quadrant, we should keep in mind that reframing requires leaders to know themselves first, because the skills they need to understand and reframe for themselves are necessary for shifting their thinking about their stakeholders. Stakeholders include employees, clients, regulators, and the external community.

Some people believe that if leaders express displeasure with them, it means these leaders will not be fair. They are convinced of the "horn effect" — a cognitive bias through which people allow a perceived negative trait to overshadow positive ones — because of past experiences or pessimism. Though the bias may be based on credible, historic information, people can change their behaviors if they are intrinsically motivated.

Self-mastery requires self-knowledge, and this means leaders need to recognize their biases (both positive and negative). This is important because biases can cause them to limit the potential of their entire teams.

So, as you reframe your employees and their needs and preferences, and become more aware of your biases, part of your contribution to team evolution can be to model the behaviors necessary for a safe, bias-free zone that allows employees to evolve their thinking and responses. This takes time, trust-building and sustaining skills, and patience, because your team members should be given the opportunity to choose to reframe their thinking about you, each other, and your organization.

Challenging Institutional Memory

Institutional memory is a perception of the past held by the people who experienced the circumstances and those who have heard stories about them. It lives beyond the employment of the individuals involved in a particular event because it is sustained by oral tradition and modeled behavior.

Institutional memory is a source of positive or negative bias and these memories can consciously or unconsciously color decisions made in organizations. Some careers are damaged by institutional memory because qualified people are passed over when there is an opportunity for a promotion. It takes the power of reframing to paint a new picture of inopportune events that limit peoples' careers.

Case Study: Reframing Phil's Misstep

Phil was promoted to a new role after the previous incumbent retired. He was appointed even though he didn't have the technical experience required for the position; it was because of his advanced leadership skills. However, after three months in the role, Phil made an unfortunate decision that cost the company hundreds of thousands of dollars, so he was unceremoniously removed from his new position and placed in his previous role.

After the incident, Phil was blacklisted. Five years later, he was not considered for another promotion despite his obvious strengths. This was because every time he applied for a new role, at least one of the decision-makers on the selection committee reminded everyone of Phil's mammoth error.

They never fully acknowledged the fact that the company shared some responsibility for knowingly placing Phil in a high-risk role without adequate support or development. Therefore, unless leaders can reframe Phil's "incident" by accepting responsibility and by being open to the fact that he may thrive in a leadership position on a different career path, Phil will either wait to be forgiven, or leave the company.

Although conventional wisdom suggests that history has predictive value, this is not always the case when it comes to institutional memory. What decision-makers need is the will and courage to challenge deeply embedded biases. To do this, you can use a disciplined questioning approach to test the relevance of the historic information and prevent it from overshadowing the current state. When it comes to a staffing decision like the case of Phil, you can ask yourself and other persons contributing to the decisions:

- Is there a current trend that supports mentioning the historic event? If not, why is it still being treated as a current event or trend?
- What evidence of employee growth is there?
- How much more is this employee capable of contributing? How has this been tested?
- How much longer should we hold this incident against the employee if it is no longer relevant?

- What part did the organization play in the crisis/event we are assigning to an employee?
- What are the associated risks with eliminating the employee? What are the benefits of inclusion?
- What are the employee's performance results since the event?
- Which other paths can we consider for this employee?
- How effective is the career coaching we provided the employee?
- Does the employee have the potential to be successful in the new position if supported with learning opportunities? Which areas of development would best support this employee?

Consider the example of Phil again. If Phil's name doesn't even show up on the short list, an IFB leader can introduce him as a qualified candidate and proceed with the suggested line of questioning if there is resistance.

Unproductive outcomes caused by the undisciplined application of institutional memory can be circumvented by letting go of the past and reframing it so decision-makers can perceive coworkers from the perspective of their highest potential.

Institutional memory doesn't have to revolve around negative memories. Sometimes positive memories are no longer relevant, but they may still color important decisions, introducing risks.

Institutional memories are not negative in and of themselves — they make cultures unique, establish competitive advantages, and provide contexts for resolving complex situations. However, when institutional memories are used unfairly to obstruct people's careers, their application should be questioned.

Reframing Institutional Memory

The top and bottom-right quadrants of the reframing tool in Table 10.1 are where you can reshape institutional memory. If you can create new narratives and put your support behind them, these narratives can help decision-makers free themselves from the limiting effects of years of undisciplined memory rejuvenation.

Because of repetition, institutional memory can be so deeply embedded within your culture that the stories can even become distorted over time. It is hard to challenge a story that is accepted as truth especially when it is based on a well-known and documented past.

Institutional memory can be likened to layers of soil. In nature, soil strata reveal the history of the impact of the elements. As with layers of soil, biases and other elements of culture are buried within layers of memory. These memories become part of a conscious or unconscious filter used (sometimes universally) to interpret events. The trouble is that these layers are sometimes difficult to detect or disprove because team members accepted them as truth for so long.

Intrinsic Motivation

Intrinsic motivation is contingent on healthy self-esteem. Leaders who possess high self-esteem can gracefully embrace both their strengths and weaknesses. They have no trouble establishing solid relationships because they care about team members, adhere to their personal values, and are in a better position to support trust-based relationships.

When leaders are intrinsically motivated they are aware of and operate according to deep-seated values. This is evident when they can stand for what is right, regardless of what's at stake. When reflecting on your motivations you should ask yourself the following questions:

- What are my motives in this situation? Are they based on my internal values or someone else's?
- Will my motives benefit both me and the people I lead in the short or long term?
- What are the risks associated with standing for what I value or believe? What are the rewards?

- What am I willing to sacrifice by taking a stand? Why?
- How willing am I to stand behind my decision, even if no one supports me?
- How is this an approach that can align me with my values and maintain my job security?

When employees and leaders are extrinsically motivated, they make decisions that are influenced by the feelings and opinions of others. This can happen when lower-level needs like safety, belonging, and security override self-actualization needs. Only when lower-level needs are met, can the higher-level needs of self-esteem and self-actualization be realized.

There are intrinsically motivated employees who are not inclined to trust others easily. They may love their work, but the politics of the organization can cause them to limit their interactions. Leaders who are not trusted but are committed to building trust will not automatically become trustworthy because of a single decision. Similarly, employees who are reluctant to trust will not become immediately trusting. Therefore, both sides need to commit to building trust and as you can imagine, this is no easy feat.

Optimism

Optimists are aware that they are empowered, even in situations that appear hopeless or pointless. Instead of buying into unproductive thought patterns, optimists are not derailed because they can tap into their positive reserves and act.

Optimism is especially valuable when leaders are building their Pillars of Trust as part of IFB implementations because progress can be exhausting. Making progress often means taking two steps forward and one step back and the step back can be quite frustrating. This is because when team members experience a step back, they can lose faith and get trapped in a disheartened, emotional loop. Those who can harness their optimism to break out of the loop know that setbacks are temporary and isolated incidents and believe it is within their power to effect changes — even though they may be incremental.

Diagnosing Emotional Intelligence

There are several validated emotional intelligence assessments that can help you diagnose your *emotional competence* as a leader, as well as the collective and individual emotional competencies of your team. I encourage you to conduct your own research into various tools to select the right one for you and your organization. As a partner with Six Seconds, the largest global emotional intelligence network, we collaborated to create the Trust Style Inventory. This self-assessment can be used to measure integrity, self-mastery and the "we" disposition of your team.

To give you an idea of the range of EQ assessments available through Six Seconds, here is a list for your consideration:

- Brain Brief Profile (BBP) — an introduction to EQ (how emotion and cognition work together)
- Brain Talent Profile (BTP) — shows respondents their "top talents" highlighting top talents from among eighteen key capabilities
- Brain Discovery Profile (BDP) — provides insight to key strengths and challenges
- EQ Dashboard — a one-page summary of a group's EQ capabilities and talents Strengths Report (introduction to the top three EQ competencies)
- Development Report (DR) — an in-depth review of emotional intelligence competencies
- Leadership Report (LR) — an in-depth review of leaders' emotional intelligence competencies in a workplace context linked to key performance outcomes
- Leader's Development Guide (LDG) — a sequel to the Leadership Report with specific, customized recommendations for improving EQ
- Group Report (GR) — an overview of a group's emotional intelligence competencies

- Comparison Group Report (CGR) — statistical data about groups or a single group over time

Once you establish a baseline emotional quotient for your team members, it is important to schedule follow-up assessments to track the growth of your team's emotional intelligence competencies both individually and collectively. The assessments can provide the data you need to make decisions about future developmental opportunities and individuals who may or may not be the right fit for your team's desired culture.

Pressing the Reset Button

Once you start working with your team to improve their emotional self-mastery, there will come a time when you'll need to hold them accountable to the desired behaviors. If they are not responding favorably to your best efforts, at some point you may need to determine their fit — no matter how much they contributed to the success of the team in the past.

Case Study: Pressing the Reset Button

During a recent job interview, a recruiter asked Raina what she would do to revitalize an underperforming team after an unsatisfactory audit. Raina answered, "I once inherited a team that was not meeting expectations. Team morale was low because of the leadership style of the previous manager." She continued, "At the time, the department had just received an unsatisfactory audit rating and despite this, we were able to significantly improve the performance of our department, exceeding the owner's expectations."

The recruiter then asked Raina, "What did you do to create a culture that could support the changes you needed to make?"

Raina answered thoughtfully, "I had to develop the team, so I modeled the desired behaviors. To do this I had to first seek development for myself. Then I pressed the reset button. I gave everyone on the team a clean slate. I sat down with each of them and told them this and then supported them with improving their performance." She added, "Those who were unwilling to press the reset button could no longer be part of the team, so we found mutually agreeable ways they could move on with their careers."

Emotionally intelligent decisions can be difficult to make, but when they are the right ones they can be beneficial for the entire team. The next chapter defines the outward-facing component of the Pillar of Trust, the "we" disposition. While all parts of the pillar are connective, the "we" disposition is outwardly focused.

CHAPTER 11

THE "WE" DISPOSITION

When you are able to shift your inner awareness to how you can serve others, and when you make this the central focus of your life, you will then be in a position to know true miracles in your progress toward prosperity.

— Dr. Wayne W. Dyer, Change Your Thoughts,
Change Your Life

The "we" disposition is an important feature of healthy relationships and networks. For leaders, it involves caring about the welfare of their teams as much as they care about themselves and their results. It is inclusive, so there is no room for "us and them" mentalities. When the "we" disposition is a feature of a culture, members of teams consider the effects of their actions on each other. Not in a codependent or undermining way, but in a way that supports collaboration and trust.

Decision-makers who lead with the intent of building or sustaining trust should possess the ability to discern between team members with a dominant "I" disposition, those with a "we" disposition, and people who achieve balance between the polarities. To differentiate, you can observe their actions or listen to the words they choose. Team members with a robust "I" disposition fall within multiple categories. Some are self-proclaimed loners, others have political ambitions and are driven by their personal agendas.

A leader's "we" disposition should not replace their "I" disposition. When a leader demonstrates a healthy "we" disposition, the "I" and "we" dispositions are in balance, coexisting so that one doesn't override the other. Ideally, the "I" resides within the "we."

We have established that leaders who demonstrate a "we" disposition are inclusive. They are sensitive to the diverse thinking and learning styles of their coworkers. Decision-makers who demonstrate a "we" disposition can engage members of theirs teams by considering the collective and individual needs of the members, making decisions that benefit them mutually. They are capable of collaboration, confidentiality, and connecting with their coworkers in meaningful ways.

Leaders who demonstrate a "we" disposition understand the importance of developing their teams and how individual growth happens in relation to others. They don't just pay lip service to developing the people who report to them, they coordinate time off for them to take advantage of learning opportunities.

"We"-oriented leaders challenge their coworkers to grow because they know individual growth, accentuated by a "we" disposition, can help organizations keep pace with changes in the external environment. This is critical because there can be times in the life cycle of an organization when the needs of the organization outpace the skills of team members. This gap can put pressure on leaders and by extension, entire organizations.

Embracing a "we" disposition goes beyond thinking about others. Leaders who are "we" oriented establish core values that are shared by their team members. These values should act as a principled guidance system (PGS) that influences all decisions made within IFB organizations. The Pillar of Trust should be part of a cluster of core values that affect the team's every thought, word, and action.

A "we" disposition is not guaranteed when only integrity is in place, because leaders can exhibit integrity and still be inwardly focused, not caring enough about others. Both integrity and self-mastery are necessary for a healthy "we" disposition to emerge. This chapter defines the "we" disposition, identifies the barriers to it, and concludes with strategies to design and integrate your organization's version of a "we" disposition among leaders (and within your culture).

Why a "We" Disposition Is Important

Mergers, acquisitions, joint ventures, and spinoffs are all major decisions executives can face during the life of an organization. When these decisions are executed, the subsequent shifting people dynamics can undermine the ability of decision-makers to realize the full value of the strategic change. There are multiple cases of failed corporate transactions attributable to clashing cultures: HP and Compaq, AOL and Time Warner, and Daimler and Chrysler, to name a few. So as you can see, tools to integrate cultures are critical in an ever-morphing corporate environment.

When leaders enter into one of these corporate transactions, conflicting cultures can impede productivity and growth. Developing a healthy "we" disposition will mitigate the risks caused by cultural collisions resulting from ineffective communication practices, unclear operational changes, out-of-control power dynamics, and strategic ambiguity.

A "we" disposition is also vital because healthy relationships are at the heart of change-based organizations — those that treat change as a mode of operation rather than a series of separate change initiatives. Change-based organizations are better equipped to respond effectively to changes in their environments because being in constant change mode makes them increasingly agile over time.

Barriers to a "We" Disposition

It is difficult for leaders to sustain or build trust if team members are unable to exhibit a "we" disposition, supported by and operating alongside integrity and self-mastery. Without these qualities and skills, interpersonal interconnectivity suffers; and this can inhibit decision-makers who have elected to build an agile, IFB organization.

Before embarking on a Pillar of Trust implementation, leaders should identify and address the barriers that make organizations ill-equipped for change — especially ones that can sabotage an entire implementation. Some of the obstacles to building a collective "we" disposition are detailed below.

Unproductive Power and Political Systems

The political landscape within and outside an organization is ever-changing. It comes together according to informal and formal rules that define and refine the acquisition and retention of power. Because political landscapes are dynamic, they evolve and collapse according to circumstances that require the constant attention of power players who seek to preserve their power structure.

Highly political players create alliances that fortify their power and put aside ones that don't serve them, cultivating loyalties wherever they can. Office politicians can spend an inordinate amount of time plotting, planning, and reacting based on personal ambitions, and unexpected events. These activities divert precious time away from strategic priorities.

Using IFB language, weak interconnectivity surfaces when overriding "I" dispositions activate unproductive political office dynamics driven by individual power agendas. At the core of highly political organizations are multiple, ambitious personal agendas that power can satisfy with more rapidity than a slower, merit-based route built on honor, trust, and competence.

In and of itself, power is neither positive nor negative—it depends on how you use it. In fact, various types of power exist that can be either empowering or disempowering, depending on intent. The following list integrates five types of power defined by John French and Bertram Raven[11] with other types of power.

- *Position/Legitimate Power*: The power inherent in the position you hold.
- *Structural Power*: The power of the structure (delegated authorities, policies and procedures etc.) to cause or sustain behaviors—this type of power is closely linked to positional and coercive power.
- *Coercive Power*: Using force to cause people to do as you desire; imposing your will on others.

- *Relationship Power*: The ability to make things happen through relationships.

- *Information Power*: The power achieved by controlling and protecting information.

- *Expert Power*: This type of power is assigned to people identified as experts. It can surface when workplace experts are few and in great demand.

- *Blocking Power*: The ability to obstruct the goal of an individual or team. It can be provoked by a perceived slight or it may be a deeply considered, necessary action.

- *Referent Power*: This type of power is based on respect for and admiration of a person. Coworkers identify with leaders with referent power for a variety of reasons.

- *Reward Power*: The ability to reward people based on fair or unfair criteria.

Politics and power can significantly lower the potential for building trust within a team. A collective mental shift is necessary to transition the focus from individuated, self-serving needs to shared goals that address the requirements of the team. This shift should start with leaders.

Personality Disorders

Personality disorders are mental disorders that cause people to demonstrate dysfunctional patterns of behavior and cognition. They are an important barrier to consider because coworkers with personality disorders can deviate from the behaviors that are necessary to build the Pillar of Trust.

As a leader, you are not a trained psychologist or psychiatrist, so your role is not to make the kind of diagnosis those professionals are qualified to make. However, it is useful to know enough to recognize these patterns so you can make informed decisions in relation to your interconnective infrastructure. Equipping yourself with this knowledge is increasingly important because some studies show that as many as one in five people exhibit personality disorders. Others reflect statistics as low as one in twenty.

There are three clusters of personality disorders. The first cluster includes people who demonstrate odd or eccentric behaviors, such as paranoid or schizoid behaviors. Paranoid leaders and employees can exhibit fear or anxiety to the point where they can seem delusional. These team members believe they are being constantly threatened or persecuted. They don't prefer human interaction, instead they can seem cold or aloof, preferring mechanical activities.

The second cluster includes people who demonstrate dramatic or erratic behaviors. This cluster includes antisocial, borderline, histrionic, and narcissistic personality disorders. Antisocial team members disregard the rights of others, and this can show up as deceit, hostility, or manipulation. Those with a borderline personality see the world in all-or-nothing terms and can be intense, emotional, and judgmental.

Coworkers who demonstrate a histrionic personality disorder like to be the center of attention and are excessively emotional and shallow, so drama tends to be present around them. Narcissists experience low self-esteem, demonstrate a sense of entitlement, and need to feel powerful and admired. They are manipulative, superficial and can be charming, yet they throw tantrums when things don't go their way.

The third cluster of personality disorders includes anxiety and fear disorders. People with an avoidant personality disorder are socially inhibited due to low self-esteem. They are hypersensitive to criticism. Another disorder that falls within this cluster is the obsessive-compulsive disorder. These individuals demonstrate a preoccupation with orderliness, and they tend to be inflexible, perfectionistic, and devoted to productivity.

While this is certainly not an exhaustive list of personality disorders, it gives you some idea of the range of personalities you will likely encounter at work—personalities that can destabilize your efforts to develop your own "we" disposition—this is especially important because you are an essential contributor to your team's "we" disposition. Personality disorders are enduring, and the interpersonal dynamics they generate are barriers to healthy work relationships and networks.

If people who display any of these behaviors are not open to seeking professional help, leaders can consider developmental opportunities—such as coaching and mentoring—for people who supervise employees with personality disorders. Depending on the damage being done to team cohesion, there are reorganizational strategies that range from changing the organizational structure, relocating difficult employees, modifying job descriptions, or eventual termination in high-risk situations.

Location

Virtual teams are now the norm. They can operate as a cohesive unit and be high performing. However, when a team is geographically separated, and members are unable to exhibit a "we" disposition, it can be difficult for leaders to create a sense of connectedness. Even when members of the team are in the same building but on different floors, or in different building on the same campus, physical separation can foster different subcultures within the same team. Sometimes these subcultures can work together seamlessly, at other times they are a source of infighting.

Resistance

There are multiple reasons why team members resist change: low trust, not being consulted, and changes in the power configuration, to name a few. For example, experts can add significant value in organizations but when they are unable or unwilling to adopt a "we" disposition because of their training, they can become barriers. This sometimes happens when experts who come from different disciplines are expected to collaborate. They are each uniquely qualified to perceive and respond to circumstances in specific, sometimes conflicting ways, so when they are unable to wear a "we" hat, they can cause stalemates that waste time and damage important relationships.

Building Healthy Relationships and Networks

When "we"-oriented leaders encounter differences among team members, they embrace, explore, and encourage interactions that serve the growth and harmony of the team. Equipped with self-mastery skills, team-focused leaders know how to transmute unproductive energy into creative tension because they can attune to latent and other types of conflict and are equipped with effective conflict resolution skills and the courage to use them.

IFB leaders should seek to refine their skills of conflict assessment so they are able to distinguish between creative tension and damaging conflict. This is essential because no matter the level of a team's conflict resolution skills, relationships are ever-changing, so cohesion should not be assumed because of an outward display of harmonious interaction.

Leaders who exhibit a "we" disposition are aware of the consequences of their actions and those of others. They consider the consequences of their own actions when it comes to their teams and know how to use "we" language. These leaders perceive their teams as extensions of themselves and this orientation helps them make decisions that consider their key stakeholders.

Inclusive decision-makers know how to get team members to buy into shared goals and values. They are also equipped to facilitate social (team) transformation by spotting and addressing the homogeneity that occurs when group think permeates various processes.

Developing a plan of action is necessary, not only for cultivating a "we" disposition, but also for building the entire Pillar of Trust. To mitigate risks, the plan should offer multiple possible options for facilitating coworker development and interaction. Additionally, as you plan you should remember to capitalize on organizational strengths. Here is a list of possible actions you can include in a plan that enhances your collective "we" disposition:

- creating and adopting shared team goals
- transforming your climate

- shifting power dynamics
- moving from an expectation of equality to fair treatment
- breaking down silos
- tackling groupthink
- deconstructing precedents
- aligning reward systems
- parting ways… amicably

Shared Team Goals

Shared goals are commonly held by all or most members of a team. Chicken or egg? It's hard to say if shared goals bring about a "we" disposition, or if a "we" disposition leads team members to open to shared goals. Whichever you think is the case, cultivating a "we" disposition involves establishing shared goals. Therefore, as you consider your team's goals, remember that when shared, they should not displace your personal goals, nor should your personal goals override shared ones. Unless there is a crisis, they should coexist in a state of balance.

When constructing the Pillar of Trust, it should be done with the tension between personal and team goals in mind. Balancing begins when leaders and their teammates gain clear understandings of their own and each other's individual goals. Then they can detect the consistencies and inconsistencies between individual and team goals and seek to address the gaps that can be closed by shifting to or deepening the collective "we" disposition.

The developmental and career goals of your team members need to be adequately addressed on an ongoing basis. Peoples' lives are dynamic and unpredictable, so their needs and priorities will shift. All you can do as a leader is ensure your team members are aware of and actively addressing their individual needs and goals, so they can be better positioned to engage and execute them.

Cultivating a team that shares goals doesn't mean all team members embrace every goal. Ones who resist some goals may be motivated if they believe in and value their team; they may be open to collaborating on solutions because of their commitment to and trust in each other and their organization. Once team goals don't violate their personal value systems, they may be persuaded to become engaged in pursuing team goals.

Transforming Your Climate

Each organization has an overlay of emotions that forms a topography reflecting the emotional landscape. It is a chart of emotion that provides insights into collective morale. A range of emotions cohabit within an organization, and these emotions are the result of personal and career realities. No matter the source, prevailing emotional themes must be understood by leaders so a relevant trust-building plan can be formulated and implemented.

The emotions of a team shape the climate. As a result, organizational climate affects the quality of interaction and vice versa. It can shift in response to conflict, leadership styles, communication quality, and reward systems. By displaying a "we" disposition, leaders have the potential to positively affect climate through their verbal contributions, body language, leadership styles, and overall tones. To assess the emotional topography of your team you should consider the following questions:

- What are the perceived dominant emotions?
- What are the primary reasons for unproductive behaviors displayed by staff? What is causing them? How manageable are they?
- What are the primary reasons for productive behaviors? How can we replicate and sustain them?
- What are the consequences of the presence of these emotions?
- What are the opportunities?
- How can you determine what else is going on beneath the surface of your culture without negatively affecting morale or trust?
- What can we do to transform unproductive emotions and related systems of behavior?

These questions can help you understand if you need to do more groundwork to strengthen your team's "we" disposition. Once you answer the questions as accurately as you can, your plan can be formulated or modified to address the priority opportunities for "we" transformation. It is important for you to ensure that your plan takes the unique attributes of your culture into consideration so you can identify the best path to deepening trust and building meaningful work relationships.

Transforming Power Dynamics

Shifting from a culture predominantly characterized by unproductive political interactions to trust-based ones requires commitment, because it is hard to integrate multiple—sometimes conflicting— value systems that drive interactions. Transformation of this magnitude requires unifying values, buy-in into those values, people development, modified systems of reward, and accountability to building trust.

Here is how you can work toward transforming unproductive political office dynamics:

- First, understand the current environment and how power is distributed, who the most powerful players are (formal and informal), and the structure of key networks.
- Identify the strengths of the political culture and determine how you can best use them. It is important to start with skills that already exist so they can be deployed constructively.
- Coach the primary power brokers at the top of your formal and informal hierarchies to start shifting their mental models.
- List the types of power that are prevalent within your organization.
- Identify opportunities to restructure your organizational chart, potentially redistributing power.
- Define how formal and informal political networks operate (similarly and differently). Identify the members of cliques

and groups, and who is in conflict. Then uncover the reason for relationships and how influence works.

- Support or even reward healthy work relationships.
- Part ways with those who refuse to or cannot collaborate.

Unproductive political office ecosystems can tip your cultural scales, so as many team members as possible should accept and endorse the new vision for interaction. To make the necessary shift, leaders should focus on reconfiguring the organizational chart, shifting employees to new departments or offering separation packages. Addressing political dynamics with soft-skill training is not enough. You may also need to change reporting lines to modify cultural norms. You may also change formal and informal policies and inspire people to be willing to use power in ways that support others.

Shifting from Equality to a Fairness Mindset

Equal treatment is not the end goal in an IFB organization because it can create imbalances. Instead, each situation should be considered based on relevant circumstances so the best possible decision can be made. The following case study further explores the adequacy of equal treatment.

Case Study: Is Equal Treatment the Optimal Approach?

Ken, a manager, is responsible for a team of five people. Reece, his top salesperson, arrives at work fifteen to thirty minutes late almost every day, but he consistently works ten- to twelve-hour days and achieves exceptional results.

The HR department introduced a policy in which all incidences of employees arriving at work after a five-minute grace period are to be documented and forwarded to the HR department, with corrective action taken after four violations. The intent of the policy is to manage attendance and the language of the policy is specific with no room for managerial discretion.

Even though Reece is a top performer, Ken feels compelled to document Reece's tardiness, so he submits the requisite reports for inclusion in Reece's file. Predictably, Reece is hurt and angered by Ken's decision, so he immediately stops putting in extra time. Reece's position is that if the organization is going to be exact with him, he will leave at 5:00 p.m. and start work at precisely 9:00 a.m. daily.

Ken managed the situation in a way that complies with the attendance policy because he felt he had to treat everyone equally. As a result, the team experienced a significant decline in team sales because he was no longer able to motivate his star performer after formally reporting his late arrivals.

What Ken didn't adequately consider was the fact that Reece was busy selling during the day and spent time after hours updating his administrative work. He kept his work up to date by staying behind and completing internal forms to finalize sales, filing documents, investigating client issues, and performing other duties that were key to the department's performance. Since Reece no longer trusted Ken to be fair, he concluded his extra work was not valued so he abruptly stopped going the extra mile (and started job hunting).

Other members of the team witnessed Ken's decision and knowing the value of Reece's contributions, they decided Ken could not be trusted to be fair. Ken weighed the pros and cons of his decisions, but he did not consider that when team morale is at stake he should use discretion. In other words, if the full context of a situation indicates that a manager should defend a team member, they should take that information to heart and undertake the team member's defense.

This case is not intended to suggest that you support the inappropriate actions of employees. It advocates making decisions by considering all the facts available to you, including the collective needs of the team. The intent is to help you to avoid inadvertently undermining your future effectiveness.

Tackling Groupthink

Groupthink is a phenomenon that occurs when people who work together think similarly, making decisions without the benefit of creative tension. This can lead to low-quality decisions because they don't allow diverse perspectives to emerge and enrich decisions and other creative conversations.

It is worthwhile taking time to determine if groupthink is present within your team because it can appear to be a "we" disposition when it is really a homogenous way of thinking and executing. The differentiating factor is creative tension. When there is no constructive tension, groupthink is most likely present, creating the appearance of cohesion. Some symptoms of groupthink are self-censorship, stereotyping, and rationalizing. Sometimes it is driven by loyalty so unquestioned beliefs are yet another potential symptom.

One indicator of the emergence of groupthink is expressed by an employee who asks, "What would my boss expect me to do?" They set out to respond in a way that reflects someone else's logic. Although this may seem to be a safe question to ask, a better one would be, "Given my knowledge of the situation and policies, how can I empower myself to resolve this situation optimally, using my unique perspective and skills?"

Groupthink can cause leaders to overlook or minimize certain trends or exaggerate them because it is supported by shared biases. You can ask the following questions to escape groupthink patterns:

- What have we not noticed about this trend in the past?
- What are other possible perspectives of this situation?
- Who can we include in this process to help us expand our thinking?
- How many ways can we redefine the challenge?
- What are our assumptions?
- What are our shared biases?
- Why isn't there any creative tension in our conversations?

- What have we not considered (because of our shared biases) that could be critical?
- What are some of the new ways we can solve this problem?
- How can we generate additional alternatives? What are the pros and cons of each one?

These questions focus leaders on creating diversity in their thinking. They also formulate a basic critical thinking path that sets the stage for an expanded view, creative tension and a more holistic conversation.

In certain organizational cultures, there is security in knowing team members think similarly. In fact, in some of these cultures it is an expectation and people attempt to preserve this safe space by using influence or even strong-arming tactics. Groupthinkers are most comfortable when decisions and the thought processes behind them are predictable, following an established framework of reason and action. Therefore, they will go the extra mile to guarantee safe space by embedding groupthink in tradition, core values, the way they lead — in almost everything they think and say. Sometimes they can go as far as attempting to make everything that does not fit into their way of thinking, seem to be wrong.

Cultivating group think among free thinkers can frustrate them and damage engagement levels. Instead, coworkers should be encouraged to access and express their authentic voices. When free thinking employees' voices are suppressed for a protracted period, some will leave the company, a few will continue to resist, while others lose their real voices, assuming one that helps them survive. In the latter example, employees may even start to believe the corporate programming is what they really think.

Remedying groupthink is difficult. To begin to help people form unique points of view, each team member will need to be encouraged to get reacquainted with their individual values and perspectives and feel safe enough to express them. Another way to make the shift is to build trust and encourage people to think freely and laterally.

Lateral Thinking: Balancing Groupthink

Lateral thinking, one possible solution to groupthink, doesn't rely on a familiar step-by-step approach. It allows leaders to resolve challenges using unconventional reasoning. Lateral thinking is nonlinear and creative and may not be immediately obvious to observers.

It involves taking time to better understand a problem before you attempt to resolve it. Lateral thinking strategies include: challenging your assumptions, considering the opposite of your beliefs, releasing judgments, using analytical tools, then using this information to generate multiple alternatives.

If you are a member of a team that has fallen prey to groupthink—which can include logical thinking—adopting a lateral-thinking approach may seem awkward at first. To stimulate this thinking style, leaders should consider diversifying their teams by awakening the diversity within their existing teams, or by changing the mix of persons over time. Keep in mind, all this would be futile if they don't lay the foundation of the Pillar of Trust so team members can feel protected enough to express divergent views.

Breaking Down Silos

Organizational silos form when teams attempt to operate as discrete, self-contained entities with little or no communication and limited interaction with other teams. Silos may be the result of damaged relationships, unproductive traditions, competition, or office politics. They can exist across geographies or in the same physical location.

Protective or territorial behavior can create silos due to different types of conflict. When protectionism or territoriality exists, the intent is to isolate or protect. Interestingly, both healthy and unhealthy team dynamics can appear within a siloed organization. For example, it is possible for healthy intradepartmental relationships to exist within a siloed team. In such cases, team members possess the skills needed for healthy intradepartmental connection but do not apply them to interdepartmental relationships—they are conditioned to selectively use their highly evolved team-strengthening and communication skills.

Sometimes members of internally cohesive departments may demonstrate overt hostility toward members of other departments. In certain situations, managers of siloed departments may go as far as instructing their direct and indirect reports not to communicate with other teams without permission. This type of directive can be detrimental to business and cause deep inefficiencies, compromising workflows.

Silos are counterproductive to building your "we" disposition because selective collaboration undermines the Pillar of Trust. Both intra- and interdepartmental connections are essential for various flows to operate as intended, both internally and externally. Therefore, after decision-makers identify silos and suss out their causes, they can plan and implement trust-building strategies designed to strengthen intra- and interdepartmental engagement as well as collaboration. The solutions suggested for neutralizing unhealthy political interactions are also applicable to breaking down silos.

Deconstructing Precedents

Some leaders use precedents as a tool to force or justify equal treatment. In law, a precedent is established when the outcome of a case is used as the basis for decisions in comparable cases. In organizations, precedents are established similarly. Organizational decision-makers can consider precedents as guidelines for future action. They might operate as undocumented policies, or they can be formalized into documented ones. In the name of equitable treatment, these precedents sometimes become strict guidelines.

Precedents are initially established when leaders encounter uncharted territory. They are used thereafter to address similar situations. If you are considering using a precedent to make a decision that can potentially affect the quality of your team's "we" disposition, you might ask yourself these questions:

- Is it optimal to apply the same solution to this circumstance because it seems similar on the surface? Why/why not?
- What are my assumptions?
- How does the current circumstance differ from the precedent-setting situation?
- What are the risks of abiding by and not considering the precedent? What are the opportunities?
- What are other ways to perceive the situation so it can be resolved differently?

Precedents should not be the deciding factor when balancing an organization. Your desired outcome should be to maintain team cohesion, not to apply policies based on past organizational decisions, disrupting engagement and collaboration.

Aligning Reward Systems

In many organizations, employees are encouraged to compete against each other and they are rewarded individually for achieving their goals. This type of reward system places higher value on individual achievement than collaboration and can contribute to toxic work environments.

Realistically, not everyone will connect with those they should work with, but team members should create what they deem to be optimal relationships. Optimized relationships are based on trust or shared goals and can facilitate problem solving, creativity, and productivity. When an optimal connection is not possible, leaders should decide if the relationship is critical and support an appropriate solution.

Parting Ways

Some team members will refuse to be aligned with your organization after you decide to implement IFB. At the outset, it is important to give them opportunities to modify behaviors that undermine the implementation of the Pillar of Trust. This means you can offer them developmental opportunities or you can initiate a restructuring exercise.

One admonition I would offer is to take a balanced approach to providing your coworkers opportunities to transform their behaviors. The longer you allow their counterproductive behaviors to persist after initiating the trust-building process, the more likely it is that your decision to leave a dysfunctional employee in place will sabotage your plan to enhance trust, thus perpetuating disequilibrium.

All in all, leaders should provide team members with reasonable opportunities for course correction. If destructive behaviors persist, and your culture is open to it, decision-makers can consider a separation package as an option. Whatever your context, the process must be perceived as a fair one when trust building is the end goal.

Competencies that Lead to a "We" Disposition

There are three components of the Six Seconds model of emotional intelligence: Know yourself, choose yourself, and give yourself (KCG). "Give yourself" is the interconnective part of model. It is also one of the essential building blocks of the "we" disposition providing the connective qualities that support collaboration.

Connecting with others requires both self-awareness and awareness of others. The ability to connect with others at work presupposes the inclination of people to care about each other—not in a boundaryless or codependent way, but in a way that engenders trust, respect, and collaboration. Leaders who can connect with others naturally possess: intermediate to advanced listening skills, responsiveness, the willingness to stand up for their team members, unwillingness to "throw their coworkers under the bus," authenticity and transparency, honesty, and an inclination to make quality time for their team members.

Because of the constantly evolving nature of the IFB Model, leaders need to constantly improve how they lead. A changing landscape demands modern leadership skills when remaining relevant and successful (however you define it) is important to your organization.

Here are a few of those skills:

- empathy and compassion
- generosity
- purpose
- your values and the "we" disposition
- using tones situationally
- coordination, *cooperation*, and collaboration
- sharing information
- embracing discomfort
- force is not an option

Empathy and Compassion

"Giving yourself" requires an ability to demonstrate empathy and take compassionate action. Empathy refers to your capacity to experience what another person is experiencing from that person's frame of reference. Empathy humanizes and connects you with your team; when present, you are very aware of the emotional effect you have on your coworkers, and they are aware of you.

When a leader makes a decision that they believe to be right, it is termed "right action." But when implementing the IFB Model, a commitment to right action is not enough if it is devoid of compassion. When a leader demonstrates strength without compassion, team members may perceive the leader to be abusive; sometimes this can take the form of bullying. In strengthening the collective Pillar of Trust, leaders need to exhibit just the right amount of compassion. The implementation of IFB can result in shifting power structures, and sometimes those who perceive themselves as losing power react emotionally.

Compassion is distinctly different from empathy, yet the two are intimately connected. Compassion motivates leaders to act with the objective of helping to transform the emotions of others. Compassion is love in action, it shows up as sensitivity toward others, and sensitivity can range from gentle to insensitive treatment.

Just to make one more distinction here, codependent action is very different than compassionate action although on the surface they may appear to be the same. "Codependence" describes a relationship in which one person relies on the other for their self-esteem, enabling underachievement. Here is an example:

Case Study: Compassion vs. Codependence

Claire is a new corporate trainer who recently completed a certification, so she can now deliver leadership seminars. She has a few students in her current class who are not new to the subject, they are seeking to refine their skills. Others are being exposed to the leadership content for the first time and struggling to become more effective. To explore the topic, Claire provided a reflection assignment, which the students were to discuss during the next class.

Todd, one of the students, was challenged by the material, so he reached out to Claire for help between sessions. Claire not only answered his questions, she virtually completed the homework for him, thus preventing him from developing his own responses to the assignment. Claire thought she was doing the right thing; she wanted to help Todd avoid the embarrassment of a low-quality contribution during the classroom discussion with his peers.

Claire perceived her support of Todd as thoughtful, even compassionate. She really felt she went above and beyond to help him avoid embarrassment. It didn't occur to her during the conversation that giving Todd the answers diminished his ability to grasp the material and transform his leadership.

To make matters worse, without realizing it, by doing Todd's work for him Claire also undermined her own effectiveness as a trainer very early in her career. Her presumed "right action" created a codependent dynamic that disabled Todd's ability to take responsibility for his learning.

When establishing the Pillar of Trust, leaders should clearly distinguish between compassion and codependence. On the surface, they may seem similar, but compassion is empowering where codependence weakens.

Codependent relationships sometimes support coworkers who are low performers. When codependent dynamics emerge, team members experiencing it can be lulled into thinking they are supported, cared for, and protected, but instead they are part of an elaborate behavioral pattern that preserves dependence and possibly underperformance.

Generosity

Generosity is yet another trait of people who exhibit a "we" disposition. It is a way people give of themselves and can be driven by compassion. It manifests in multiple ways, including within a team, when people are willing to contribute time and other resources to the goals of their coworkers.

Truly generous people give from their hearts when they sincerely value the people in their circles. They have no expectation of receiving anything in return. Like compassion, generosity shouldn't be confused with codependence because when considering generosity in the context of IFB, it is tied to healthy appreciation and is manipulation-free.

If a leader's giving is motivated by a personal agenda, the leader will give, but their giving is part of a quid pro quo arrangement that may be clearly articulated or assumed. This is not generosity when the motive is to preserve existing power dynamics or create new ones, it is manipulative.

On the opposite end of the generosity spectrum is tight-fistedness. Tight-fisted leaders are selective about who they support—if anyone—and how they support them. They deprive employees of what they need to remain engaged because of cost considerations, and the potential outcomes of tight-fistedness are disaffected employees and the emergence of an "us and them" dynamic.

Being selective when giving can mutate into favoritism when choices are primarily based on perceivably unjustified positive bias. Giving to and supporting only those you favor, can be counterproductive to building a connected team capable of agility and maintaining balance.

Purpose

Leaders driven by purpose don't only believe in what they are doing, they are doing what they are passionate about. When members of a team are doing what they were born to do, they use their talents regularly and are likely to be engaged.

What is even better is when coworkers are passionate about what they do, trust is present, collaboration is possible, and the organizational structure adequately connects work flows. In cases like this, the "we" disposition can transcend individual effort because people are connecting organically, facilitating flow — even optimized flow states — as a unified entity.

In an IFB organization, leaders attempt to ensure more people are aligned with their respective talents, and these talents are aligned with the vision and mission of the organization. By doing this, leaders can position the entire team for growth and engagement.

While some decision-makers are more disciplined about ensuring fit than others, there are organizations in which employees occupy positions that aren't quite right for them. In fact, some of these employees may be completely disinterested in their current roles. When building and strengthening the Pillar of Trust and placement emerges as a significant challenge, it's not practical or feasible to immediately terminate team members who are in roles that are not aligned with their passion and inherent talents.

You can tell if employees are aligned with their purposes when they automatically light up about their work. Their alignment with purpose shows up as irrepressible happiness, sometimes even when they are working in a toxic environment.

Some employees have a good idea of how their interests, talents, and abilities come together and support their purposes early on in their careers. Others embark on a path of self-discovery that reveals their purposes incrementally, over time. Then there are those who may never uncover it.

The search for purpose is a personal path with no definable timeline. It can be perplexing for people who work for many years in an organization and are unaware of the path that will take them to their highest potential.

A person's unique purpose is not something that can be imposed, yet leaders make decisions about where people should be placed on a regular basis without knowing their aspirations. The following questions can provide you with information you can use to help your team members define their deep-seated ambitions:

- What lights you up?
- What type of work ignites your passion?
- What are your strengths?
- How are your values aligned with the values of the company? If they are not, why not?

When your team members don't immediately connect with their why, you can help them by assigning projects that take them outside their comfort zones in relevant ways. When assigning stretch projects, you shouldn't automatically discount a person's ability if they don't successfully complete it. Stretch projects are developmental tools that facilitate insight by trial and error. Therefore, you should dig deeper into a failed developmental project to determine if you delegated too much too soon, if the person was pushed beyond their limits, or if this may not be the right direction for the person being developed. Another direction may be more appropriate.

Your Values and the "We" Disposition

According to research in neuroscience, values are both emotional and cognitive. They undergird goals and serve as intrinsic, driving forces. When values are internal, they shape opinions and can stimulate emotions that affect decisions. From an organizational perspective, values form the collective filter members of a team use to perceive their environment, so it makes sense to take steps to ensure values are aligned within the team and those collective, intrinsic values are aligned with those of the business.

A value system is a set of values that guide a person's behaviors. Value systems are not always easy to detect because sometimes they are situational. Situational value systems operate according to a fluid prioritization system that can lead to unpredictability when team members are motivated extrinsically or when a life event or decision shifts their value prioritization. Here is an example of how value systems can work:

Case Study: Shifting Value Priorities

Quinn recently accepted a position as senior manager. He is more than capable of performing in his new role, but not interested in long-term employment because he is quietly building his own business on the side. He accepted the new role because he values the experience and exposure he can receive in a senior position in a successful and structured organization. He knows he can make good use of any new skills he develops.

From his perspective, Quinn's long-term goal to start his own business aligns with his short-term decision to continue working for an employer so he can save. Quinn places high value on a freedom lifestyle, but the value he places on learning the skills he needs to run his own business outweighs his need to be free in the short-term. Once Quinn is satisfied that he has achieved his developmental goals, his freedom value will become his highest priority.

If Quinn is interested in developing himself in preparation for his departure, he can meet his long-term goals while being employed for the near term. When he starts to lose interest in working for an employer he will focus on his exit strategy.

In some organizations the true values and goals of decision-makers can be hard to detect due to the lack of cohesion among senior leaders. This can result from each leader having a different value system that guides their actions. Some have values and goals that contradict the organization's values; others are aligned with them. Mixed core values among decision-makers is a source of disconnection and low trust within an organization and as we have already established, there are tangible costs associated with low trust environments.

Using Tones Situationally

For our purposes, "tone" refers to how you manipulate your voice or choose your words and nonverbal language to project an attitude or create a mood. There are different tones you can experience or project: excited, curious, friendly, pretentious, angry, anxious, or sad. Whether you are opening a meeting or greeting someone in the hall, your tone will cause coworkers to be attracted, unaffected, or repulsed by you. Approachable, authentic tones are necessary if you intend to create an inclusive environment that is safe enough to facilitate creativity.

Mastering tone is important when you intend to cultivate a "we" disposition within your team. Leaders who exhibit self-mastery in this area can project the right tone regardless the circumstances. They are attuned to others and can adjust their tones to suit a variety of situations. They are also familiar with the responses each tone will generate. For instance, they know when they use a critical tone, it can lead to *blame*, excuses, cover-ups, or minimization, so they use tones that invite ownership, problem solving, and truthfulness.

Various tones can reinforce employee value and support psychological safety. A curious tone can achieve this, so can wise or appreciative ones. A friendly tone can also lead to a positive shift if friendliness doesn't change into a casual tone that invites impaired boundaries. A firm tone may also be necessary at times, and when used appropriately, it can preserve safe space. Adopting any of these tones can build or strengthen trust and collaboration.

Even when used appropriately, supportive tones will seem suspicious if historically, your first reaction has always been critical, dismissive, or frustrated. In cases like these, employees may interpret your attempts to change your tone as inauthentic if you don't take a realistic, authentic, and incremental approach to making the change.

Coordination, Cooperation, and Collaboration

Coordination, cooperation, and collaboration are all necessary for teamwork and are strengthened by a "we" disposition. Each of these three actions has a distinct purpose, even though some authors choose to use the words "cooperation" and "collaboration" interchangeably. I will adhere to definitions by Jesse Lyn Stoner, coauthor of *Full Steam Ahead! Unleash the Power of Vision in Your Work and Your Life.*[12]

- "Coordination is sharing information and resources so that each party can accomplish their part in support of a mutual objective. It is about teamwork in implementation. Not creating something new."
- "Cooperation is important in networks where individuals exchange relevant information and resources in support of each other's goals, rather than a shared goal. Something new may be achieved as a result, but it arises from the individual, not from a collective team effort."
- "Collaboration is working together to create something new in support of a shared vision. The key points are that it is not an individual effort, something new is created, and the glue is the shared vision."

In healthy work environments, leaders use coordination, cooperation, and collaboration to attain their goals. In other cultures, internal competition can be the primary driver of goal achievement. Keep in mind the notion that even when it is couched as "friendly," competition is the antithesis of coordination and collaboration because it creates tensions that can become unproductive when coworkers opt to use low-integrity, competitive strategies. This strategy also has the potential to lower morale when results are made public, shaming low performers.

While cooperation can be less effective in achieving team goals than collaboration, cooperation can be effective because people in different departments have a variety of deadlines that may not always align, but they can still help each other by working around interdepartmental workflows.

Collaboration differs from cooperation. With cooperation, team goals are not necessarily shared, and if they are, they may not be assigned the same level of priority. Some decision-makers assume collaboration exists within their teams because of clear evidence of productivity. The difference between cooperation and collaboration is in how teams work. Collaboration is based on shared goals and vision. When they are collaborating, people take ownership and care about the team's results. Above average productivity is possible when team members cooperate, but sustainable, high productivity is possible when coworkers collaborate.

The differences between cooperation and collaboration can be muddied when employees care about the success of their team and collaborate within the department, but don't collaborate with other departments. This is conditional and cannot be fully considered as collaboration.

Leaders need to attune to their teams because sometimes people on the same team should be collaborating, but instead they are cooperating. This can happen in competitive work environments. It can also happen when incompatible coworkers are forced to work together. If they are not able to establish healthy relationships, the quality of communication is most likely compromised, possibly affecting team output in both the short and long-terms.

Collaboration is not only dependent on individuals being predisposed to working together; it also requires sound structures — such as organizational charts, policies, and procedures — unencumbered by emotion, incompetence, or resource challenges. The IFB Model is collaborative, so it is important to make distinctions between coordination, cooperation, and collaboration.

Case Study: Aidan Cares

Aidan is a senior officer within a government agency. He is an active member of his team and represents his country at multiple international meetings. He forged strong work relationships with international stakeholders over the years because of his integrity, readiness to constructively challenge others, professionalism, and willingness to do work no one else wants to do. Aidan's commitment to excellence and the "we" disposition positively affect his local team as well as international stakeholders.

He is organized and thoughtful, and he applies high standards to his work to ensure quality outcomes. Aidan will push back whenever his team inadvertently veers away from the goals of a project. He has no problem being a leader who challenges others respectfully. His commitment to team goals is balanced with his commitment to his own goals and those of his individual team members.

Aidan's first step in any collaborative effort is to understand the goals of the project; if the goals are not well defined, he helps to clarify them. When he buys into a project, he will support it and use his skills of influence to persuade others to do the same. Depending on his role, Aidan will also assist with coordinating projects because he knows sound practices are essential to successful outcomes.

His coordination aligns with his deployment of people on projects, so where possible, their assignments are aligned with their individual career and developmental goals. He knows their aspirations and seeks to support their motivation.

Sharing Information

In cultures where a "we" disposition is evident, leaders share information as a form of team empowerment, enabling informed action. Sharing information is also an effective tool of connection and support that can create and sustain balance.

As with developing other competencies contained within the Pillar of Trust, sharing information should not be forced but facilitated instead. It is more likely that team members will share information automatically when leaders

- are trustworthy;
- are competent with communicating relevant information;
- develop the team so each member communicates more effectively;
- implement an appropriate communication framework; and
- care about their team members.

Communication, or sharing information, is a critical part of the interconnective infrastructure explored in Part I of this book. Communication is everyone's responsibility, so all team members need to participate in the system of communication ensuring appropriate balance between transparency and confidentiality. This requires everyone to strengthen their communication skills and make time to employ them.

Embracing Discomfort

When it comes to individuals, discomfort is a natural part of the transformative process. Because the IFB Model is designed to establish change-based organizations, IFB leaders need to be able to adequately address their own discomfort with change and that of their team members. There will always be varying levels of comfort.

At a macro level, there should be a sense of uneasiness with the status quo before change takes place. However, discomfort is not enough. Some leaders and employees experience discomfort and only chronically complain about their organizations. Therefore, because they lack an influential voice, and resources, vision, or a plan, they remain immobilized.

Sometimes executives don't recognize that they are operating in a mode that may be nonbeneficial because of cover ups. For instance, an organization may be in the midst of a people crisis, but decision-makers are unable to recognize the risks because of manipulations of language and metrics designed to minimize the crisis state.

During a crisis, leaders and their teams should pay close attention to key performance indicators even if a business remains profitable. Profit and productivity can create a false sense of security, obscuring leaders' abilities to identify potential long-term risks. Their short-termism can cause them to overlook degenerative indicators such as declining employee engagement or cultural shifts.

Force Is Not an Option

The Pillar of Trust requires leaders and other employees to build relationships. While building the Pillar of Trust may trigger transfers and promotions, employees shouldn't feel forced into "getting along". Even if people are on the same team and workflows connect them, you cannot force healthy working relationships into being.

Conversely, people cannot be forced out of relationships. For example, when employees are transferred from one department to another to separate them, it probably won't disrupt their relationships. If a relationship is deeply rooted, the team members in the relationship will adapt.

When considering relationship architecture, leaders should attempt to orchestrate interpersonal connections using skills like impact and influence. However, if the chemistry isn't quite right, there may be little to no relationship-strengthening potential, no matter how influential the leader may be.

To understand relationship potential, you should be aware of the dynamics between your team members. To achieve this, you can seek firsthand knowledge and not rely on narratives from people who may intentionally or unintentionally distort information. Also, you should be aware of your own biases and seek to be as objective as possible. Your own observations can give you an understanding of naturally or abnormally occurring relationship architecture so you can identify the least invasive ways to transform the team.

Empowering Teams Using the "We" Disposition

Leaders who demonstrate a "we" disposition can focus appropriately on their teams. They are skilled at creating the feeling that "we are in this together." These leaders operate from a place of authenticity by being themselves and allowing members of their teams to do the same.

An empowered team can focus on change as a constant, both in the present and the future. These teams are empowered to make decisions and they have a tested communication framework in place that facilitates the movement of information throughout organizations.

Empowered team members are not trapped in the behavioral loops of the past. Rather, they can challenge tradition and are willing to let go of what no longer serves them. Leaders facilitate this when they are attuned to their perpetually changing environments and know that agility keeps them relevant. Empowered team members who possess a "we" disposition adopt shared goals. Their personal and professional goals coexist, but both are being adequately addressed, allowing them to focus on success through collaboration.

The IFB Model is a framework that facilitates change as a constant with growth as an anticipated by-product. The model depends heavily on establishing a "we" disposition within the Pillar of Trust because inclusion strengthens relationships and makes collaboration possible.

Empowerment is essential in change-based organizations because it also facilitates agility and sustainability, delegating power to allow people to make decisions on the spot. Empowerment should be evidenced throughout an organization for it to have maximum effect. Organizations that rely heavily on policies and procedures as controls can shift toward empowerment through rewriting those formal and informal policies and procedures so there is more discretion allowed in the new policy framework.

Becoming a Changed-Based Organization through Development and Design

One of the most important leadership skills necessary for strengthening the entire Pillar of Trust is the capacity for restructuring relationships. Of equal importance is developing team members as relationships change. Both skills depend on the outward-facing characteristic of the "we" disposition underpinned by integrity and emotional self-mastery.

When it comes to the Pillar of Trust, it is not enough to schedule employees for training sessions and expect them to modify their behaviors without being provided complementary developmental opportunities. They will need additional support including (but not limited to) establishing accountabilities, upgrading job descriptions. Other important support elements include providing coaching, mentoring, cross-training, rotational learning experiences, and stretch assignments to reinforce your team members' developmental goals.

Part III

IFB by Design

Envisioning a change-based organization founded on IFB principles is no mean feat when leaders are accustomed to treating changes as "projects." In transactional organizations, decision-makers tend to regard change mandates as discrete processes, especially when daily routines have programmed their thinking because of unrelenting deadlines. When employees in transaction-dense cultures are under pressure for exceptional results, the skills and mindsets they need to treat change as a constant have virtually no opportunities to emerge.

Part III provides guidelines for designing, planning, and implementing the IFB Model within your organization. In this part of the book, we'll take a deeper dive into how you can create an IFB organization. You can refer to it whenever you are considering change. In addition to molding agile leaders IFB can contribute to the implementation of ongoing learning and continuous process improvement while integrating ongoing change into your entire organizational agenda.

Part III assumes decision-makers have not yet implemented IFB for the first time, so the initial IFB change process will start out as an initiative. Thereafter, it becomes an integral part of your normal operations. The leadoff chapter in Part III offers an overview of the change framework for IFB design and implementation. This same framework will be replicated in subsequent chapters.

On a final note, as you read Part III, remember that although we continue to explore the IFB Model and Pillar of Trust as though the components are disconnected, they are all intricately linked. The elements of each of the models contribute to overall organizational stability because they are continually interactive and reliant on each other.

CHAPTER 12

IFB BY DESIGN

Design creates culture. Culture shapes values. Values
determine the future.

—Robert L. Peters, graphic designer and educator

Interconnectivity, flow, and balance are three dynamics that operate within any active ecosystem. Restructuring these dynamics to establish change-based organizations requires carefully crafted IFB design. The design stage is predicated on your vision and precedes plan implementation. It adds depth and breadth to a vision and allows decision-makers to conceptualize new ways of interacting within their ecosystems using a mix of new and existing skills, systems, and frameworks.

When IFB leaders focus on design they should consider what is important for their ecosystem(s). The design ought to incorporate features that motivate their teams, and it should adhere to their core values. It should also consider how the ecosystem (culture) works, who defines it, and which resources are available—including time.

In most organizations time operates like cryptocurrency, where a fixed amount is available, and people access this resource within established parameters. One of the keys to the success of the IFB Model is to find ways to maximize the use of time within available hours. Mastering the use of time is critical because for an organization to be change-based, leaders need to achieve balance between time spent executing duties and projects, and time spent developing the team and strengthening relationships.

Leaders should approach IFB design as an integral part of their perpetual balancing activities. If a flaw in design becomes apparent, it should be solved at the causal level, not patched. As with buildings, IFB design flaws can have catastrophic consequences when they're just papered over.

IFB design requires both technical know-how and innovation. As an IFB designer, you should establish as many design teams as you need to enrich the brainstorming, visualization, planning, and implementation processes.

IFB requires leaders who can cultivate the strengths of their team members helping them increase their capacity to produce. Consequently, wherever possible, you should place people on design and planning teams based on diversity and their demonstrated and potential strengths. In this way you can maximize the effectiveness of your design.

Human interactions are sometimes connected, other times they appear not to be; they are dynamic and unpredictable. They drive interactions between the layers of the interconnective infrastructure and as a result, they directly affect internal and external flows, and what your leadership team can (and cannot) do to keep your organization in a healthy state of balance.

Establishing trust-based interactions can be challenging when unproductive relations are tolerated for a long time. Sometimes these dynamics are observable, and when these counterproductive patterns contradict espoused core values, they may go "underground" to survive in stealth mode. A shift like this can happen in response to a change initiative that confronts people's comfort zones.

When your IFB design is effective, it can cause individual reactions to emerge in different ways, ranging from predictable and healthy to unexpected or agitated. Regardless the emergent states, once they materialize leaders have information they can use to facilitate balance and further transformation.

While design is an important part of the IFB change process, this chapter also provides an overview of the entire change process.

It explores a framework that starts with diagnosing your existing environment and visualizing your future circumstances. The next step is design, the focal point of the IFB change model. Then you begin the planning, and execution processes. The final stage is adjustment — or, in IFB language, it is the balancing phase.

Why the IFB Design and Implementation Processes Are Important

IFB design involves visualizing the new state, collecting data relevant to your goals, and then analyzing that data. Out-of-the-box thinking and exploration allow potential designs to address arising and existing priorities of key stakeholders. Ideally, designers should develop more than one solution to ensure decision-makers can select or integrate the designs so the final solution can optimize return on investment of their time, money, and other resources.

IFB design requires leaders to create a blueprint for their vision before planning begins. Many leaders skip a step, shifting from visioning to planning. They should include design as a separate step, detaching it from visualization and planning, thus allowing leaders to add important detail to the vision while creating a structure before starting the plan. Establishing design as a distinct part of the change process will help ensure critical components of your vision and values are built into your plan.

Forming an IFB Design Team

Before commencing the change process, decision-makers should appoint an IFB design team. This may be the same team that creates the plan and implements it, or it may include people who have innovative and other relevant strengths. Once they complete various design options, the appropriate team should reassess the organization's readiness for adopting the qualities of a change-based organization founded on the IFB framework.

If an organization is not in "ready mode," the senior team is responsible for getting the organization poised for change. This means leaders should also possess persuasive skills because board members may need to be convinced that a delay is the best alternative.

Members of the IFB design team should be selected based on the following criteria:

- strategic thinking capabilities
- advanced communication skills (including persuasion skills)
- visioning skills (creativity and innovation)
- cultural change experience
- scenario thinking (because there should be multiple design scenarios)
- problem-solving skills
- relevant technical and analytic skills
- planning and execution skills (some members of the planning team need to be able to translate the design into reality, so it is important to include planners and implementers)
- influence within the organization and resourcefulness
- mastery of IFB principles

As part of the pre-design phase, members of the design team will need to distinguish between "important" and "urgent" priorities. Important actions are critical but there is no particular time pressure, whereas urgent priorities require immediate action. By distinguishing between the two, the design team can consider right timing when they get to the planning stage. This is important because poorly synchronized plan execution can lead to premature gap closure and other circumstances that trigger unexpected imbalances.

The IFB Change Process

The beauty of the IFB change process is that it takes dynamics into account that are already in motion. In other words, the framework is integrative, so it can accommodate tools and systems already in use by your organization. It also shifts perceptions, creating new ones that can drive meaningful changes.

IFB is not something organizations do—it's who they are. IFB organizations can lead the way as the external environment becomes increasingly unpredictable. Change powered by IFB is unrestrictive; it is comprised of daily, incremental adjustments.

Readiness for IFB Change

Research consistently suggests 70 percent of change initiatives fail. This is a sobering statistic that indicates how important it is to be fully prepared before you tackle any type of change. Change readiness assessments provide information organizations can also use to determine the relevance of their change vision, the best timing of an initiative, costs, benefits, risks, and opportunities. This information can provide valuable insights leaders can use to help ensure there is a higher probability of change success.

After decision-makers identify their organization's state of readiness for IFB implementation, change leaders should apprise the design team, keeping them in the loop so they can understand how to integrate readiness considerations into the IFB design. Overall design should also help organizations to better facilitate strategic planning and implementation, ensuring an integrated.

The timing of a change readiness assessment can be determined by decision-makers. Some decision-makers conduct readiness assessments before they plan for change, for example, when a team's culture is so toxic that it will negatively affect the potential for success of any change plan produced. Others test readiness after change is planned so they can understand change readiness needs using the plan as a determining factor.

Some leaders jump head-first into change processes without assessing the team's readiness. In IFB organizations, periodic change readiness assessments can be useful. These four approaches have their respective pros and cons; Table 12.1 explores these advantages and disadvantages in greater detail.

Conduct Your Change Readiness Assessment before You Plan Your Change	
Pros	**Cons**
• This will allow you to create a change readiness plan and implement it prior to the design and planning cycles. • It may help to reduce the thinking limitations (groupthink and biases) that can affect the design and planning phases before planning begins. • Your organization can be better positioned for change and the plan can focus more on the intended change, rather than readiness for it. • It reduces the risk of change failure. • It encourages team members to embrace IFB change (change as a constant) and planned initiatives.	• Organizational decision-makers may not have the luxury of time to conduct a readiness assessment. As a result, pressures may cause leaders to create and execute a suboptimal change readiness plan, leading to the risk of a failed change initiative. • There is no guarantee it will improve long-term outcomes. Any plan can take a different direction than initially intended. • It may be too early to plan for readiness without knowing the plan, its related costs, and potential risks. • Team members can experience change burnout.
Conduct a Change Readiness Assessment after You Plan Your Change	
Pros	**Cons**
• The intent behind this approach is to reduce the potential for change failure. • The right change sponsors can emerge after change is planned or while changes are being implemented.	• There is the risk that the organization is not ready for change or is unable to become ready while it is already in the process of change.

• Once IFB is implemented and your leadership team has already transformed your organization into a change-based organization, this is an unavoidable path.	• Employees can become overwhelmed because not only do they have to learn new technical skills, they may also need to learn new behavioral skills while experiencing the stress of implementation. • It may cost your organization if readiness is assessed too late.
Conduct No Change Readiness Assessments	
Pros	**Cons**
• Your organization may speed up the change process if decision-makers are already attuned to barriers to change and can build strategies to address these barriers into the implementation process.	• Your organization runs the risk of not detecting critical, uncompromising readiness challenges that act as barriers to successful implementation. This can retard the process or worse, cause change failure.
Conduct Periodic Change Readiness Assessments	
Pros	**Cons**
• Once your organization adopts the IFB framework, it has become change-based. It makes sense that leaders would want to ensure their teams are always poised for change. By building change competencies and mindsets within your team, you can improve organizational agility.	• There are costs associated with this approach. Positioning a team for change requires investments of time and other resources, even sacrificing revenue generation opportunities.

Table 12.1   *Making a Change Readiness Decision*

As suggested in Table 12.1, it is conceivable that decision-makers won't have the luxury of time to remove obstacles to readiness before a change initiative is undertaken. In cases like this, leaders can design their plans to remove obstacles and execute changes concurrently. Sometimes this means they will have to make dramatic decisions regarding staffing and the like to avoid delays.

If change leaders assess readiness and decide an organization is ill-equipped to proceed, the next step is to understand why and then create a plan to position the team. If an organization is not ready and change plans proceed, several outcomes are possible: a) the change fails; b) the change appears to have worked, but the success is illusory; or c) because of advanced change and technical competencies of employees executing the plans, the initiative can still be a success.

Obstacles to Readiness

The list below outlines some of the obstacles a change readiness assessment can be used to uncover:

- a vulnerable Pillar of Trust
- office politics
- incompetent staff
- an inadequate organizational chart
- weak strategic planning and execution competencies
- inability to adequately finance capital projects
- insufficient financial capacity to underwrite change
- ineffective communication channels
- inflexible policies and procedures—inflexibility and control leave no room for engagement, creativity, or innovative problem solving
- an unclear vision for change

As already emphasized, just as layers of stone and sand reveal the Earth's story, there are layers within organizations made up of individual and team memories resulting from corporate decisions, culture, traditions, systems, hierarchy, and politics. These layers form an organization's history and this information can either enable or inhibit flow. Therefore, when appropriate, leaders should attempt to understand the organizational history, so it can be used (or mitigated) for maximum effect.

The Change Readiness Assessment

Change readiness surveys can be created and facilitated in-house. If trust is low, an organization may obtain more accurate results through external assessment providers who offer proven tools that can define your organization's state of readiness for change from the following perspectives:

- clarity of the vision for change
- change leadership skills
- communication effectiveness
- capacity and willingness to change
- organizational design
- internal and external events
- culture

Once you facilitate a readiness assessment, the following questions can help you analyze the results and make decisions based on the data:

- Which obstacles, if resolved, will yield the most return?
- Who are the key stakeholders in this change? How can we strengthen their support?
- Which single solutions can resolve multiple obstacles to change?
- Who are the right leaders to champion the change readiness solutions? How can they be held accountable? How well equipped are they to deliver the solution(s)?

- What is the state of our Pillar of Trust? What are the strengthening and weakening agents?

- What resources do we need to get ready for change? If there are limited resources, how can we creatively use what we have or can access?

If it makes sense, while leaders ready their teams for change they can use this time to create buy-in for the changes to come. This means executives who were not part of the decision-making process will have an opportunity to express their commitment or concerns before they announce changes to middle management. The same opportunity should be given to management before they make announcements to the general employee population; otherwise, potential pushback can come from those expected to lead changes.

The IFB Change Process

The IFB change model is different than other change models because it emphasizes design and balance as ongoing processes. It operates as a perpetual change loop, because the IFB Model both drives and responds to perpetual cycles of change. It incorporates some traditional change-related steps, but the integral elements of interconnectivity, flow, and balance distinguish it from other change models.

As IFB leaders guide their organizations through change processes, they are diagnosing, visioning, designing, planning, implementing, and balancing. The rest of this chapter is dedicated to defining these steps.

STEP 1: DIAGNOSTICS

The purpose of the diagnostic stage is to conduct research that will inform visioning and design activities. Diagnostic undertakings include assessing interpersonal relationship quality and the effectiveness of communication practices. Relevant policies can also be reviewed to determine how they are being administered and if they are effective or potentially counterproductive to anticipated changes. According to Table 12.1, readiness surveys are yet another diagnostic tool.

Priority flow dynamics are next on the list. As part of the diagnostic process, IFB change leaders should be intimately familiar with them, so they can understand the potential for achieving and sustaining future balance. Decision-makers should also seek to define how their organizations naturally bring themselves into balance. Here are a few questions you can use to find the answers you need:

- How do imbalances manifest in your organization?
- What skills and tools do leaders typically use to balance and rebalance?
- How effective are your balancing actions? What needs to stop, start, or continue?

Some leaders use scoping exercises to gather information and diagnose their current state before starting a change initiative. A scoping exercise is an activity where experts identify and evaluate the strengths and challenges of a team and the productivity of the operation. As a data-collection effort, scoping clarifies the parameters of a project or supports decision-makers with design and planning.

Scoping exercises should involve as many key stakeholders as possible so they can integrate their perspectives into the vision, design, planning and balancing steps. When used optimally, the results of a scoping exercise can contribute to the formation of a relevant plan and reduce the chances of project failure.

Scoping has at least two purposes: to confirm what is already known and to discover the unknown. Decision-makers often deploy subject matter experts to collect this information, so whenever possible, a scoping team made up of people with diverse skills and perspectives should be dispatched to facilitate a comprehensive view of the current state.

In summary, when scoping exercises are effectively executed, they provide decision-makers with critical information that can inform the visioning, design, planning, and implementation phases of IFB change. Scoping also provides leaders with data they can use to make informed decisions about the resources required for intended changes. It reveals both potential obstacles and facilitative elements within an organization and offers decision-makers a better understanding of the team's potential to undertake a change process.

Diagnosing the Pillar of Trust

While some types of scoping can provide anecdotal information about people dynamics, qualitative information isn't necessarily precise or representative. It doesn't provide an unobstructed view of the pervasiveness of beneficial and unproductive people dynamics within teams.

Quantitative diagnostic instruments for understanding trust and the nature of people dynamics include climate and other team assessments, trust profiles, engagement surveys, and leadership assessments which include 360-degree multi-rater surveys. The diagnostic instruments you choose to use to define the current state of your Pillar of Trust should define trust, relationship quality, engagement, culture, and your climate.

The IFB Model depends on organizational leaders endeavoring to achieve a high level of team trust. Improvements in trust opens doors for higher-quality communication, improved structures, and a collaborative approach to strategic implementation. In other words, it is a foundational quality for developing higher-performing teams.

When an inadequate foundation of trust exists within an organization, leaders have a good starting point for strengthening their relationship architecture (you will be provided additional tools for this exercise in the next chapter). If trust levels are still not high enough to meet a minimum standard needed for change success, decision-makers can first establish a developmental plan for building their Pillar of Trust—starting with themselves.

This learning plan should ensure that decision-makers and all other employees develop the interpersonal skills they need to construct the Pillar of Trust throughout the organization. It should also identify whether change leaders possess the capacity and determination to make "trust-friendly" changes in their leadership styles. From a structural perspective, these leaders should also take active measures to be sure the structures don't contradict their trust-building goals with ineffective policies and imprudent organizational chart modifications.

STEP 2: CREATE YOUR VISION FOR IFB

The visioning stage is the second step in the IFB change process. It comes after the scoping and other diagnostic exercises. Diagnostics can expose elements of your organization that are not readily per-ceived by decision-makers, uncovering limiting biases, and bringing information to the design and planning processes that needs to be seriously considered. This is especially useful the first time IFB is being implemented.

The IFB vision is different than and connected to the overall strategic vision of a change-based organization. The IFB component of the vision defines the desired state of interconnectivity, flow, and balance: the entire operating system. Therefore, as you visualize your plan from an IFB perspective, you should envision your culture from the standpoint of how you want interpersonal relationships to operate, how the internal communication grid will work, what the best structures would be, and of course, how IFB will integrate with the strategic plan. You can also avail yourself of the opportunity to use the visioning process to redefine your culture.

Core values can have universal benefits, both within your team and outside your organization. Each organization should define their core values and when implementing the IFB Model, and the Pillar of Trust should always be non-negotiable. Non-core values are not universal, so they only benefit some stakeholders. They are likely present but should not override core values. Where possible, they can be reinforced if they can optimize the effects of the core values.

Core values should play a starring role in your visioning, design, planning, implementation, and balancing phases of the IFB change process. This is because leaders should always seek to maintain alignment between core values, decisions, and actions.

Visioning Guidelines for IFB

As you embark on the IFB change journey, remember that IFB is not a linear model. Although the IFB visioning process illustrated in Figure 12.1 appears to be linear, your execution of it will more likely be cyclic, requiring you to create an overall vision for the IFB implementation then separating out the components. This is because when you visualize interconnectivity, you need to know what flow and balance will look like in relation to the connections you foresee.

New relationships are unknown quantities, so known connections can be used to mitigate the risks of potentially counterproductive interactions. Sometimes a lone individual cannot adequately support integrating a new coworker the same way a team can—it can "take a village" to onboard and orient new team members.

This is an important reason why connections between team members should not be visualized as dyads—two-person relationships. Instead, network coordinators/designers should visualize the architecture of the network (teams, hubs, power distribution, etc.) at a macro level while also understanding the patterns and pervasiveness two-person communication patterns.

Change leaders may need to recalibrate their vision during the design phase. This is one of the benefits of adding a design phase before planning starts because as diverse ideas are put forward

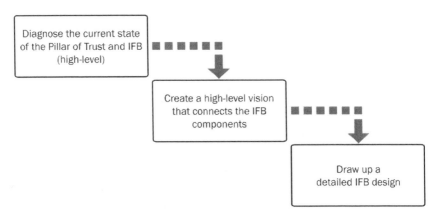

Figure 12.1   *The IFB Visioning Process*

during this stage, your team may identify flaws in your vision or different versions of the vision.

By following the IFB visioning process defined in Figure 12.1, you can develop a macro perspective of how you will implement and institutionalize IFB within your organization with the goal of becoming a change-based organization. As I mentioned previously, even though you may envision each component of the IFB Model separately, creating an overarching vision for IFB operation provides a unified view you can use to design, plan, and implement changes.

STEP 3: IFB DESIGN

In architecture, there is a process called predesign that happens when an architect outlines a project before starting the drawings. They consider zoning and building codes as well as long-term goals and expected difficulties. During this phase, architects produce summaries and conduct research to understand the design parameters. This involves site visits and data review.

The next step is to create schematic designs. In architecture, schematic designs are informal sketches that illustrate multiple concepts, each with a unique feature. Developing a variety of schematics adds breadth to the creative conversation. By brainstorming alternative structures, architects can explore potential opportunities and complications and remedy them in their plans.

IFB design should be approached similarly. Before plans are made, the diagnostic information should be analyzed in much the same way it is in the architectural predesign phase. As already mentioned, data collection may include scoping and collection of survey data. It can also include available internal metrics such as retention statistics, risk reports, succession plans, strategic plans, audit reports, and efficiency studies.

Once architects start their schematic designs they attach rough cost estimates to each option. When their client selects a design, the architect refines it. Similarly, the IFB design team can provide a minimum of two, change scenarios. Each option should also incorporate a budget as well as nonfinancial costs or risks. The selected alternative can then be refined in preparation for or as part of the planning process.

STEPS 4 AND 5: IFB PLANNING AND IMPLEMENTATION

While different organizations possess varying degrees of competence when it comes to planning and execution, multiple authors provide adequate resources that can help you in these areas. Part III of this book emphasizes what makes the IFB change process different; in it, the diagnostic, visioning, design, and balancing components of the change process are more developed than planning and execution. These are the more creative parts of the process.

STEP 6: ADJUSTMENT AND BALANCING

This is the part of the process that ensures change operates as a constant. When change happens as part of an enterprise initiative, leaders can't possibly consider everything that will go wrong, so it's probable there will be missteps during the planning phase and other parts of the process. Adjustment and calibration are natural phenomena in any ecosystem. When there is a change project, adjustment happens during and after any of the phases and is dependent on an effective *feedback loop* that conveys reliable information through communication channels to the right people.

Adjustment is a balancing action that ensures that the intended rate and quality of flow are in accordance with change plans. Adjustment kicks in when change plans don't adequately consider potential obstacles (or fail to implement processes to address them). Adjustment is also a critical tool for dealing with the unexpected.

When change leaders are committed to achieving balance by using adjustment tactics, they listen carefully to feedback, investigate without bias, and modify action plans based on vital information. For adjustment to be effective, there must be a multidirectional information flow and feedback loops that are clear of obstructions. When something counterproductive to your change plan happens, the information needs to be communicated through the appropriate channels so leaders can make the necessary decisions.

If change leaders push back with blame or retaliation when vexing feedback moves up communication channels, the flow of information can grind to a halt. No one wants to have their careers negatively affected by being labeled as a resistor when their intent is to offer or refine a solution.

Adjustment and balance are contingent on the capacity of change leaders to listen and make the best possible decisions given the information available. Leaders who take too long to make decisions, or ones who consistently make the wrong ones, compromise the ability of their teams to execute change successfully hindering organizational growth.

The adjustment and implementation phases should entail multidirectional communication, so in addition to their obvious functions these phases can also be used to build trust and strengthen work relationships when well-orchestrated.

As introduced in Chapter 11, research in neuroscience reveals that changed behaviors and attitudes result from doing things differently, not through rote training. Therefore, shifting attitudes and strengthening engagement are best accomplished through effective communication practices and employing the principles embedded within the Pillar of Trust.

CHAPTER 13

MAPPING YOUR INTERPERSONAL RELATIONSHIP ARCHITECTURE

At their core, organizations are just a giant network of relation-
ships. So, if you fail to build those relationships, your chances
of succeeding are not very high.

— Tom Rath, employee engagement consultant and author

Relationship economics refers to how people form, grow and let go of relationships based on whether they are viewed as costs or benefits. In daily workplace interactions, considerations about the pros and cons of relationships can act as a filter for strategic, transactional, and other decisions.

Even when leaders and employees are unaware of the economics of relationships, they are part of the ecosystem. When relationships are destabilized, and interactions are poorly coordinated, they have the potential to adversely affect results. Therefore, network coordinators (who are also leaders), should observe relationships on an ongoing basis to proactively mitigate risks or preserve the strengths of the networks.

According to authors David Ehrlichman and Matthew Spence at Converge (a team of strategists and designers committed to social and environmental impact), "The effectiveness of any collaborative effort — whether it's a network or an organization — depends primarily on the strength of the connections that exist between the participants involved." Similarly, in the IFB Model, the strength of the connections can drive team performance, but this is dependent on whether goals are shared or if there is trust.

In certain organizations, relationship economics operate with the currencies of power and influence, and these currencies are fueled by and have outcomes that affect the emotions, thoughts and actions of people within complex networks. Others operate based on the currencies of integrity, and trust. Serving the greater good, rather than individual agendas.

Mixed emotions typically coexist within an organizational ecosystem. These emotions (and related thoughts) create an emotional topography that overlays an ecosystem. Organizational leaders refer to this topography as climate or morale, and both are affected by trust. The emotional topography of an organization is characterized by peaks and valleys and exists within a culture and its related subcultures, sometimes shifting in response to internal and external stimuli.

The emotional topography of an organization is active and therefore fluctuates. Both internal and external dynamics affect it. When influential members of a team are focused on building power structures for themselves, the more likely they will be to form relationships that serve their individual agendas, further affecting team climate.

The Relationship Architecture

Networks of relationships that exist within organizational ecosystems configures themselves into the relationship architecture. Effective network coordinators use a mapping process to first understand, then reconfigure (if necessary or possible) interpersonal dynamics in alignment with strategic priorities.

In addition to formal structures that resemble organizational charts, relationships can configure themselves into informal structures that may or may not be hierarchical, with some existing within and others that extend outside organizations. Relationships can organize as networks, though they may not. They can enhance or detract from the status of a person within a relationship, making some people powerful by association.

When leaders are interested in using IFB to create a change-based organization, they should first seek to understand the form and function of organizational relationships and networks. In companies where balanced and focused leaders can strengthen trust and engagement, these leaders should take care that changes don't create or reinforce unproductive imbalances.

Relationships are at the heart of the IFB Model, and as you know, the Pillar of Trust is what improves the quality of these relationships. Multiple relationships coexist and operate within and outside organizations as dyads, triads, or networks that may (or may not) effectively facilitate communication and other important flows.

As you design your IFB relationship architecture, keep in mind that relationships cannot be forced. As with any other type of relationship, there needs to be an element of chemistry or an openness to it. Sometimes neither one is present. This is compounded by the reality that some relationships can be unpredictable or fragile. Nonetheless, connections can be coordinated when there is perceived mutual benefit.

Each relationship or network has a purpose. Some are closed, others have porous boundaries that allow people to venture in and out. There are relationships and networks that are aligned with the goals of the organization, others are not. At the individual level, a person can lead in certain networks and follow in others. These distinctions are important to understand as you seek to define relationships and networks within your organization and how they work.

Relationship Intelligence

Whether from a leader's bird's-eye view of network dynamics or an employee's perspective, *relationship intelligence* is built on foundations of emotional and social intelligence. Relationship intelligence involves understanding why relationships and networks exist, how they operate, why they unravel, and how they are powered. It also requires understanding who your informal leaders are, how they affect your business, what their communication norms are, and how they establish and manage boundaries.

Leaders who possess relationship intelligence can connect as effectively with the entire team (as a group) as they can with one-on-one conversations with team members. They know what they need to do to stimulate team cohesion and how to sustain synergies.

Leaders who possess advanced relationship intelligence competencies know they can't force people into relationships. Instead, they have powerful skills of influence and can coordinate networks without imposing their will on others. They know that coercing relationships between people contradicts the principles of the Pillar of Trust and can generate harmful interpersonal dynamics.

Designing Relationship Architecture

Organizational charts are a great starting point for reconsidering your relationship architecture. They provide a useful framework for plotting people dynamics because they can be used to identify optimal work and other flows, and to pinpoint obstacles.

Once you identify informal relations and the associated qualities of work flows you can consider restructuring your organization, if necessary. When you restructure your organizational chart, you may believe strategic considerations, rather than relationship dynamics, should drive the design. I was a purist initially, and, I shifted my perspective on this because I realized that if organizational chart designers don't adequately consider relationship dynamics during the design process, the new structure can inhibit flow and balance, and consequently restrict results.

When designing relationship architecture, you should consider the quality of flow — or lack of it — caused by damaged relationships. For example, if placing two people on the same team will polarize a department, this pairing will make it difficult (though not impossible) for the team to achieve its results.

When a rift exists within a department, circumventive flow patterns can emerge. As a reaction, decision-makers who work toward unifying a department may transfer one of the polarizing employees out and bring in a replacement who may not be as technically skilled as their predecessor but can help unify the team.

In this chapter, we will explore how to diagnose and map the architecture for relationships and networks. Based on IFB principles, the new relationship architecture should facilitate continuous change, healthy networks founded on the Pillar of Trust, and be based on your organization's unique core values.

Why Mapping Relationship Architecture Is Important

According to researchers Ehrlichman and Spence, "Mapping a network can also help a network coordinator to identify patterns of connection in a network, intentionally weave connections, facilitate conversations that increase a group's awareness of itself, and maximize its potential for collaborative action. And organizations can benefit from SNA [Social Network Analysis] by identifying gaps in communication within or between departments, supporting the critical information hubs within the organization, and identifying opportunities to improve connections across silos." In other words, there are multiple benefits relationship mapping can provide that can boost the performance of an organization.

Mapping your relationship architecture is important for providing a macro view of your existing architecture and for designing new alternative maps intended to provide decision-makers with alternatives for future relationship and network configurations. Since relationships and networks include and transcend formal interconnections, mapping them allows change-makers to make informed decisions, thereby reducing the potential for failed change initiatives. Charting your existing relationship architecture also gives leaders opportunities to troubleshoot before time and resources are wasted. It is especially important to consider external stakeholders during the mapping process.

For instance, when employees resign from one company and join another, they may have enough referent power to continue to influence the behaviors of their former coworkers if they were influential power players. This is a risk because people who resign are no longer part of a company and may be unaware of or in disagreement with IFB principles. As a result, their ideas and opinions could be based on historic or uninformed biases irrelevant information, causing low quality decisions, unnecessary costs, and missed opportunities for a company.

Mapping relationships is an indispensable activity when diagnosing your current circumstances, but it is equally powerful when evaluating future relationships and networks. In multiple organizations, relationships and networks form organically, without an overall plan that deliberately connects them with team goals. When leaders decide to use the IFB Model to establish a change-based organization, other members of their teams should participate in relationship architectural design because there can be multiple unknowns that may remain concealed that can sabotage designs.

STEP 1: DIAGNOSE—MAPPING THE CURRENT RELATIONSHIP ARCHITECTURE

The point of a diagnostic exercise is not to use the collected data to manipulate circumstances for individual gain, nor is it to create a utopian environment—it is for you and your team to take the team to its next evolutionary level.

When diagnosing the configuration and quality of your relationships and networks, one of the first steps is to identify influential relationships and networks at every level within your organization, and then define how they work and why. Impartial observation can help with this, but so can constant, invested, constructive connection with staff—outside the range of the grapevine—using productive information collection methods like focus groups and surveys. While grapevines can be sources of useful information, tapping into them may lead to diminished trust levels.

When it comes to using your powers of observation for diagnosis, some relationships are exactly what they seem, others are not. One important reason why observation should be used in conjunction with more scientific methods is that other methods may not adequately explain the emotional topography. This landscape is important because hidden emotions may indicate deeper connections and allegiances, impaired relationships, or opportunities for deeper interconnectivity. When observing relationships and networks, it helps to pay attention to workplace artifacts like photos on desks, souvenirs gifted to fellow coworkers after travel, or memorabilia from local events.

Artifacts are not proof of informal connections, but they may be indicators. If the potential for an informal relationship is identified as a risk, once identified, additional information should be gathered — it is premature to draw conclusions at this stage. This means leaders may have to balance known facts with their intuition; they will also need to discern between facts and very convincing opinions.

IFB Relationship Mapping Diagnostics

The previous exploration focused on how you can gain an understanding of relationships from the inside out, but sometimes leaders need to understand relationship dynamics from the outside in. When adopting this approach, their aim is to diagnose situations by observing external manifestations of behavior so they can map current and future states. These patterns may be the only source of information available in some circumstances.

In attempting to understand the current state of relationships and networks by canvassing relevant team members, leaders can begin to appreciate why observed interpersonal dynamics exist. If they're lucky, decision-makers will uncover information that is typically hidden from view. As they progress through the diagnostic process for relationships and networks, they should remember that relationship coordinators will never uncover all relevant aspects of these connections. Despite this, it is still important to seek the information they need to make informed decisions, being careful not to cross into the domain of gossip.

Having diagnosed existing relationships, it is time to map the current state either manually or using software. Decision-makers should consider:

- Which relationships are critical to the success of the team? Why? (Use the relationship prioritization information collected in the diagnostic phase to inform this.)
- Who or what is affected most by these relationships?

- What are relationship dynamics? How do they affect performance?
- Why do the more influential relationships coexist, and how does the ecosystem sustain them?
- Which relationships are personal (informal)? Describe them.
- What do the metrics reveal about the potential for reconfiguring our interpersonal networks?
- What are the power/political dynamics? Who holds the power? Who benefits, and who doesn't? How do various power structures interface with each other?
- Which relationship challenges are contributing to bottlenecks? What can be done about it?
- How protective are team members of productive and unproductive relationships? How does this affect overall results and the potential for change?
- Which types of relationships are executives modeling, and how do we contradict or support desired interconnectivity? If there is a contradiction, what is our willingness to do something about it?
- What is the quality of intra- and interdepartmental communication?
- How is relationship quality affecting communication quality or vice versa?
- What are the loyalty dynamics?
- Which relationships have the potential to positively or negatively affect the entire team? Why?
- What are the risks and benefits associated with addressing unproductive relationships and productive ones that require refocusing?
- Where are the cliques (closed networks)? What purpose do they serve? How do they affect the bottom line?

- Which relationships are healthy and what are the risks if these relationships are weakened?
- What are the relationship and network norms that contribute to culture?
- How do relationships and networks operate and what are the patterns of connection?
- Who are the most influential people (formal and informal)? Where are the hubs of influence? How would you describe them?
- Which healthy and unhealthy relationships have significant influence on the team?
- What are the strengths and weaknesses of the most influential relationships and networks? What value do these relationships and networks bring?

The point of this line of inquiry is to collect and analyze relationship and network data to not only define your current map, but to inform all versions of possible future maps. These questions are a guide for diagnosis, analysis, and design of viable solutions for coordinating relationships and networks—feel free to add your own questions.

The descriptors below are drawn from Chapter 2 and can be used in conjunction with the list of questions to characterize or contextualize relationships and networks. Think about whether relationships and networks are:

stable	formal/informal
compromised	internal/external
situational	inclusive/exclusive
circumventive	loyal/disloyal
too new	nonexistent

Analyzing Diagnostic Information for Mapping the Current State

Analyzing relationships and networks involves identifying patterns in interactions. For instance, if a person is considered a gossip, they will likely magnetize others who gossip. However, it is important to perceive patterns responsibly and wisely; people shouldn't automatically be believed to be guilty by association, things may not necessarily be what they seem. Therefore, you will need to collect additional information to understand the context to diagnose recurring relationship patterns from a balanced perspective.

While assumptions are not ideal, informed assumptions may be your only option when analyzing some relationships and networks since facts won't always be readily available. Assumptions should be clearly identified as such and tested over time to strengthen your understanding of your relationship architecture and make informed decisions. Assumptions are useful for closing information gaps but only relying on them can be risky.

No relational network is without its idiosyncrasies; each has uniquely defining characteristics that reflect its rhythm, what keeps it in flow, what it accepts, and what it rejects. Therefore, when analyzing relationships and networks, designers and planners should honor these distinguishing characteristics. Your analysis of data related to your relationship architecture should help you identify opportunities for deconstructing, establishing, or reconfiguring relationships and networks and map the current state.

As one last consideration in the diagnostic process, you should make use of the Relationship-Strengthening Potential Tool introduced in Chapter 3. This resource can indicate which relationships should be prioritized during the visualization, design, and planning steps.

STEP 2: VISUALIZE YOUR RELATIONSHIP ARCHITECTURE

Envision your relationship architecture by integrating multiple considerations. You will need to take the diagnostic information from the current state mapping exercise into account. Visioning exercises are future-specific and for IFB purposes, they should project more than one desired scenario. Gaining buy-in and alignment with a shared vision is critical to the success of your change process so influencers should be involved in the initial stages of the visualization process because you will need their support during the design, planning, implementation, and adjustment phases.

Visualizing your relationship architecture involves generating a visual representation either manually or by using relationship mapping software. There's a full spectrum of applications available, ranging from free to quite expensive. Software is more useful for complex maps and for generating multiple versions.

It is also important to consider how your vision for workplace relationships and networks aligns with the individual relationship agendas of your team members. This doesn't mean you should diminish your plan because of conflicting personal agendas; rather, it suggests you should identify potential obstacles, so you can create a vision for a structure that can transform, and work in tandem with, or remove hindrances to performance networks.

The questions below can help you envision multiple versions of your relationship architecture:

- What can relationships and networks look like if they were to better support the strategic goals of your organization?
- How will coworkers interact with each other in each scenario? Which behaviors are acceptable and which ones aren't?
- What do we need the level of trust be to improve performance?
- What will our company look like when it is operating based on the Pillar of Trust?
  - How will leaders lead?
  - What will engagement look like?
  - Which complications or complexities will we consider? What are the opportunities?
  - How will coworkers interact with each other?
  - How will intra- and interdepartmental communication work?
  - How will people feel as members of the team?
  - What will the team's performance distribution look like?

○ How will we gain buy-in?

○ What mechanisms will we have in place to sustain trust friendly behaviors?

○ Which behaviors should executives model? What plans will we put in place to develop others?

• If individual and organizational goals contradict each other, how can decision-makers resolve this?

STEP 3: DESIGN THE NEW RELATIONSHIP ARCHITECTURE

Designing your relationship architecture requires preparation. Steps 1 and 2 explain how this can be done. Some designers start their masterpieces at the end state and work backward. Others take a more conventional route. Regardless of where you start, keep in mind that you should have envisioned multiple scenarios, so you should design multiple, differentiated relationship maps that each integrate various perspectives: the organizational chart, informal relationships and networks, power structures, your strategic plan, etc. This practice intimately connects the intricacies of the designs with reality, keeping them relevant and realistic.

Like artists who paint by going with the grain of the canvas, IFB designers who are responsible for future relationship mapping should go with the natural tendencies and strengths of relationships, harnessing these qualities for new, constructive purposes.

Mapping Your Design

This step may require returning to key stakeholders for additional information as you formulate your design. You may want to test your design ideas with these stakeholders before you commit to them. By doing this, you can learn more about the opportunities and limitations within your existing relationship framework and the general openness to change.

As you create your design for your relationship architecture, it will have a better chance of success if team members are intrinsically motivated to participate in the changes. Intrinsic motivation is critical here because when people experience changes directed at relationships, their connections can be strengthened if these relationships are meaningful to them. They need internal motivation for openness to change and the stamina necessary for building and sustaining trust-based, reconfigured work conditions.

In addition to the diagnostic and visioning information you collected and created in steps 1 and 2, you can use the list of questions below to help you configure design options for your proposed relationship architecture:

- Which relationships will best facilitate team flow, and how can we optimally configure them?
- Who are our most effective connectors? How do they operate, and can they add value differently?
- Which strategic priorities should the relationship architecture design options support?
- How can our designs sustain relationships and networks?
- How can relationships and networks dismantle silos?
- How can our designs neutralize the ivory tower?
- How can our designs neutralize unproductive power dynamics?
- How can we configure interpersonal connections to ensure that strategic priorities are adequately addressed?
- How can we reinforce already healthy relationships and networks that contribute to the bottom line? What do they have in common and how can we replicate them?
- How can we create open, inclusive relationships and networks?
- How do our designs minimize conflict and the potential for it?
- How do our designs facilitate organizational agility?
- Which circumventive measures do we need and why? How should they work?

- How can we stimulate productive relationships and networks?
- How should leadership styles shift to support future relationships and networks? Which competencies do we need most? (Additional training and development may be necessary at this and any other stage — the model is flexible.)
- How will we facilitate the envisioned communication through the design?

Leaders and environments change over time, so networks need built-in versatility. As you progress through the relationship mapping process — to define the desired future state of relationships and networks — you should carefully consider the obstacles to flexibility. This is because one purpose of the IFB Model is to facilitate organizational agility, so it is vital that relationships and networks meet this standard.

Design thinking also requires considering the potential for relationship growth. For instance, if a new relationship exists to achieve the goals of an organization and for no other reason, it may have increased potential to produce results if the relationship dynamics can be deepened. If a goal-based relationship exists between family members who work in a family-owned business, there are an infinite number of factors that contribute to the quality of interactions within those relationships. This can be attributed to the complexities inherent in family owned businesses.

Establishing Goals for Your Design

Goals should be defined for the overarching network. Your goals may include: developing people and leaders, improving operational efficiency through people, opening channels of communication, sustaining balance, and facilitating flow. When establishing IFB goals and principles of trust that align with strategy, be sure to consider the following:

- how you can establish sustainable interconnectivity based on the Pillar of Trust
- how you can use relationships to facilitate flow

- how relationships and networks can support balance in the long term
- how this all comes together to create a change-based organization

Moving to Empowered Relationships and Networks

Regardless of your organizational structure, when left to its own devices, power will establish itself in a configuration that serves the dominant values of the powerful members of a team. Unproductive political systems include several types of people who have different orientations toward power: ones who long for power but can't access it, those who possess power and use—or abuse—it, and ones who don't perceive their power and don't aspire to it.

In an empowered environment, power is distributed, not hoarded; those with power use it to develop others, so people around them can step into their personal versions of empowerment and use it respectfully and collaboratively, stimulating opportunities for mutual growth.

During the design phase it pays to carefully consider how an empowered work environment will operate in your organization. Your relationship and network designs should consider your existing or potential empowering patterns and seek to replicate them. Conversely, the design should have a built-in accountability system (like a regular 360-degree multi-rater assessment) to help you identify dysfunctional power dynamics and take corrective action before or, as they reemerge.

Here's a list of strategies you can use to support your team when your goal is to shift to empowered interactions. These strategies are based on the understanding that change happens by doing and they provide ideas for tackling some of the commonly encountered, unproductive power dynamics:

- When team members use relationship power to manipulate others, decision-makers can restructure the organizational chart if this action will likely neutralize this behavior.

Leaders can transform power dynamics by transferring, promoting, or coaching employees to help them adopt appropriate behaviors.

- Neutralizing expert power can involve developing additional experts, so leaders no longer have to rely on a single source of expertise. Executives can also offset expert power plays by keeping them happy. One way to do this is to create multiple expert career paths that provide them with opportunities to grow professionally and increase their base salaries.

- When political actors are incompetent, non-political employees ought to be equipped with the skills they need to successfully navigate political environments, and then placed in positions where they can create positive change if this is possible or prudent.

- When people withhold information that their coworkers need to complete their work, improve your internal communication structure so information can flow freely through multiple, accurate sources.

- When patterns of unfair treatment emerge because of abuses of relational power, leaders should become aware of the dynamics they are contributing to by listening carefully and openly to others. Not only to what they have to say, but also what they *are not* saying. This means leaders will need to hone their skills of meta listening to help them read between the lines. Meta listening requires leaders to understand themselves so they can understand others. Self-mastery requires them to be responsible with that information and to be open to strengthening compromised relationships.

- Create an accountability system designed to highlight unproductive power dynamics and address them when they attempt to reorganize. This system should also identify empowered dynamics, so they can be replicated.

The design of your maps should address unproductive power dynamics in a way that will allow — not jeopardize — existing empowered dynamics to persist.

From a macro perspective, your design team can map informal or formal networks across multiple departments, so they can eliminate silos. To achieve this, leadership teams can take steps like holding integrated team meetings or transferring team members to each other's departments — particularly those who are influential in their current posts and are open to working in another department.

Whichever solution you choose, the design should address the root causes of your challenges in conjunction with your organization's strategic priorities. Of course, silos are only one example of mutated power dynamics. As indicated in the list of potential strategies, multiple fluid approaches can be taken when neutralizing other patterns of behavior related to power abuse.

STEP 4: PLAN

Action plans are powerful accountability tools that provide a detailed view of activities. An effective relationship strengthening action plan is well thought out and flexible enough to allow unforeseen circumstances to be addressed fluidly. Planning requires usage of the selected design(s) and continued references to the information produced in the diagnostic and visioning exercises, especially if the design and planning teams are different.

Different companies have different practices when it comes to assembling a planning team. Some get all staff involved, others have one team that does the visioning, design and planning then they attempt to involve others. Some even get anticipated early adopters involved. There are pros and cons to using potential early adopters on the planning team. You can make the choice based on your unique circumstances. If you choose to engage them, consider enrolling adopters who are respected by others and earmarked for succession. Alternatively, they can be influencers, top performers, or experts.

Decision-makers can also consider assigning fence-sitters and late adopters to the planning team if there is high potential for them to convert and support the proposed changes. They can be even more influential than those who are usually early adopters.

Creating Your Relationship Reinvention Plan

The following guidelines can help you with your relationship and network reinvention plans:

- Use the designs mapped in the previous step to inform the plan. If you have more than one design, decide if you will choose one or plan—in whole or part—for multiple scenarios because of the volatility of your environment.
- Be sure your plan doesn't inadvertently contradict the selected design(s).
- Create a plan with built-in accountability to strategy and IFB principles.
- Use the plan to take advantage of opportunities and mitigate risks.
- Review policies to determine if they are counterproductive to your plan for your reinvented relationship architecture.
- Create a training and development plan focused on building technical skills and behavioral competencies that support trust, interconnectivity, flow, and balance.

Leaders can make imprecise calls when considering how to reinvent relationships and networks—or during any other planning process. This can happen when they don't have adequate information or perhaps they may have elected to plan for a scenario that was rendered irrelevant by unforeseen events. Curve balls are a guaranteed feature of change; your IFB plan should heighten your awareness for the need to plan for them and your leadership team should continue to build the skills they need to adapt.

STEP 5: IMPLEMENT

Drawing once again on the comparison of architectural design and IFB, in the architectural world, plans are designed based on the vision of the property owners, the contours of the land, the infrastructure, and other considerations. Once funding is available and a contractor is selected, the plans are used to construct the building.

Those who have experienced the construction of a home or other type of building know that construction work can deviate from the plans. Building owners sometimes experience unexpected costs, plan changes resulting from interpretative differences (aka "creative license"), and subcontractors who execute their part of the plan with varying degrees of skill. Sometimes it all somehow comes into alignment with the overall vision, other times it's way off the mark.

Effective implementation skills aren't always resident within an organization—while some organizational cultures support effective execution, others don't. The ones that don't, tend to have complex decision-making processes, inadequate communication practices, excessive bureaucracy, and counterproductive behaviors such as blame that replace accountability.

Competencies such as action orientation, effective communication, execution, flexibility, empathy, and balance can better support plan implementation processes and the principle of change as a constant because unplanned circumstances can surprise teams, no matter how well a change is planned.

Relationship coordinators and other IFB plan implementers should possess the acumen they need to recognize when employees are not implementing relationship and network changes as prescribed by their plan. It may be that employees are reverting to comfortable habits because they don't understand or accept the changes. Regardless the reason, reverting to familiar patterns is safe and predictable, especially when it comes to relationships.

Flow is quite possible even when an interconnective infrastructure is not grounded in trust, but when trust is absent, the sustainability and quality of flow and balance may be at risk. Implementing trust-centered relationship architecture is ideal for reducing the risk of project failure and the resulting skepticism—or even apathy—that can materialize as a by-product of failed change attempts.

STEP 6: ADJUSTMENT AND BALANCE

Balancing relationships requires trust and leader dexterity. This is because relationships and networks fall in and out of balance when there is conflict, a shift in power, or movement in and out of a network. As with the implementation phase, leaders should remain continuously attuned to the status of the reinvented architecture to be sure they can address expected and surprising conditions.

While attunement to relationship dynamics is vital, it is not enough; leaders should also be able to innovate solutions to emergent challenges and implement those solutions on an ongoing basis. This is especially important in change-based organizations.

Relationships and networks are constantly morphing. Some characteristics are enduring, while others are short-lived. Adjustment through balancing action is everybody's business. It comes together better when managers and employees take ownership of and become adept at keeping their fingers on the pulse of relationship dynamics.

CHAPTER 14

DESIGNING YOUR COMMUNICATION INFRASTRUCTURE

Communication always changes society, and society was
always organized around communication channels.

— Vinod Khosla, engineer and businessman

The communication infrastructure is another component of the glue that holds the IFB Model together. It facilitates the flow of information and is more effective when strengthened by trust. With effective communication practices, teams can plough through bottlenecks and break down silos.

The communication infrastructure is also important for achieving balance. When operating at its peak, it is the conduit that allows necessary information to flow through an organization, expediting decisions and encouraging timely actions. It bolsters cohesion, prompts creativity, and sets the stage for a flexible, agile organization to do its thing.

In the previous chapter, we explored how you can facilitate changes in relationships and networks in a way that supports the creation of an IFB, change-based organization. The interconnective infrastructure has three more relational elements to be integrated into the design: communication, organizational structure, and strategy.

This chapter integrates communication into the IFB change process. It is a guide for designing the communication infrastructure for your change-based organization. As with other chapters in Part III, it adheres to the change framework defined in Chapter 12 and is intricately tied to relationships and networks because, as I have noted, without healthy relationships, the quality of the information and communication channels will be compromised. If you need a refresher, you can refer to Chapter 3 for additional ideas you can use to create the right communication infrastructure for your organization.

Why Design Your Communication Infrastructure?

Communication infrastructure design is integral to the IFB Model. Without productive internal and external communication channels and practices, it is difficult for an organization to maintain healthy connections, promote action and flow, support engagement, or sustain balance.

When you consider change as a constant in the context of communication, remember that communication shouldn't flow in only one direction. Unidirectional communication flow limits decision-makers to a narrow perspective and they run the risk of making poorly informed decisions. It can also become difficult to gain buy-in. If plans to make changes are compelled, change implementation might fail or underperform.

The Communication Infrastructure

In various organizations, communication takes shape only when it occurs to a leader that it's needed. Leaders in these organizations may not have a robust internal communication infrastructure in place because quality communication practices are not their priority. When an organization has underdeveloped communication channels, important messages that require clarification through conversation can be transmitted via email, or perhaps not at all.

Sometimes organizations do have a well-thought-out internal communication infrastructure, but it's not adequately used. For instance, messages communicated to middle management fall through the cracks because managers are swamped by transactional priorities that distract them from communicating effectively or at all.

A robust communication infrastructure depends on effective communication channels that facilitate both internal and external communication. This book and chapter focus on how you can build optimally operational internal communication channels. You can use some of the same principles to expand your relationships, networks, and communication systems beyond the boundaries of your organization once you get an effective internal infrastructure in place.

STEP 1: DIAGNOSE YOUR COMMUNICATION CHANNELS

Leaders should use the diagnostic process to understand the quality of internal communication channels and how information moves through them. An internal communication audit can expose the strengths and weaknesses of the infrastructure—it can identify where the blockages are, where high- and low-quality information flow exist, and how cultural norms and other factors contribute to the communication patterns of your team.

For instance, in some organizations, leaders use a tone that makes everything seem urgent. To get employees to adopt a sense of perpetual urgency, they may also use threatening language to impose a sense of fear or anxiety. While the team may step up and deliver, the low connective quality of their communication damages relationships because when threats are a communication staple, they tend to communicate the message, "I don't care about you or your well-being, just get it done."

Another important consideration is the generational makeup of the workplace has shifted, and as a result, millennials are the largest group of employees in the global workforce. A constantly urgent tone doesn't motivate millennials; in fact, it has quite the opposite effect. Most millennials prefer cultures that support meaningful learning and career progression, not ones that rely on threats and fear to drive results.

Diagnosing Internal Communication Channels

A formal communication channel should activate when an executive team communicates a decision. Ideally, in a hierarchical organization, a formal channel starts with an executive communicating a decision to senior and middle management. From there, middle management communicates the message to supervisors, and supervisors share the information with frontline staff.

Sometimes messages move through layers of an organizational hierarchy (channels) as expected, though they can be delayed by middle managers and others who are too busy to disseminate messages in a timely manner. This asynchronous timing tends to activate the grapevine and degrades trust. Dips in morale occur when some teams receive information intended for everyone before others.

Communication channels can be direct, involving face-to-face conversations or emails. Some direct channels can appear to be direct, but they are really indirect; for example, when two coworkers who don't trust each other are communicating digitally, they may copy (or blind copy) numerous others. In circumstances like this, the words are carefully chosen for the carbon copied crowd, not for the recipient.

Another challenge here is that when carbon copied recipients have no clear stake in a conversation, other than to be a witness to a strained relationship, they can become annoyed by email bombardment, especially when the infamous "Reply to All" selection is made on every response between all persons who choose to respond.

Indirect communication channels are effective at moving information through paths that are not a straight line. Consider: a corporate decision is secretively communicated to someone outside an organization, who tells someone on the front line, who tells a manager, who tells another person who is external to the organization, who tells another employee. This zig-zagging can distort information and affect trust when people start to wonder why their supervisor didn't tell them instead of one of their peers or worse, an outsider.

Sometimes employees lament the inadequacies of communication within their organizations, but their supervisors will say that employees are receiving the information — they sent out emails and had informal conversations with them. What some leaders don't consider is that effective internal communication is more than just sending out information or having informal chats; it requires ensuring that targeted employees receive the same information, and once they receive it, that they understand so they can act on it. This can only happen with two-way or multidirectional communication. The effectiveness of one-way communication is typically lower.

Below is a list of questions you can use to diagnose your internal communication channels and practices. These questions are designed to stimulate your thinking at a macro level because by thinking about communication strategically, you are setting the context for the diagnosis of the current state of your unique communication framework.

- How effective are decision-makers at timing communication?
- How effective are leaders at ensuring that information is disseminated?
- How do employees align their communication with the values of our organization?
- Who are our audiences, and how do they prefer to receive information? How do our communication channels and practices align with these preferences?
- How well does our internal communication plan support our overall strategy?

Internal Communication Channel Questions

Your channels are the infrastructure of your communication framework, they facilitate the movement of information—not unlike an urban water distribution system. The water is in the pipelines and when it is needed, it is immediately available, so long as the pipes and plumbing systems are operating as they should. The questions below will help you think about the efficacy of your communication channels.

- What are the strengths and weaknesses of our internal communication channels? Why are they effective (or not)?

- How open are our communication channels? How effective are they at facilitating top-down, lateral, and bottom-up flows?
- Overall, how effective are our communication channels? (Why do the channels work, or why don't they?)

Leadership & Communication Questions

Leaders are responsible for selecting communication modes, crafting messages and facilitating meetings. They are owners of the overall effectiveness of the communication infrastructure. You can ask:

- How trusted are decision-makers as messengers? If decision-makers aren't trusted, who is?
- Do employees trust information from leaders to be correct/true? Why or why not?
- How well-timed are communication flows?

Messaging Questions

Crafting the right message is one of the most important aspects of communication. Different audiences require specifically targeted messages. Here are a few questions you can ask to diagnose your messaging framework:

- What are our different target audiences and what level of information do they need?
- How do we ensure our messages contain the right information?
- What is the overall tone of our messages?
- How clear and consistent are our messages? How do we know?
- How do we gain buy-in? Why does our approach work (or not)?
- What level of skepticism do we perceive when making an announcement?

- How well do our messages align with our vision for communication?

Communication Mode Questions

Once you decide on your target audience you should be sure they are receiving the message in a mode that contributes positively to their engagement. The following questions can help you determine if your communication modes are a good fit for your stakeholder groups.

- How effective are the communication tools we deploy within our own organization (meetings, newsletters, podcasts, social media, etc.)?
- Which communication modes work best?
- Where is communication flowing or constricted? Why?

Questions about the Effectiveness of Meetings

Meetings are a very important communication mode; the larger ones can disseminate information to complete networks at the same time — they can be creative or informational. Meetings are essential to the IFB Model, so it is important to get them right. They need to operate optimally, regardless the size of your organization. Here are a few questions to help you diagnose the efficacy of meetings in general:

- What is our overall meeting quality? What do we do well? What do we need to improve?
- How many meetings happen within our organization? Are they the right meetings? Do we need to add any? If yes, how many? Can any of them be combined or eliminated?
- Who attends these meetings? Are they the right people?
- How effective are our agendas?
- How effective are meeting chair persons at managing discussions?
- How do we ensure our meetings aren't a waste of time?

Team/Network Communication Questions

You can't leave your people out of the diagnostic process. Here are a few questions you can use to help you think about team communication:

- How does our culture influence how teams communicate?
- What is our team's communication style? Is it formal or informal; does it utilize specialized language or communication skills?
- Describe our regular departmental meetings. What works, what doesn't?
- How does our relationship architecture (formal and informal) affect the quality of communication?
- How effective is our intra and interdepartmental communication?
- Where are the silos and how do they affect communication?
- How willing are team members to speak up?
- How does our grapevine work? How does it affect trust?
- How do power dynamics affect interpersonal and network communication?
- How willing are team members to trust leaders? Why (or why not)?

Individual Communication Questions

We started from the perspective of the big picture and worked our way down to individuals. These questions are different than the team questions from the standpoint that they focus on how people relate to each other.

- How does relationship quality affect how individuals communicate?
- How willing are coworkers to trust each other?

This information can be obtained through surveys, interviews, and focus group sessions. To maintain the integrity of the IFB framework and its ability to facilitate a change-based organization, decision-makers should conduct internal communication assessments periodically.

Analyze Your Data

The next step is to analyze your diagnostic information. If quantitative data exists, you can add it to your analysis, so you can better understand the qualitative diagnostic information you collected during the scoping process. But before you start your analysis, be sure you have the data you need. You don't want to be paralyzed by information overload.

When you collect both quantitative and qualitative data, the quantitative data may be collected first and then the qualitative information can help decision-makers understand the what the numbers mean. The following questions can guide you through your analysis and help you synthesize the data so you can inform visioning and design phases. Feel free to add questions to this list (and to any of the lists) to deepen or customize your exploration:

- What is working well? What isn't?
- What are your opportunities, constraints, and risks?
- If you have conducted surveys, what are the results telling you?
- How does this information impact your overall vision for IFB?
- Who are the relevant internal stakeholders? How do they affect the quality of communication and the openness of your channels?
- Why are your communication channels operating the way they do? (Evaluate resources, skills, reward systems, political dynamics, processes, etc.)

The scope of information analysed during the first phase will help designers better appreciate the dynamics of information flow. Designers should be involved with deciding which information should be collected, how it will be gathered and which stakeholders to target. The collated information can then be organized using a prioritization tool.

One last note on diagnostics: IFB designers should attempt to obtain top-down, lateral, and bottom-up perspectives on existing communication dynamics (to the extent possible). Perspectives will most likely differ as information moves up, down, and around an organization, and varied points of view can provide clarity and depth.

STEP 2: VISUALIZE THE PURPOSE OF THE COMMUNICATION INFRASTRUCTURE

To envision designs for your communication channels, you should visualize relationships, networks, communication norms, culture, organizational structure, and strategy. The quality of relationships will affect all aspects of communication.

When you envision the future state of your communication channels, take care to define the purpose of its framework and specify your definition of effective communication. You can ask yourself:

- What should effective communication look like in our organization? (Define too much or too little communication.)
- How often do we need to communicate the same message for people to recall the message?
- How many times do we need to repeat the same messages before they sink in?
- Which communication modes operate more effectively in our organization?
- How will our communication channels work when they are operating optimally?

- What are the key messages that should be integrated in all communication?
- Who owns the effectiveness of internal communication channels?
- How will we check the efficacy of our communicative structure?

Use these visioning questions to prompt your imagination, and while you create, remember that perfection is not the goal: the goal is optimized communication.

STEP 3: DESIGN

At stage three, the design team should transfer the vision for communication channels into an outline. In fact, the team may decide to create several designs for the communicative infrastructure because the relationship architecture may be unpredictable and interfere with attempts to open the channels.

Communication channel design should minimize contradictory elements in the plan. For instance, if decision-makers plan to implement an initiative to ensure that people speak up and share their views, the plan should not include policies that contradict psychologically safe space.

When visioning the future state, you might consider these elements for your potential designs:

- How will leaders facilitate the movement of information through the channels?
- What are the channels, and how do we keep them active?
- Which communication modalities work best?
- Which mechanisms should we put in place to ensure that effective communication remains a priority?
- How should we structure meetings for success?
- How should we communicate with our key stakeholders?

As with the visioning process, you can use the diagnostic questions to prompt additional ideas for communication design. Chapter 4 provides insights into how to unblock communication channels and stimulate flow. It also explains how to use appropriate communication modes when establishing your framework and provides insights into how you can improve meetings.

STEPS 4 AND 5: PLANNING AND IMPLEMENTING THE COMMUNICATION INFRASTRUCTURE

The usual steps should be followed when planning and executing a communication channel design. As with relationship building, one component of the plan should address how to detect emerging, unproductive communication patterns. The plan should also provide clear steps to correct relapses in individual communication habits, which include tone and language. The communication accountability system should also have built-in versatility to address macro-level and individual communication challenges that can emerge as circumstances change.

The plan should be based on the design and therefore should include the following:

- identification of communication modalities that will effectively disseminate information
- development of leaders to communicate more effectively
- built-in mechanisms to periodically measure the effectiveness of the internal communication framework
- an external communication component (branding, for example)
- consistent messaging

Planning and execution should be flexible because as relationship and network growth plans are implemented, people may not be open to trust-based communication immediately, if at all. If resistance surfaces during your execution phase, recalibration may require recalibrating or reimagining potential future states.

STEP 6: ADJUSTMENT AND BALANCE

Sustaining a productive communicative infrastructure requires performing periodic assessments to test the continued effectiveness of your framework, so the right adjustments can be made. This is especially useful in change-based organizations. In these organizations, the communication channels should facilitate work, but they should also encourage creativity.

Creativity can only happen when your people are engaged with the communication modes. Therefore, once in use, the communication infrastructure should be regularly monitored. In fact, it should be assigned to an executive who can ensure that the framework is not only working, but also evolving.

When change happens, dysfunctional power structures can be tested. During turbulent times, people who perceived themselves as being powerful before a change, will do whatever it takes to hold onto their power. Whether their perceived power is informational, expert, or even positional, change initiatives can cause them to withhold critical information, blocking communication and other flows. Leaders should be attuned to power dynamics before, during, and after IFB implementations to ensure unhelpful patterns don't sabotage their best-laid plans.

Some people who execute change plans can be destabilized by curve balls because they are counting on predictability. When unplanned events happen or there is ambiguity, stress levels escalate. Some authors—such as Virginia Satir—define the unpredictable stage of the change implementation cycle as the "chaotic phase." This stage starts soon after the change announcement and lasts as long as it takes for new competencies to become skills. This is when adjustment and balance are most important. It is also where it can be most complex.

To progress through this stage to stability and successful change, team members need to be able to safely engage each other and their leaders. More specifically, they need to be free to speak up about perceived obstacles without being labeled as resisters. To achieve this, change leaders should project themselves as trustworthy and their leadership style should be empowering. Structural changes are also helpful. Ones that involve organizational chart modifications, job description alterations, work flow changes, and delegated authority enhancements can help to distribute power and improve communication norms.

CHAPTER 15

DESIGNING THE ORGANIZATIONAL STRUCTURE AND STRATEGY

Design is not just what it looks like and feels like.
Design is how it works.

—Steve Jobs, designer and visionary entrepreneur

While some relationship change models emphasize people development, the IFB framework places equal emphasis on people development as well as operational and strategic activities, taking a holistic view of connection and change. The interconnective infrastructure introduced in Chapter 2 defines a matrix of networks, facilities, and systems necessary for connection. Your organizational structure is an important part of this infrastructure because it defines connections and the parameters within which your organizational activities occur. As a reminder, your organizational structure is also made up of your corporate governance guidelines, organizational chart, job descriptions, reward systems, and policies. It also encompasses procedures, delegated authorities, strategy, and other formal — and informal — structures.

In addition to formal structures, informal organizing influences also make up your organizational structure. They operate concurrently, and sometimes invisibly. Depending on the organization, one type or another may dominate, or they can operate with equal intensity.

Official and unofficial organizational structures are directly influenced by formal and informal relationship networks. The quality of operational execution considered in conjunction with the absence of policies can drive the need for informal policies, procedures, and other unofficial structures as circumventive or sorely needed evolutionary measures. Any of these informal solutions can occur when an organizational structure is inadequate for the business or when office politics gets in the way of effective practices.

Some decision-makers prefer less confining organizational structures, so they can emphasize flexibility and innovation; others require a structure that is rigid and controlled. The balance points between formal and informal, and innovation and control are defined by your vision and strategy, and should be featured in your design.

This chapter is a guide that leaders can use to design the last two parts of the interconnective infrastructure: the organizational structure and the strategy. Before digging deeper into the IFB change process in relation to these two topics, it is useful to reinforce the central utility of interconnectivity, and the fact that all parts of the interconnective infrastructure should work together to support outcomes of the entire IFB Model. Therefore, as the infrastructural design comes more clearly into focus, you should continuously consider all elements of the IFB framework in relation to each other.

Why Structure and Strategy are Important

Structure, an important element of organizational success, is a multifaceted construct. When businesses grow without adequate structures, leaders will find it increasingly difficult to keep their finger on the pulse of everything the same way they did when the organization was smaller and less complex. As organizations grow, structures facilitate standardization and quality, serving as risk-mitigation and performance tools.

Strategy is based on the vision for the organization. It undergirds the plan to achieve a desired future state based on an organization's vision, mission, core values, and goals. Together, strategy and structure support organizations throughout their life cycles. Both should evolve simultaneously, otherwise structures will be underutilized or become obsolete, or strategic plans will be constrained by inadequate structures. An example of a structure becoming a constraint happened some time ago when there was once a burgeoning business that grew to multimillion dollar revenue status within a relatively short time. The owner of the business didn't understand the value of strengthening and evolving structures during the growth phase. His philosophy was *if it ain't broke, don't fix it!*

Soon, the inadequacies of a structure that was suitable at the inception of the business—that was being used during the growth phase—started to materialize. One example of this was that the owner was trying to operate a business with two hundred employees as though it was a business with a ten-person workforce. As a result, important deliverables fell through the cracks, HR issues mounted, inventory was stolen, and employees were unenthusiastic about coming to work.

In fact, employees felt their input wasn't welcomed or valued because the owner micromanaged all aspects of the business. While some businesses survive under these conditions, this one didn't. After three years the company met its demise; one of the main reasons was the owner's lack of understanding of how to ensure the existing organizational structure doesn't limit growth his business. He didn't understand that using a structure that was suitable at the inception of the business could not be used to grow the company.

The Organizational Structure and Strategy

Positioning your organization to be change-based is not easy, but it can deliver rewards. To achieve them, you begin by keeping relationships and people networks at the top of mind by giving them the learning and developmental opportunities they need.

The next priority in your relationship infrastructure is your organizational structure. This can also have a profound effect on the success of team performance. As you consider the design of your overall structure, be sure there is sufficient built-in flexibility to help your organization to become a dynamic IFB entity.

Before you implement a change plan, operating within the parameters of your organizational structure is second nature to your team members — because structures contribute to culture. Your coworkers may be so comfortable with them, that they may even adopt some version of your workplace structures in their personal lives.

This type of structural migration is sometimes evident when employees leave one organization and join another. They are trying to recreate familiar or safe space by reestablishing the cultural norms they experienced previously. Sometimes this enhances the new company's culture, sometimes it is counterproductive.

Structure supports the execution of strategic plans, and sometimes strategic plans change structures. Some structures promote agility while others can be quite limiting because they have not evolved in tandem with shifting internal and external influences.

Another important consideration is that change can be overwhelming when there is constant, wholesale replacement of strategies, technology, policies, and procedures. This is not feasible financially or otherwise. Instead, cyclical, carefully timed improvements of team effectiveness and efficiencies, followed by larger investments in appropriate intervals, is a more fitting pursuit when you're positioning your organization for sustainable change and viability.

As you are aware, strategic plans are tools leaders use to achieve their respective visions. Strategy is connected to relationships and structure because together, the right skills, sound relationships, effective communication practices, and flexible organizational structures can underpin strategic innovation, planning, and execution. The IFB Model supports strategy in the short and long terms. When it is implemented effectively, the framework facilitates interconnectivity, flow, and balance that supports sustainable engagement, performance, innovation, agility, and many other strategic benefits.

As with the previous chapters in Part III, diagnosis is the first step of the IFB change process. Step 1 outlines detailed suggestions you can use to assess multiple organizational structures as well as your strategy. It may sound like a waste of time to diagnose your strategy if scoping and diagnosis were already part of your strategic planning exercise, but it is not. The point of diagnosing your strategic plan is not to duplicate the project plans or to change scoping process, it is to analyze the strategic plan through the lens of IFB to gain additional perspectives on its viability and likelihood of execution success.

STEP 1: DIAGNOSE THE ORGANIZATIONAL STRUCTURE AND STRATEGY

When diagnosing the effectiveness of your organization's structure, you should review each component (corporate governance structure, organizational chart, job descriptions, reward systems, policies, procedures, delegated authorities, strategy, etc.) from multiple perspectives:

- the effectiveness of each structure
- how the structures affect and communicate trust
- the strengths and weaknesses of each structure
- how each structure, formal and informal, interacts with others (e.g., how the organizational chart affects decision-making)
- the configuration of formal and informal relationships associated with structure
- how people relate to different aspects of structure

These are questions you can use to assess the structures from a macrocosmic perspective. The rest of this section is dedicated to guiding you through the diagnostics of each type of structure — then we'll explore strategy.

When considering best practices as part of your IFB pursuits, keep in mind the possibility that these practices (which apply to policies, procedures, and other structures) will work successfully in some organizations but not in others. This is because each organization has unique cultural features that can contribute to the success or failure of these practices. Therefore, best practice applicability should be carefully considered during the diagnostic phase, especially if you are researching best practices for use in the design and planning phases.

Because it may be difficult to replicate or sustain a best practice in companies where the practice didn't originate, IFB leaders should either seek to understand the culture necessary for that practice to work optimally or create their own best practices that align with their culture, resources, and collective skill levels. Also keep in mind that just because a practice may have worked well for you in the past, that doesn't mean you should continue to use it. On a final note, if your company is not able to fully implement a best practice used in another organization, that practice can still serve as creative inspiration for your team.

Diagnose the Governance Structure

The governance structure is the ultimate responsibility of the board of directors; its purpose is to balance the interests of multiple stakeholders, such as shareholders, employees, regulators, clients, etc. The governance structure also provides a framework for policies and strategy. Using the IFB framework as an organizing tool, the following questions will help diagnose your current state:

Interconnectivity

- How does our board ensure accountability for ethical behavior (e.g. code of conduct, policy on conflicts of interest and corruption)?
- How effective is our board's oversight of the strategic plan?
- How effectively is our board managing organizational risks?
- What is the quality of communication between our board of directors and executive team?
- How does our governance structure ensure there aren't any conflicts of interest and other ethical infractions?
- How effective are our board committees?

Flow

- How does our governance structure facilitate the introduction of fresh, relevant ideas?

- How does our board measure organizational performance?
- How does our board measure its own performance?
- How does the board hold itself and the executive team accountable for establishing an adequate succession plan?

Balance

- Which skills and experience are necessary for a high performing board? Are they represented here?
- How is our governance structure supporting or hindering the organization?
- Which areas of the business does our board focus on the most? How ideal is this?
- How effective is our board at balancing its responsibilities?
- How does our board ensure appropriate delegation of duties between it and the executive team?
- How does our board measure its success? How often is this reviewed?
- How well is our board performing? What are its performance indicators? What are its contributions, and what are the obstacles to stellar performance?

Whether you use the questions above or create other relevant ones, you should then choose the most effective data collection method to collate information. As a reminder, collection methods include surveys, interviews, and focus groups. You may also choose to research best practices.

Diagnose Your Delegated Authorities

Some decision-makers fail to establish delegated authorities for the board or executive team. A variety of risks can exist when authorities are not delegated or when they are not clear. Operational, customer, people, and strategic risks can all result from bottlenecks related to failure to properly assign decision-making authorities.

Bottlenecks are especially risky because multiple areas can be directly or indirectly affected by delayed decisions or actions. Additionally, employees who are forced to wait for backlogged decisions tend not to take responsibility, even though they may possess the skills necessary for taking ownership.

Properly delegated authorities ensure that leaders and employees know which decisions they have the authority to make. This clarifies daily duties and longer-term requirements. When you are scoping your organization's decision-making process — whether authorities are delegated or not — the decision-making cycle should be analyzed. When diagnosing the effectiveness of decision-making authorities, the diagnostic team should seek answers to the following questions:

Interconnectivity

- What are the established authorities?
- How relevant are the authorities to our organizational chart and related workflows?

Flow

- Where are the bottlenecks?
- If authorities exist, how far down the organizational chart is authority delegated?
- Which authorities, if delegated, will reduce bottlenecks?
- How are delegated authorities and related policies (together) facilitating or impeding flow? For example, a policy that is currently in place might require multiple layers of authorization that create overkill.

Balance

- Which authorities, if delegated, will increase risks? What can we do to decrease these risks?
- Which authorities effectively mitigate risks?

- How often should we revise our policies related to delegated authorities to ensure our practices are evolving with the business?

- How can we ensure employees are qualified or experienced enough for their assigned authorities?

- How compliant are employees with their established authorities?

When decision-makers delegate authorities to enable flows, they can minimize risks by ensuring that those who are being tasked with a given level of authority receive the developmental opportunities they need to assume the responsibility. Delegating authorities is a capacity-building activity, so diagnosing the quality of and practices related to your authorities should include determination of how authorities (or the lack of them) affect overall performance.

Diagnose the Organizational Chart

Organizational charts provide the framework that houses multiple structures (workflows, policies, procedures, succession, etc.). As a decision-maker interested in IFB, you should create the most appropriate organizational chart for your strategic execution. It should be designed to ensure that the interconnectivity, flow, and balance it facilitates are operating at their peak.

As I mentioned previously, I thought organizational charts should be designed based on the strategic goals of the business without regard to interpersonal dynamics. Over time, experience led me to modify my approach to organizational chart design due to limitations with this type of inadequate chart design combined with resource constraints. Now I integrate considerations related to strategy and interpersonal dynamics because personalities and power dynamics can create very real obstructions to workflows.

The questions below were crafted to help you diagnose the effectiveness of your organizational chart from both perspectives:

Interconnectivity

- How well is our organizational chart aligned with our strategic priorities? If it's out of sync, what do we need to do to bring it into alignment?

- Was the organizational chart built based on office politics, the strategic needs of the institution or some combination of the two? What is the evidence of this? How appropriate is this to our existing circumstances?

Flow

- How effectively does our organizational chart facilitate succession? How well-defined are the paths?

- How is our organizational chart supporting or hindering workflows?

- What are the anomalies within our organizational chart (placements that seem counterintuitive or counterproductive to flow)?

Balance

- Which employees within the organizational chart have we deemed "untouchable"? (Untouchable employees are protected at their pay grade and are not performing.) How does this serve the untouchable employees and the organization? Do the benefits outweigh the costs?

- How balanced is our work distribution? Are more responsibilities delegated to a particular department or person than others? If so, why?

- What are the criteria for promotions? What are indications of employees being promoted or overlooked unfairly?

- What are the dysfunctional team dynamics caused by difficult personalities?
- What are the anomalies in the chart that create imbalances? (For instance, there might be political roles designed for a person who serves no significant operational purpose or hybrid roles created because a person has a unique skillset that no single person can replace.)

In an IFB organization, the organizational chart should be reviewed periodically to ensure there are no new or underestimated opportunities for enhanced relationships, better flow, and improved balance. There should also be a decision-making accountability system put in place to ensure imbalances are not introduced to the chart based on flawed solutions.

Diagnose Job Descriptions

Job descriptions are directly linked to both organizational charts and delegated authorities. Whenever an organizational chart changes, the corresponding job descriptions, related work flows and delegated authorities should be modified to reflect those changes. For a job description to support a balanced work environment, it should: contain essential duties; outline the qualifications and experience necessary; itemize the knowledge and skills needed; segregate duties; and clearly articulate workflows.

Now that we have established that job descriptions should change as roles evolve, consider the practicality of wholesale change, since updating job descriptions is time consuming. This type of project usually requires already burned-out subject matter experts to rewrite them.

I would be remiss to leave out a very important consideration related to organizational chart and job description change initiatives, one that many leaders underappreciate. It is the emotion that is triggered when these types of changes are announced. Without the right messaging and other effective communication practices, decision-makers can get bogged in a mire of resistance, passive and otherwise.

Given the time and volume of work associated with properly revising job descriptions, it is not always a priority, especially in smaller, growing organizations with limited manpower. However, updating job descriptions as the organizational chart evolves is central to expanding the capacity of your organization, so something has to give. Otherwise, engagement will decline and future growth can be jeopardized because people are continuing to do what they used to do before the changes were put into effect.

When job descriptions don't reflect changes in workflows, reporting lines, and duties, this is an indicator there may be an imbalance in a department or potential for future imbalances. In some organizations, job descriptions are viewed as too rigid or confining and leaders prefer some role ambiguity so persons can help out wherever they are needed. In other organizations, they don't make the time to change these performance tools because everything seems to be working fine. Outdated job descriptions may be linked to obsolete organizational charts, and as we've noted, outdated organizational charts can lead to multiple imbalances when growth is a strategic priority but the structure can't adequately accommodate it.

Here is a list of questions you can use to diagnose your job descriptions as part of the redesign of your organizational chart and other related structures:

Interconnectivity

- How effectively do our job descriptions segregate duties?
- Are there any behaviors within our departments that suggest potential conflict due to overlapping duties?
- How well do the duties defined in interrelated job descriptions reflect workflow connectivity?
- How can job descriptions better support ongoing change and agility?

Flow

- How representative are the duties listed in the job descriptions of the actual work being done?
- How well do job descriptions reflect the essential duties of each role? Are job descriptions really only task lists?
- Are there job descriptions are based on a person's unique skills rather than optimal workflows? If so, why?
- Which essential duties are being performed that are not recorded in any of the job descriptions?
- Which essential duties are not being performed that should be? Why?
- How effective are our job descriptions at creating or inhibiting flow?
- How do you ensure that job descriptions reflect a full day's work?

Balance

- What systems do we have in place to evaluate job descriptions? How effective are they?
- How many hybrid roles did we create based on the unique skills of the person in the role? If there are any, how can we mitigate long-term balancing risks associated with this?
- How balanced is the work distribution in our department/organization? How do we ensure that employees have enough work to do each day? How can we verify if our best employees are overloaded?
- Are we creating positions to reward employees for reasons other than performance? How is this impacting balance within our organization (i.e., performance, engagement, etc.)?

Diagnose Policies and Procedures

Multiple, granular policies can coexist in tightly controlled work environments, with policies for as many circumstances as can be imagined. The intent behind granular policies is usually to reduce risks by increasing standardization, minimizing errors, limiting the use of discretion, and promoting predictability. Depending on how oppressive the controls are, some may call this micromanaging. In contrast, decision-makers who value innovation may intentionally keep policies unrestrictive, so leaders and employees can maintain creativity.

Some organizations have weak or nonexistent procedures. This can lead to nonstandard practices and though not immediately apparent, it can also produce people, operational, and customer risks. Nonstandard practices are especially troublesome because when errors occur, it can be very difficult to backtrack.

Weak or nonexistent procedures can also lead to nonstandard circumstances in which departments within the same organization perform the same processes in different ways, based on an oral tradition featuring liberal, creative license. Addressing this practice with well-documented procedures and a planned roll-out is not enough. Effective implementation requires cultural change. This means there needs to be buy-in for the new policies. To achieve this, the policies may need to allow enough discretion so they won't be completely ignored.

Here is a list of questions you can use to scope the current state of your policies and procedures:

Interconnectivity

- Which formal (documented) policies and procedures exist? What's missing?
- Which informal (undocumented) policies exist?
- How do formal and informal policies work together (or not)?
- How are our policies and procedures aligned with our vision?
- How compliant are our employees with policies and procedures?
- How effectively do our policies and procedures connect with each other? Which ones are contradictory?

Flow

- How restrictive are our policies? Should they be as granular or flexible as they are?
- How do our policies affect our ability to be agile, flexible, or innovative?
- How much decision-making discretion do our policies provide employees (at all levels)?
- How do our policies and procedures affect priority flows?
- How accessible are our documented and undocumented policies?

Balance

- How do our policies and procedures affect our culture? Or how does our culture affect policies and procedures (i.e., compliance vs. noncompliance, multiple interpretations of policies, informal policies overriding formal ones, resisting change, etc.)
- How do informal policies and procedures affect work relationships and our bottom line?
- How many (connective or conflicting) versions of the same policy are active within our organization?
- How effective is our system of updating policies, communicating the changes, and gaining buy-in?
- How compliant are employees with our policies and procedures? If there is low compliance, why and what are the perceived risks?
- How do our policies and procedures contribute to balance and imbalances?
- How often are exceptions made to our policies and procedures? Why would exceptions be necessary? Do exceptions trump policy compliance or vice versa? What are the overall risks associated with the way we make exceptions?

Policies and procedures should support your vision for your IFB implementation, not contradict it. Understandably, leaders in growing companies don't have much time to spend on updating policies and procedures—still, they should do what they can. In larger organizations with leaders who have established IFB as a priority, they should dedicate resources to keeping these guidelines current.

Diagnose Your Strategic Plan

The suggestion here is to review your strategic plan to verify that it's aligned with the principles of interconnectivity, flow, and balance. You should also establish whether your strategy can sustain these principles within your organization in the long term or not. You can use the following questions to diagnose the IFB alignment of your strategic plan:

Interconnectivity

- Is there a formal or informal (undocumented) strategic plan? How accessible is the plan to the general staff population?
- How aware are employees of our strategic plan? Is there overall buy-in? Why or why not?
- How is our existing strategic plan aligned with IFB principles (or not)?
- How does our strategic plan facilitate connectivity, both within and outside our organization?
- How do our stakeholder relationships affect the effectiveness of our planning, design, and execution?
- How does our strategic plan facilitate connectivity?

Flow

- What is the quality of the collective execution skills within our organization? How do these skills support or inhibit flow and balance?

- How effective is our team at achieving the results defined in our strategic plan?
- Which flows do our strategic plan create, obstruct, or complement?

Balance

- What are the inherent balancing qualities and imbalances within our existing strategic plan?
- How balanced is our strategic plan? Which key factors or tensions need to be brought into or remain in balance?
- How does our strategic plan ensure interconnectivity, flow, and balance in the medium to long term?

STEP 2: VISUALIZING THE ORGANIZATIONAL STRUCTURE AND STRATEGY

Visualizing your organizational structure and strategy involves envisioning the structures separately and as an integrated network. All aspects of structure are driven by people and affected by cultural norms.

To envision your organizational structure, start by envisioning your network of structures in a way that is unconfined by resources. Paint a picture of your optimal state that's free from constraints. Pull out your wish list, diagnostic information, and best practices and use all this information to innovate. Brainstorm different scenarios and don't initially analyze or get too granular—just record your ideas.

Then review the ideas you've collected and determine which ones can be implemented incrementally over time and which can be tackled immediately. Your strategic priorities will help you decide which structural improvements will have the greatest impact on your strategic objectives.

So let's explore this. If your strategic priority is to differentiate your organization and improve results by transforming your culture, you can visualize different structural scenarios that would help your organization achieve this. For example, an executive team decides to institutionalize a service culture. They set three priority objectives. One that reviews policies, processes, and technology to determine their alignment with the goal of creating a service culture. Secondly, they know that policies that establish multiple layers of approval will need to be revisited. And lastly, they will develop a talent development plan that will support the creation of a service culture.

Given budgetary parameters, decision-makers can create different scenarios that emphasize one or more of these three critical areas to determine the best way forward. So one scenario may address policy changes but place less emphasis on talent development initially. Another scenario may place equal emphasis on each scenario and a third option can focus on talent development as the primary driver of the service culture. It is important to weigh the pros and cons of each scenario before deciding.

When envisioning how your strategic plan can be successfully executed, you should consider how relationships can support achieving your strategic priorities, create projected flows, and keep your entire ecosystem in balance. You can envision how this will work during the design, planning, implementation, and ongoing balancing stages. Here are two lists of questions that can help you visualize your future structural state and strategic success:

Create a Vision for All Your Organizational Structures

- What should our organizational structures look like? How should they interconnect and operate when the structures are performing as designed?
- How are we considering room for growth in our design?
- How often should we make changes to our organizational structure to ensure we maintain change-based organization status?
- Which structures have the potential to obstruct our goals and objectives?

- Which structures are most useful for successfully establishing a change-based organization?
- What is our vision for our organizational culture and how should our structures support it?
- How does our vision for structure align with our strategic vision? Can it adequately support our strategy?

Create a Vision for Strategic Efficacy

- What principles of IFB should we include in our strategic plan to improve its chances for success? What should the goals and objectives of a strategy include?
- How can we ensure our strategy does not have unintended effects on flow?
- How can we use IFB principles to strengthen flow and facilitate balance?
- How should people be trained in IFB principles to create a strategy that adheres to IFB principles?
- How can we define strategic effectiveness using IFB principles?
- How can we use IFB to improve the potential for success of our strategic implementations?

STEP 3: DESIGNING THE ORGANIZATIONAL STRUCTURE AND STRATEGY

In organizational structural design, each part of the infrastructure (governance, organizational chart, policies) should align with others with as few contradictions as possible. For instance, if decision-makers want to create a culture of innovation, the organizational chart, policies, procedures, and other structures need to align as best as possible to promote creativity.

You may involve multiple stakeholders in the diagnostic, visioning, and design processes to ensure adequacy of design given the reality that structure affects everyone. Here is a list of questions to help you think about the design of different aspects of your IFB, organizational structure:

Interconnectivity

- How can/did we best utilize our diagnostic and visioning information to inform our design?
- Given what we know now, including the probable scenarios, do we need additional information that was not previously collected?
- Which individual and team behaviors do we need to modify to optimize our structural design?
- How do all parts of the proposed structural design interconnect? In addition to IFB, which other principles apply to all our structures?
- How can we design organizational structures to create or safeguard cohesion? How flexible should they be? How should they facilitate innovation?
- How can we design our organizational structures to minimize conflict and reinforce inclusion?
- How do our organizational structures facilitate or detract from interconnectivity?
- What do the relationships between each organizational structure need to be to enable seamless operation?

Flow

- How can we design our structures to close performance gaps and introduce efficiencies and other beneficial outcomes?
- How will employees contribute to seamless flow through structures?
- What are the obstacles to flow that we need to neutralize in our designs?

Balance

- Should we redesign our entire structure, or can we use parts of the existing one? Why?

- What mechanisms can we put in place to test our structures periodically and ensure continued balance and effectiveness?

- How can we ensure our organizational structures coexist without contradiction?

- Which mechanisms should we establish to help us take pro-active measures to maintain equilibrium within the overall structure?

- How do our structures contribute to organizational balance or imbalance?

- What does agility mean for us? How can we design our organizational structures to set the groundwork for organizational agility?

Governance Design

Governance is the framework within which other organizational structures operate. After envisioning the interpersonal interconnective infrastructure, the next step is to design a governance structure that will support your vision. As you evolve your governance design and other non-personal structures, you will need to develop your relationship architecture simultaneously.

Here is an example of one type of need for governance redesign: The board of directors of a medium-sized company gets overly involved in the firm's operational details. They are so active in daily business transactions that the executive team feels undermined; employees have been trained to circumvent certain executives, seeking direct approvals from various board committee members, preempting the executive team. A consultant was hired by the executive team to facilitate the IFB change process. During the diagnostic session it was clear the practice of board overreach was creating a deep divide. In this circumstance and others, the design phase can include:

- relationship mapping of multiple future states (that is, maps that consider redistribution of power within the organization among other interpersonal factors.)
- rewriting board governance documents
- envisioning the mix of skills needed on the board (with the goal being reconfiguring the composition of the board)
- development of the directors and executive team (sometimes boards step in because of their competency gaps and the perceived skill gaps of executive team members)

Some boards maintain the same structure and members for decades, but in an ever-changing environment, this can mean the board can become incrementally irrelevant. When used effectively, the IFB Model can contribute to board evolution and relevance to ensure it delivers meaningful oversight. Author and consultant Doug Macnamara coined the term "return on governance" — an activity used by boards to set the stage for increased relevance.

In his article entitled "The Real Work of Governance," Macnamara explains: "If the Board isn't contributing benefit back to the organization at least as much or more than the costs of having a Board, then what is the Board doing and how is Management listening to the Board?" By doing the work of the executive team, the board is incurring costs that can have far-reaching, damaging effects.

He continued, "If the Board isn't actively pursuing the five areas [Network Scanning; Future Relevancy and Community Engagement; Oversight; Perspective, and Ethical Reflection; Risk Management; and Diplomacy/Influence Leverage] — effectively, efficiently and with clarity — then one must wonder if they are truly fulfilling their fiduciary duty and living up to the trusteeship standard of care expected today."[13]

Designing Your Organizational Chart

Organizational charts can be connective. But they can also be a mixed bag: they can have enhancements to interconnectivity and flow as well as obstructions to productivity built into them. This can be exacerbated by the natural turnover cycle — where employees come and go, and departments evolve (or devolve).

If decision-makers don't maintain an objective macro view when redesigning organizational charts, the intended design can begin to exhibit anomalies that can be detrimental to the company's strategic priorities. As with any structure, when the design of a component of IFB is faulty, the entire framework can be put at risk.

Some organizational chart designs don't consider the reality that not everyone is interested in a leadership path or will thrive on one. To meet their teams' diverse needs, other organizations provide a variety of career path choices. For example, there can be expert paths, leadership paths, lateral paths, and nonlinear ones. Wherever possible, IFB designers should take the full spectrum of possible career goals into consideration when redesigning organizational charts and interpersonal relationship architecture.

Any changes to your organizational chart design should ensure workflows associated with the modifications make sense both inter- and intradepartmentally. Otherwise, undetected imbalances can lead to unforeseen risks in the new design. The steps below serve as a guide to creating an organizational chart design aligned with IFB principles:

- consider the strategic direction of the company, the existing organizational chart, and related workflows
- consider the people dynamics associated with the chart (the three P's — power, politics, and personalities)
- analyze the workflows and make changes to the organizational chart to better support them where necessary
- build in a process for periodically evaluating the relevance of the organizational chart

- Modify job descriptions to reflect the organizational chart
- include a robust communication plan that ensures information is effectively disseminated after changes are announced

In summary, when designed with IFB in mind, the organizational chart is one of the structures that supports agility, performance, collaboration, strategy and even engagement. It serves as a framework for the entire organizational ecosystem, so it affects multiple other structures, including policies and procedures.

Designing Policies and Procedures

Once leaders decide on a vision of how policies and procedures should shape culture and performance using IFB principles, any existing policies and procedures that get in the way of the new vision need to be replaced, recalibrated, or abolished. New ones should also meet established standards.

A thorough design process should consider how changes to targeted policies and procedures can potentially interact with other policies and procedures, reducing the risk of unintentional fallout. Here are a few guidelines for policy and procedure design:

- Designers should establish parameters for changing and creating policies and procedures.
- During the diagnostic stage, leaders should identify linkages between policies, procedures and other structures that emanate from different functional areas. Once they progress to design, leaders can use this information to inform the creation of new policies and procedures. The design phase should also test how the proposed changes will affect related policies and procedures and overall performance.
- When designing policies, it is important for policy-makers to enable enough flexibility within policies to allow leaders to use their discretion where necessary. In highly controlled

cultures, granular policies are used to reduce risk, but this approach also negatively affects employee engagement and can reduce the capacity of an organization for agility.

- Think about what you will do about informal policies. Should they be formalized in your design? How will that affect your overarching goal of building a controlled or innovative culture?
- Consider how you can make policies accessible.
- Leaders should define how they want people to interact with policies. Should they be compliant, should they be given discretion, or some combination of both? Clarify the relationship between polices and the people who are affected by them.

These guidelines are to be used in conjunction with the questions outlined at the beginning of Step 3 (Design) in this chapter.

Strategic Plan

If decision-makers have decided to implement IFB and have already planned and started executing their strategic plan, the plan can be modified to address IFB gaps. If you have no strategic plan and creating one is a priority, then IFB principles should be integrated into the plan. Here are a few tips to help you with integration once you review your diagnostic and visioning information. You should

- identify whether work relationships and skills are supporting or inhibiting plan execution;
- be sure the entire interconnective structure is adequately considered in your strategic plan;
- review how your plan affects the flow of transactional activities that are key to short-term performance and make changes to address obstructions;
- take steps to ensure your strategic plan isn't causing unintended imbalances;

- take advantage of unplanned balancing caused by the strategy;
- adequately space the timelines in your plan to be sure they don't create imbalances; and
- consider the flows (intended and actual) created by your strategic plan and how they affect each other.

STEPS 4 AND 5: PLANNING AND IMPLEMENTING ORGANIZATIONAL STRUCTURE

IFB is a framework that integrates existing tools and plans so leaders have the flexibility to maximize or change what they have. Changing a company's organizational structure is a major undertaking that can unfold incrementally, be pursued as an urgent priority, or some combination of the two. Because of the number of structures that coexist, leaders will need to decide which structural changes are a priority and how to integrate those changes into IFB planning and implementation to optimize ongoing initiatives.

Depending on the scope and complexity of change you require, structural changes can be added to your strategic plan integrating them into various goals like talent development, risk mitigation, and improved operational efficiencies.

STEP 6: ADJUSTING AND BALANCING YOUR ORGANIZATIONAL STRUCTURE

Your structural framework should be flexible enough to allow your organization to make immediate and long-term changes. Your IFB structural plan should include a balancing component that facilitates regular checks of your structure to ensure it doesn't threaten the integrity of your Pillar of Trust, or your achievement of strategic goals.

IFB balancing actions should ensure that your structures are connecting and facilitating flow and balance. In larger organizations, this responsibility can fall within the scope of a department dedicated to policies and procedures. In smaller organizations responsibility can be delegated to the leadership team.

On a final note, as you progress through Steps 4, 5, and 6 in relation to organizational structure, keep in mind that no structure should be considered sacrosanct or untouchable when it comes to IFB. They can all be subject to recalibration.

CHAPTER 16

DESIGNING FLOW

Everything flows and nothing abides; everything gives way and
nothing stays fixed.

—Heraclitus

F low is nourished by the layers of relationships both within and outside your organization. Flow not only operates inside these layers of relationships, it also moves between them. An example of this happens when workflows operate within and between three departments, and decisions about these departments are made by the executive team. The executive team communicates changes to these flows through the hierarchical layers of the company, with the intention of stimulating changes to flows through and between departments.

Just like relationships, not all flows are discernible; they can be hidden for a variety of reasons. When considering your flow design — as with other parts of the IFB Model — you should uncover as many flows as you can, then prioritize them.

The Interconnectivity and Flow Tool introduced in Chapter 6 identifies three states of flow: blocked, intermittent, and steady. Depending on the states of multiple flows, you can tell which interconnections need to be strengthened and vice versa. In other words, the states of interconnectivity and flow can also help you determine which relationships to prioritize so you can improve flows in a way that helps you achieve your strategic goals.

The strategic direction of your organization determines which flows are priorities and how they should move. As we emphasized in our explorations of the Pillar of Trust, it's important to establish or reinforce relationship cohesion, regardless the types of flow required. Some organizations establish strategies based on a vision of steady flow, but since organizations experience cycles of natural ebbs and flows, flow should be defined within the context of strategy and these cycles.

For example, the demand for consumer goods can be driven by calendar seasons, the cycle of customer tastes and preferences, or both. If steady revenue flow and cost containment form your profitability goals, decision-makers can synchronize external and internal cycles with plans that drive the attainment of business targets.

This chapter provides a process, tools, and strategies you can use to design your envisioned states of flow. Some aspects of flow seem to operate on autopilot and can be highly productive, but because of the everyday nature of the underlying processes, your routines may not inspire optimized flow. In circumstances like this your plan may focus on attaining optimized flow states. As a reminder, optimized flow states are ideal when innovating or problem solving, so keep this in mind as you use this chapter to design flow for your team or organization.

What Is Flow Design?

The term "flow design" refers to the design or patterns of flow that move through your internal and external interconnective infrastructure. It requires clarity about your vision for all types of flow within your organization. Your flow design should incorporate the options that take your interconnective structure into consideration because of the intricate linkages between interconnectivity and flow. As part of the change process, you will also need to decide on flow patterns for priority flows, whether they are optimized, steady, unsteady, blocked, and so on.

Sound flow design also requires you to consider your drivers of flow. If talent development is required to strengthen your drivers, then talent development and management plans should form an important part of your design solutions.

As you design various flow scenarios, you should consider the probability that the interconnective structure will not always maintain high-quality connections because relationships are fluid. To address this, your flow design can include features that neutralize obstacles to healthy relationships, dismantle unproductive patterns, and remove existing impediments. One good example of a solution that can achieve these three objectives is an effective internal communication structure that can reduce the possibility of unplanned disruptions to flow.

Why Flow Design Is Important

Flows operate within a complex, network. They are like a network of wires — entangled, separated, connected, or disconnected, and existing for different purposes — that channel electricity behind the walls of a building and guide the flow of electrical currents through it. Similarly, in your organization, various states of flow coexist, in different states of effectiveness and order.

The purpose behind designing flow is to be sure it operates as intended. Your design can include attributes that facilitate sustainability, agility, and alignment of the flow states embedded within your strategy. Design allows you to deliberately orchestrate your flows, rather than standing by and witnessing organic or even disorganized flow, both of which can diminish the probability of achieving your goals.

Flow: A Brief Review

Organizations establish goals as tools for achieving outcomes. Understandably, some are more adept than others at tracking external patterns and creating goals that respond to the trends that affect internal flows.

In Chapter 5 I explained configurations of flow, how flow is facilitated, and the rates and drivers of flow. Initially, I provided this information with the intention of helping you diagnose flow; now you can use the same model to inform your design.

Flow can occur in both internal and external cycles, and understanding these cycles provides an additional perspective for decision-makers to better forecast business fluctuations and manage key stakeholders' expectations. Taking time to design flow can also reduce wastage and support team collaboration. You might want to revisit Chapter 5 to recap the list of the variety of types of flows that exist within and outside organizations.

STEP 1: DIAGNOSE FLOW

As with interconnectivity and balance, diagnosing flow needs to go beyond a superficial assessment. It requires an understanding of cycles, patterns, and movement as well as an appreciation of the flow drivers — in other words, the *why* behind the what and how. When diagnosing flow, select the flows that are priorities for your organization, then you can characterize their current flow states by answering the following questions:

- Which internal and external cycles affect our priority flows?
- What are the priority flows? (Use the types list.)
- What are the configurations of priority flows?
- How are priority flows facilitated? What are the rates of these flows?
- What are the primary drivers of priority flows?
- Considering the flows of different types of information, what are the patterns? How are these patterns related to interpersonal relationship dynamics?
- How would we characterize our workflows, and how effective are they?
- What are the risks inherent in priority flows?
- What are the opportunities related to priority flows?
- How can we describe our emotional climate? How do morale and the general emotional state of the team affect flows?
- How can we execute change fluidly?

- How does change flow in the context of daily business demands? What takes precedence: long-term goals, or our daily routines? Why? How are we managing them both?
- How are our decisions and decision-making processes facilitating flow or creating obstacles?
- How do we define our revenue flows?
- How do we describe customer flows?
- Which cycles of our organization and external environment affect our flows (e.g., the life cycle of the business, the market preferences, seasons, consumer tastes, and market trends)?
- How do our relationships (internal and external) facilitate flow? Which ones facilitate it, and which don't?
- What plans do we have in place for succession?
- How do we describe the flows of succession, development, and growth?
- How well does communication flow through existing channels?
- Does communication facilitate other flows? How? What are the gaps?
- How effectively does our team facilitate innovation?
- How do our policies and procedures facilitate flow? How do they not?
- How does our organizational chart facilitate flow?
- How do our delegated authorities support or hinder flow?
- How does our governance structure contribute to or detract from flow?
- How does strategy facilitate flow? How does it obstruct it?
- Which flow dynamics seem to be out of balance and require adjustment?
- For each flow prioritized, is it optimized, steady, unsteady, blocked, or a combination of these characteristics?

- How should we characterize flow within and between departments?
- What are our cycles of flow (the natural ebb and flow) within your organization?
- How does our relationship architecture support or impede flow?
- How does our relationship architecture support the possibility for long-term sustainability of flow?
- Who can help strengthen our relationship architecture? Who is weakening it?

While observation and institutional memory may partially determine the answers to these questions, metrics, survey results, one-on-one interviews, and focus group data can also supplement your research. For further support, you can refer to the macro IFB solutions you developed in response to the guidelines in Chapter 13 and the introduction to flow in Chapter 5.

Diagnosing Drivers of Flow

The drivers of flow are the impetus behind flow dynamics. After diagnosing the symptoms of your flow states, you should attempt to identify root causality. At this stage of diagnosing flow, you have defined what is going on with various flows, now you can identify the drivers behind patterns and outcomes. Since multiple drivers are usually at work simultaneously, it's useful to identify as many as possible so you can map patterns in causality as well. Drivers related to flows include:

- your emotional climate
- values of the organization and values of individuals within the organization
- the effectiveness of your communication infrastructure
- innovation/ideas
- relationship quality

- your configuration of networks and silos
- trust
- loyalty/obligation
- the quality of policies and procedures
- your strategic acumen
- execution skills (competence)
- ability to execute plans
- collective knowledge/skills/abilities
- internal and external power and political dynamics (personal agendas, ambition, the desire to grow)
- desire/vision/purpose
- climate/emotion (fear, purposefulness, freedom)
- leader competence
- decision-making quality (based on fact/emotion/intuition)
- intent (personal agenda vs. team agenda)
- cultural norms
- quality of meetings
- accountability framework for the organization

A key question decision-makers should ask about every driver is "How does this driver facilitate flow?" Another necessary question is "How does this driver inhibit flow?" Even though drivers should support flow, sometimes relationships change in quality and become obstacles. Additionally, a driver can facilitate flow, but the flow created may not be *optimized* flow. So you can ask, "What is our potential for achieving optimized flow?" and, "How can we optimize important flows?"

Other Diagnostic Resources

Organizations collect data over the years that can be added to their diagnosis of flows. The following list provides additional resources and other analytical tools that can aid this exercise of discovery and understanding:

- strategic (action) plan
- efficiency studies
- compliance reviews
- internal audit reviews
- financial audits
- other metrics and analytics
- regulatory audits
- expense controls
- climate assessments
- engagement surveys
- leadership assessments
- performance statistics
- industry reports
- IFB survey
- enterprise risk reports
- map of relationship architecture
- status of implementation of the Pillar of Trust

A significant amount of information can be uncovered by your diagnostic process, so as with other parts of IFB change, it is critical for designers to prioritize these diagnoses. Otherwise, you can fall into the trap of analysis paralysis.

STEP 2: VISUALIZE FLOW

Now it's time for your design team to envision future flow states. After reviewing the information collected, you can invite members of your team to visualize your optimal states of internal and external flow. A baseline understanding of the strategic plan will allow the team to determine whether entirely new flow states or modified ones are necessary to achieve your goals.

Be sure to include your priority flows in your vision, describing them in their ideal states in the present tense. Be as detailed as you can because as with others, this visualization exercise will serve as the foundation of your flow design. You can have someone record the session in a diagrammatic format (as an interconnected map), in writing, or a combination of both. Also, remember to take time to envision desired states of flows that were less easy to perceive.

Sometimes organizational strategies require intentional deceleration or stoppage of flow. This can occur when a product or service is discontinued, or when decision-makers want to deliberately manipulate the demand and supply of a product or service. As a result, designers should consider some flows in terms of cycles and include these cycles in the visualization process.

STEP 3: FLOW DESIGN

Your design should include the leadership and team competencies you need to build within your team to better facilitate flow, encompassing both technical and soft skills. Start with the competencies for building and maintaining the Pillar of Trust. Your flow design should also include competencies to help your organization honor its core values and other important skills such as developing team members, recognizing opportunities, and thriving in ambiguous circumstances.

An important benefit of flow design is that organizations can become more deliberate about influencing priority flows. Flow is largely powered by technology and interpersonal systems. And as we have already established, people dynamics are constantly shifting, so consider the following as you use your diagnostic and visioning information to inform your flow design:

- Which behaviors or cultural norms do we need to change for the design to be most effective?
- Do we need entirely new flow designs, or should we modify existing ones?
- With an understanding of how all parts of the structure interconnect, what are some of the considerations that should apply to flow within each structure?

- How should our flows operate to overcome performance gaps? How can they be strengthened?
- How can our flows be designed to minimize conflict and create inclusion?
- How can flows better support sustainable balance?
- How can our flows be tested periodically to ensure movement is happening as planned?
- How can employees facilitate flows seamlessly through the structures?
- Which mechanisms should we establish as proactive measures to maintain flows?
- How can our priority flows facilitate or detract from interconnectivity?
- How can our flows contribute to organizational balance or imbalance?
- What should the configurations of flow be for priority flows (loop, linear, nonlinear)?
- How should the priority flows, facilitate movement (managed, forced, organic)?
- What should the rates of flow (steady, unsteady, blocked) be?
- What are the benefits and consequences of our flow designs?
- What features should all our flow designs embody?

Your designs can be used to reinvent or strengthen flows. You can also employ them to circumvent or dismantle unproductive flow systems and remove blockages. Whether you plan to create a new system of flows or redesign existing ones, these questions should be explored.

Final flow design should encompass multiple interconnective layers, so consider the potential interaction of flow within and between these layers. When working with the IFB Model, the design and planning phases can overlap; complete separation is not necessary, or even possible when teams are executing adjustments to flows for balancing purposes.

STEPS 4 AND 5: PLANNING AND IMPLEMENTING FLOW

Having designed priority flows through your interconnective infrastructure, your next steps should be planning and implementation. Depending on the current state of your flows and the strategic direction of the business, your selected design(s) will guide planners, helping them to create a plan that will enhance flow or reinvent it completely.

Circumventing or Removing Obstacles to Flow During the Planning and Implementation Stages

Obstacle circumvention requires your leadership team to sidestep obstructions in the design (sometimes it isn't possible to remove an obstacle), creating an alternative path of flow. Circumvention can be useful, as it may carve out an even better path. However, it can also highlight deficiencies within an organization, especially if it happens because of a damaged relationship that's key to a team's performance.

Ecosystems can be self-correcting and one way it achieves this is through circumvention. Self-adjusting steps like this may not be easily perceived, but decision-makers should become adept at detecting them so they can proactively address potential challenges whenever possible.

Removing obstacles during the planning process can be complicated if the source of your blockage is a person. The same applies if removal is associated with a high cost. In cases like these, it's important for you to set reasonable expectations because, depending on your leadership team and its planning and execution capabilities, it can be a lengthy and risky process.

Implementation

Execution success depends on the diversity and relevance of the skills of leaders and other team members who are required to implement strategic goals using IFB principles. Some leadership teams possess advanced planning skills but weak execution abilities, some are not so strong with either, and still others are very strong at planning, execution, and adjusting to new information. The adjustment mechanism is the balancing process; it both facilitates flow and flow enables balance. These elements of the IFB Model operate in a reciprocal relationship.

Implementing plans for flow requires familiarity with the structure and feel of your flow designs and how to implement them — in much the same way that a contractor constructs a building using the architectural drawings. Successful implementation depends on effective messaging and communication channels, the skills to detect minor or significant variations in flow, an understanding of the consequences of those shifts, and awareness of the actions needed to appropriately address variations.

STEP 6: BALANCING AND ADJUSTING FLOW

Balancing and sustaining flow requires a keen sense of attunement and observation. But this isn't enough. Leaders should understand the goals and objectives for achieving desired flow states and detect when those flow states are behaving as expected, without coercion.

If a particular flow is not operating as planned, change leaders should track it to discern patterns and causes of the unplanned configurations. Once leaders ascertain the root causes of an aberrant flow state, they can determine if the unplanned pattern can be managed to a better outcome and if so, take action. If solution management does not yield positive results, an alternative approach should be identified and implemented in an effort to bring your ecosystem back into balance.

When a newly implemented flow is not performing to expectation, leaders responsible for coordinating balance should also seek to understand how and why the flow pattern is performing the way it is and if appropriate, create a plan to address the factors contributing to the less than satisfactory results. Unacceptable results may be attributed to resistance to change, flawed change plans, or inadequate communication and training.

When balancing flow, change leaders have several options. You can

- track flows, beginning before the noticeable departure from the desired flow state (exact timing is the leader's judgment call);
- track priority flows to identify and address trends in flow modulation;
- determine if gaps exist between the planned balanced state (using priority balancing spectra) and the actual balance state. If gaps are evident, determine causation;
- establish which changes can occur based on modifications in another category (leveraging stronger flows), thereby reducing the need to address all out-of-balance situations;
- engage employees to achieve successful adjustment; and
- monitor progress, which may involve assigning responsibilities for close monitoring and evaluation.

Once you consider these questions and any others you can formulate, you can modify or create your flow (and any related) designs, adjusting plans where necessary. But before adapting, you should first consider if time will take care of imbalances.

While in balancing and adjustment mode, change leaders should pay close attention to the impact of shifts in flow on engagement and vice versa. Even if planned flow changes operate as expected in the short term, employees can become demoralized because changes can cause stress and burnout. Sustained pressure tends to lead to retention challenges over time, particularly among top talent.

CHAPTER 17

YOUR BALANCING ACT

*In a balanced organization working toward a common
objective, there is success.*

—Sir Arthur Helps, writer and dean of the Privy Council

A ll facets of the IFB Model are in constant motion; therefore, maintaining balance isn't an event, it's a process. The balancing component of the IFB Model is what can potentially transform companies into change-based organizations. It takes a shift in mindset, the capacity to remain in change mode, even after the initiatives have been successfully or ineffectively executed. When operating according to IFB principles, leaders and team members are in perpetual change mode, ready to deal with the constant state of flux produced by environmental influences.

The IFB Model has two, built-in balancing mechanisms. One is the Pillar of Trust, which promotes intrinsic and interpersonal balance and connection. The other mechanism is the balance component of the model, which gives decision-makers a bird's-eye view of multiple aspects of their respective organizations, so they can take proactive steps to ensure their operations are in an overall state of equilibrium.

Leaders who facilitate balance as part of an IFB implementation exercise ought to deliberately surveil the current operational state, so priority dynamics can remain in balance. The observation process should also detect emerging priorities and long-term ones that are no longer contributing significantly to the overall well-being and sustainability of your organization.

You can use this chapter as a blueprint for achieving and sustaining your desired state of balance, keeping multiple, shifting tensions in equilibrium. Like the previous chapters in Part III, it's a roadmap that will support you with navigating the path through your diagnostic phase and on to the adjustment stage. Like interconnectivity and flow, balance can be part of a cultural change plan and should be compatible with your strategic plan.

Why Facilitate Balance?

Balancing is a skill that supports organizational sustainability and agility. In a global environment that's increasingly unpredictable, the economy, social challenges, climate change, and contentious political forces are only a few of the external factors that affect your ability to achieve your goals. If decision-makers are out of touch with their external environments, balancing can become a predominantly reactive exercise.

Internal and external environments should operate in synchronization. Your external environment affects internal considerations such as strategy, staffing, resources, and other areas. Conversely, depending on the leadership teams' capacity for innovation and the influence of an organization, internal actions can affect the external environment.

Facilitating balance can mean the difference between a growth-oriented, relevant, and successful business and one that remains static or eventually meets its demise after operating in an isolationist bubble.

Like the other features of the IFB Model, balance is everybody's responsibility but there are different roles within the practice. For leaders, it is important to attune to emergent external and internal opportunities. By doing this you can plan for multiple possible scenarios and respond quickly and appropriately.

For instance, if a change in your external environment has the potential to negatively affect your organization, IFB decision-makers who planned various change scenarios are better positioned to respond to the event and maintain balance with minimal drama.

Getting to Balance

The condition of balance is unique for every organization because multiple attributes called "organizational dimensions" need to be managed to achieve it. Attaining balance differs from one organization to another. In fact, thanks to subcultural differences, sometimes leaders of various departments within the same organization use completely different methods to achieve balance. They do what comes naturally.

Decision-makers can seek to manage balance as they implement change initiatives or during routine day-to-day activities. Some leaders first implement a change, then focus their resources on bringing the situation into balance. The ideal approach is to keep balance at top of mind from the strategic visioning and goal-setting stage, through implementation, and adjustment—throughout the process, in an unending loop.

Once leaders establish strategic goals, they can seek to bring priority areas of their organizations into balance. For instance, an executive leadership team decides to address employee engagement because they identified a strong correlation between engagement

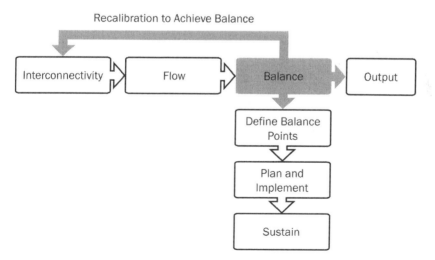

Figure 17.1   Balance in the Context of the IFB Model

and productivity. The company's existing engagement levels are low, so the balancing process involves a plan to enhance productivity and profitability levels by implementing engagement and talent development plans.

Figure 17.1 depicts the balancing process introduced in Chapter 7. It starts with defining or establishing your balance points, about which you might obtain quantitative and qualitative information. The next step is for decision-makers to create a plan, followed by the implementation of the changes. Finally, the key players apply fine tuning, or balancing actions, as needed for sustainability. Balancing, or recalibration, may require revisiting your interconnective infrastructure and flows.

Calibrating Balance

When decision-makers achieve balance in simple, dynamic, or complex systems, they may view their achievement as an event rather than an ongoing process. In reality, the state of balance within an organizational ecosystem is constantly shifting because relationships are interlocking, releasing, and reconnecting unceasingly as flows move along multiple coexisting paths. Within evolving institutions, various characteristics of the organization are in constant motion, moving with varying degrees of momentum.

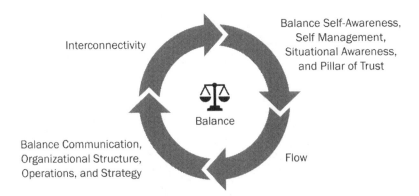

Figure 17.2 Calibrating Balance

Figure 17.2 illustrates balance calibration in the context of interconnectivity and flow, highlighting the constant motion that includes balancing actions. It also shows how balance is achieved through internal self-regulation, but this alone is not enough. Leaders who operate within the scope of the Pillar of Trust, use information they gather to manage and maintain healthy team environments and engagement with multiple structures.

False Balance Appearing Real

The underlying purposes of balance include growth and evolution. You should take proactive steps to ensure what you are perceiving as balance is actually balance, and not a staged representation of it. False Balance Appearing Real—or FBAR—materializes when your organizational ecosystem assumes the appearance of stability by resolving superficial symptoms of imbalances while the root causes continue to erode balance, triggering new challenges. So as you set out to define your balance goals and objectives, be vigilant about discerning your true state of balance.

Attaining and Maintaining Balance

Balancing action can be organic or managed. When working toward balance as part of IFB implementation, there is room for both. This is because organizations have multiple moving parts and systems that should be managed from both macro and micro perspectives.

These systems are concurrently self-regulating and self-managing. When multiple, coexistent changes are introduced to the landscape, leaders may find themselves consumed by transactional activities—putting out fires while attempting to overlook the strategic consequences of their nearsighted decisions that affect balance. To prevent this from happening, leaders should be adept at sustaining balance both from a bird's-eye view as well as up close.

In Chapter 7 I introduced the balancing process illustrated in Figure 7.2. It is a framework you can use to attain and maintain balance within your organization and forms the outline of the remainder of this chapter. It is slightly different from the IFB change model used in the rest of this chapter as it places an emphasis on balance points and calibration throughout the process. As a refresher, the process is: define the current state; define new balance points; plan, implement (achieve new balance points), and sustain balance.

STEP 1: DIAGNOSE THE CURRENT STATE OF BALANCE

As with all other diagnostic processes introduced in this book, the first step is for executives to define the current state by identifying balanced dimensions as well as tensions that are out of balance. They should consider that the presence of a tension doesn't automatically signify an imbalance. Additionally, before collecting relevant information they can decide on the best tools to accurately define their current contexts: like focus group sessions, data collection, analysis of survey results, and so forth.

In addition to identifying circumstances that lead to disequilibrium, leaders should identify balanced conditions and determine how these conditions might be affected by bringing out-of-balance dimensions into balance. Bringing certain conditions into balance can lead to positive or negative domino effects, causing other priority flows and dimensions to come into or slip out of balance.

Consider this example: a company has outgrown the technology that drives their production, sales, and customer service. Employees using the technology are knowledgeable, and the IT team is capable of maintaining the hardware and troubleshooting software errors. While the company's priority balance dimensions are mostly in equilibrium, changes are necessary in the near term for the organization to remain relevant to its customer base in the long term.

In their plan for long-term balance and sustainability, leaders of the company upgraded their main software, but they encountered challenges with the solution. Not only did the new software fail to sustain the previous standards of customer service, this solution didn't yield the functionality decision-makers thought it would. Unfortunately, this meant the prospects of the new software adequately meeting the company's future needs were slim.

The executive team's decision to purchase software to meet the company's future needs was not thoroughly researched; as a result, an incompatible software solution was purchased. This decision had multiple effects on balance: it impacted morale and engagement levels, and this led to deficiencies in client care which in turn eventually compromised revenue levels.

This is a case in which a seemingly balanced situation was destabilized by a single decision. A diagnostic workup will involve

- understanding the technological deficiencies and how they affect people, sales, customer service, IT and any other relevant areas;
- appreciating the people challenges brought about by the decision: trust, engagement, client care, team competence, power dynamics, personalities, *institutional memory*, communication effectiveness, etc.;
- conducting a cost, benefit analysis;
- researching how your company can resolve the imbalances introduced by the decision; and
- contemplating the affect your decision had on flows (e.g., number of transactions, quality of those interactions, etc.).

Using information obtained through the diagnostic process, the design and planning team can then shift to the visualization and design phases.

Diagnostic Questions

Here is a more wide-ranging list of questions to help you identify balancing challenges so you can prioritize the dimensions of your organization that require it. Remember, the intention of this exercise is not to bring all aspects of your organization into balance, it is to bring the priority or selected tensions of your business into balance.

- What are the organizational performance gaps?

- What are all the tensions in our organization? Which ones are priorities?
- Which tensions need to be brought into balance, or sustained in a state of balance?
- Where are the discernible occurrences of False Balance Appearing Real? What are they?
- Which characteristics of our business need to be brought into balance?
- Which characteristics of our business need to remain in balance?
- Which dimensions are out of balance and can remain out of balance given the low risk associated with it?
- Using the balance dimensions (tensions) in Table 7.1 or your knowledge of the needs of your organization, which dimensions of your business are strategic priorities? What is your criteria for selection and prioritization?
- Which flows are in and out of balance?
- What are your relationship dynamics that contribute to balance and imbalance? (Use your relationship maps.)
- How does culture contribute to balance and imbalance?
- How do you characterize overall balance?
- Which risks did you create with your current balances and imbalances?
- Which opportunities created by our existing balances and imbalances?
- How effective is your organization at managing imbalances created by change execution?
- How does decision-making affect balance? How do decisions avoid or create obstacles?
- Which cycles of your business and environment (e.g., life cycle of business, life cycle of market, seasons, consumer tastes, market trends) affect balance?

- How does your communication infrastructure facilitate balance?

Selecting Balance Dimensions

As a reminder, Table 7.1 outlines a number of balance dimensions that can have a significant effect on balance within an organization, both internally and externally. While the list is not exhaustive, it provides a starting point for your diagnostic process.

When establishing your unique list of balance dimensions, you should identify only the tensions that have the power to compromise your strategic goals and contradict your core values now and in the future. As part of the diagnostic process, once leaders identify priority balance dimensions — tensions — they can plot the dimensions (tensions) on various spectra as illustrated in the next section.

Plotting the Current State of Balance on a Scale

After identifying which priority organizational dimensions you plan to bring into, or keep in balance, you can plot them on scales to provide visual representations of your individual and collective balance states. These scales should represent critical tensions of your organization that are in and out of balance. As you plot your dimensions, keep in mind the fact that if priority tensions are in balance and important to your business in the present and future, this doesn't mean they should be excluded from your list of priorities.

As we have discussed, a balance point is the point on a balance scale that represents either the current or future state of organizational tensions. When plotting future states, the balance point represents the proposed optimal point necessary for meeting your organization's strategic (and other) goals. You can get creative and also use the scales to reflect what will happen in the future if corrective action is not taken.

Here is an example of the current state: The manager of an administration department is interested in bringing balance to her department. She identified several tensions as priorities and plotted them for her department. Figure 17.4 illustrates how she plotted one of the priority tensions: technical competence versus incompetence.

Figure 17.3   Sample Team Technical Competence Scale

In Figure 17.3, the value 0 is equivalent to no competence in the required technical areas, 5 represents 50 percent technical competence, and 10 represents 100 percent required technical competence. The scale can be adjusted to include above-average competence if preferred. To modify the scale, 10 would now mean above average competence, 0 will still equal no competence, and 5 would indicate that an employee or team possesses the required competence. Whichever scale is used, each point on the spectrum will need to be qualitatively and quantitatively defined by the organization.

Based on the scale in Figure 17.3, the manager assigned her team a current state (CS) balance point of 2.5/10 or 25 percent, which represents the current state of the team's technical competence. Despite the low competence level, she does recognize the potential to improve their technical skills with development.

The manager rated the technical skill gaps the way she did because she observes errors by tracking team and individual results. She also takes note of knowledge gaps by recording the types and frequency of questions being asked by her team members. Despite the inherent gaps within the team, the department is meeting its goals. This is because the manager is a consummate micromanager, often staying behind to complete unfinished work herself because she believes she is more qualified and experienced than anyone else.

Figure 17.4 represents an engagement scale for a different organization. In this example, the placement on the engagement scale is based on the collective outcome of an engagement survey.

Figure 17.4   Sample Engagement Scale

The current goal or benchmark for the engagement balance point is 65 percent, but the actual CS balance point is 5/10 or 50 percent.

To achieve the targeted balance point, the team needs to take a deeper look at its internal dynamics to identify opportunities for improving engagement levels. Based on feedback from employees, they decided to put a plan in place that establishes relevant career paths, implements engagement initiatives, and facilitates cultural change.

STEP 2: CREATING A VISION FOR BALANCE

Envisioning balance requires leaders to analyse the critical tensions diagnosed as being in or out of balance. To achieve this, leaders will need to first consider them from a macro perspective, determining how they interact with each other and how their strengths can be leveraged to turn around important dimensions that are weak. A macro perspective will also provide insights into whether important tensions are missing from your priority list.

Figure 17.5 is an example of an IFB balance wheel. The balance wheel is a qualitative measurement tool that can be used to define and analyze your current state of balance; you can also repopulate it to envision future scenarios. Figure 17.5 provides a depiction of the current state of an organization and takes you through a process that shows you how you can use it to define your vision.

Mapping Your Current Satisfaction State

Once leaders prioritize the critical balance dimensions and plot them on separate scales, they can map these dimensions collectively on a balance wheel. In this diagnostic mapping exercise, the purpose of the balance wheel is to understand the current state.

Figure 17.5 represents an example where decision-makers identified eight dimensions that are most relevant to their strategic goals and sustaining IFB. The leaders of this company decided on a satisfaction rating scale from 1 to 10 − 10 being the highest possible satisfaction with the current state and 1 being the lowest.

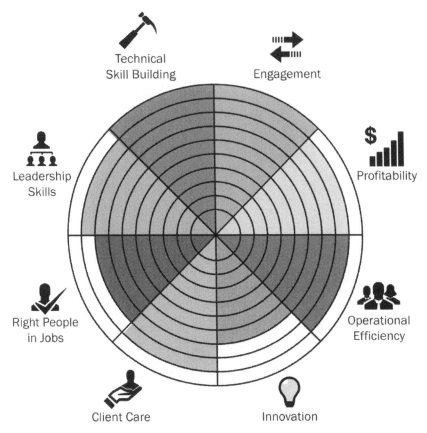

Figure 17.5   *Example of a Balance Wheel*

This balance wheel represents the current state of a high-performing company whose executive team established goals to achieve industry leadership through enhancing innovation and building client loyalty. The company has a history of commitment to sustaining high trust levels; it is goal driven and profitable.

After analyzing their map, the leadership team concludes there's additional capacity to grow their innovative abilities by restructuring the organization, getting the right people in innovation roles, and harnessing the advanced technical skills of the team and high trust levels behind engagement.

Sometimes a balance wheel like this—with every dimension highly rated—can show up when there is rater bias or when the evaluators are not comfortable expressing themselves authentically. To reduce the possibility of inaccuracies that come along with rater bias, you can consider using measurable criteria for each dimension.

Creating Your Vision for Balance

Once you map your current satisfaction levels on your balance wheel(s) representing the current state of your priority tensions, another IFB balance wheel can be created to map the future state for the same, or new priority dimensions. Designers can again use a 1–10 rating scale, but this time 10 represents the highest desired satisfaction with the future state and 1 the lowest. When using the balance wheel to define or refine your vision, here are a few questions you can use to ensure that you integrate pertinent information:

- Are there priorities in the future state that weren't priorities in the current state? Why or why not?

- How many future priorities should we consider? (Based on resource, and other constraints.)

- What is the current balance wheel telling us about strengths we can leverage in the future? How can we use this information to establish our vision and design?

- What can we reasonably do about weak dimensions that are critical for achieving our future state?

- Which dimensions (that weren't included on the balance wheel of critical tensions) may emerge as being critical in the future if we only focus on dimensions highlighted as priorities? How can they affect our vision?

- What are the future opportunities and threats that the vision for balance should address?

- Which dimensions, if strengthened, will help our organization to become a resilient, change-based organization?

- Which dimensions, if strengthened, will help us to become more agile?
- What are the possible external events that can affect balance within our organization?
- Which internal decisions or events can affect balance within our organization?

This visioning exercise is strengths based, focusing leaders on how they can shape their organizations using existing advanced competencies. The overarching intention behind balancing is to capitalize on your strengths to grow your business — and one of the anticipated by-products of this type of exercise is enhanced results.

Leaders should consider various possible scenarios during the visioning process. As a result, should produce several balancing scenarios that require different strategies. Production of multiple future scenarios supports the organizational agility; it is a practice that is essential to creating a change-based organization supported by IFB principles.

STEP 3: DESIGNING BALANCE (DEFINING THE NEW BALANCE POINTS)

Your designs for balance should have built-in accountability to ensure teams achieve and sustain balance according to your vision. Designs for balance should incorporate priority trust, interconnective, and flow elements, identifying new balance points or refining the reasons behind maintaining the status quo.

In Step 1, we used the balance dimensions and scales along with the balance wheel to define the current state. Now we are revisiting the tools to create a design (or designs) that will inform the planning phase. When using the envisioned balance points in your design, you will need to clearly define the desired future state of each priority tension with the goal of ensuring your entire organization remains in a state of equilibrium as you evolve. Initially, this should include critical tensions; however, some noncritical tensions may also need to be added because they have the potential to become critical if left unattended.

Once you achieve the balance points featured in your design, it is possible that it will not be sustained without effort. Sustaining balance requires effort and an effective support system because people environments are active and diverse.

Your team can create design options for balance using the vision(s) you created in Step 2 and the following questions as a guideline:

- Which visions for balance (scales and balance wheels) are most fitting for our organization?
- How can we achieve balance between our organization and our environment?
- What are our success measures for balance?
- What are our opportunities for balance?
- What are our risks if we don't achieve or maintain balance?
- What are some of the ways we can get the most out of our priority tensions? What are they?
- What are the priority tensions that if harnessed or addressed might drive even better results?
- What happens if we continue with the same priorities as before? How will our organization continue to grow and remain in balance if we choose this route?
- What are the criteria for designing balance on scales for the future? What are our guidelines for establishing future balance points?

Ideally, your design for organizational balance should consider the long-term implications of your creation. As with all other parts of the IFB Model, several scenarios should be created: for example, one of your designs might reflect business as usual. This would be growth along your current trajectory, all things remaining equal. Another scenario can consider a change in your external environment, while a third may consider a change in your strategic direction.

It doesn't have to stop there—a fourth scenario can consider a combination of internal and external changes. By including various scenarios in your design, your leadership team can decide how it can prepare for these scenarios and by thinking them through; you may gain valuable insights.

Designing Balance Using Scales

Designing balance using scales requires defining new balance points; it is a process that starts after the design team conducts diagnostic and visioning exercises. The design process should yield future balance scales and wheels for multiple tensions, especially the high-priority ones identified in Stage 2.

Keep in mind that as you develop your designs, you may identify new priority dimensions for the future while some of the existing dimensions may diminish in priority. This is a natural part of the process and you can decide how this will affect other priority dimensions.

It is also important to think about the number of priority dimensions you have identified and ask, "Do we have the resources to effectively manage this number of priority dimensions and achieve our strategic goals?" You don't want your balancing process to inadvertently create an imbalance, shifting too much focus away from your strategic priorities because balancing has become a distraction.

Plotting Your Desired State

Figure 17.3 revealed how the current state of competence can be plotted on a scale and Figure 17.6 shows how you can plot your design goal for the same scale. So previously, the manager diagnosed the collective technical competence level of the team using a balance point of 2.5 (25 percent) on a scale of 1 to 10. The manager arrived at this rating by reviewing career development plans in conjunction with the overall performance of the team.

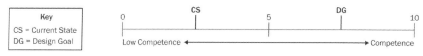

Figure 17.6   *Modified Sample Team Technical Competence Scale*

In Figure 17.6, the plan is to move competence from 2.5 (25 percent) to 7.5 (75 percent) over a period of three to five years. To get there, designers should determine if the current manager can take the team where it needs to go, and if so, which developmental opportunities does the manager need? Designers can also take past performance evaluations and existing workforce development plans into consideration, along with projected organizational charts. In this way, they can holistically assess the viability of their future targets.

Figure 17.7   *Modified Sample Engagement Scale*

Figure 17.7 is a continuation of Figure 17.4. In Figure 17.7, decision-makers established a goal of a 10 percent improvement in engagement over the next three years; the design team is aware trust levels and other factors that contribute to the current engagement level take time to improve. Additionally, designers (along with the appropriate decision-makers) are planning staffing changes to further improve engagement.

Sometimes remaining in the current state is a valid option. This can be appropriate when a critical dimension of an organization is already very strong and requires little to no support for sustainability. A dimension may also be left in its existing state when it is not a high priority and neither slippage nor increase are inconsequential.

Before moving to the planning stage, designers should plot all the priority dimensions in their proposed future states, and then consolidate them for review in a balance wheel. To test the validity of your prioritization, you may plot the future state of some of your non-critical tensions and can ask your team critical questions. Before moving to the planning stage be sure to consider the answers to the questions provided in the diagnostic phase to ensure your design is as well thought out as possible. The next section outlines how you can use the IFB Wheel in your design phase.

Using the IFB Balance Wheel for Design

The IFB balance wheel you used previously to map your current state should now be used to map your future design. The priority dimensions may or may not change but before you make that decision you should consider your strategic plan. The dimensions you choose to leave as priorities should endure because of your strategic goals, not a sense of loyalty to those tensions.

Mapping the dimensions on your balance wheel (or wheels, if you draft more than one) during the design exercise also requires using a scale from 1 to 10. In this integrative exercise, 1 represents the lowest possible desired level of satisfaction, and 10 represents the highest possible desired level of satisfaction. Once you and your team complete the balance wheels that represent your future state, you can compare the current and future wheels so you can devise a plan to close the gaps.

Once you complete your balance scales and wheels, you will need to merge the information into a consolidated design. Some change leaders may choose to represent their design in the form of a report, tying it all together. Others may use visual representations in the form of a video or a two-dimensional map of a journey that charts the course.

However you choose to represent it, your path starts at your current state of balance or imbalance and as it progresses, it should identify important processes, milestones (timelines linked to measures that progress in intensity), tools, and celebrations. For your design for balance to be IFB compatible, it must contain considerations for both interconnectivity and flow.

In IFB organizations, people are a critical component of any design (relationships, networks, and communication). Therefore, you should strive not to get lost in process (flows) and content, leaving people considerations as an afterthought.

Feel free to use the following questions stimulate further thinking about your designs—remember you will need multiple designs:

- Which scenarios should we design for inclusion in the plan? What are the conditions for scenario viability?
- What are the people considerations?
- How can we leverage the strongest dimensions of the business to change compromised priorities or strengthen other strong ones?
- How should we differentiate the scenarios?
- What are the most important dimensions of our organization that we should keep in balance in the various scenarios? Which dimensions are represented in all scenarios?
- Based on our balance wheel(s), which dimensions of our organization require a sustainability strategy?
- Given our critical balance dimensions what are the barriers to balance? How can we overcome them?

STEPS 4 AND 5: PLANNING AND IMPLEMENTING BALANCE

Once decision-makers diagnose the current and envisioned states of balance, establish priorities, define new balance points (assuming an understanding of where both balance and imbalances exist), and create an integrated design, they can develop a balance plan that addresses the dimensions identified in the designs while at the same time strengthening relationships and facilitating flow.

As with the designs, the plan for balance should encompass all aspects of the IFB Model. Most importantly, the plan for balance should be balanced (it should balance consideration of priorities and non-priorities adequately) so be sure to consider any potential imbalances that may be hidden in your plan.

Implementing Balance Plans

The best-laid plans cannot address every possible eventuality. So unexpected outcomes are guaranteed to arise along the way. One of them can take shape when a plan is carefully researched and developed but the people responsible for execution are unable to implement the plan as intended, causing confusion, tension, or other types of imbalances that may not be immediately detected or fully appreciated. IFB change leaders should be particularly attuned to the balance implementation processes — especially if the readiness for change survey identified clear risks.

While change can be stressful for anyone, it is particularly important for change leaders to navigate their own stress levels with self-awareness, because a leader's stressed-out approach can cause resisters to push back with renewed fervor or turn to passive resistance. As a foundational principle, IFB leaders who facilitate change should work toward mastering their own interior and exterior balance.

When executing IFB balancing plans, leaders involved in implementation should manage their activities in a way that not only delivers based on strategic expectations, but they should also ensure that execution is IFB compatible. Imbalances during a change process can affect the success of an initiative, so everyone involved should attune to and participate in balancing activities. Since force can lead to passive resistance, true balance cannot be achieved using coercion. All this will do is trigger additional imbalances.

Because balancing is an active state, achieving it requires leaders to identify imbalances on the fly, to know when action is needed and when it would be counterproductive. In some organizations, leaders notice imbalances, but all they do is complain. Sometimes this lack of response can be cultural, or it can happen because they don't possess the skills they need to resolve ambiguous challenges.

Attaining balance requires you to be competent at perceiving the forest and the trees simultaneously, understanding the interconnectivity of the entire organizational ecosystem. Therefore, when balancing your organization, whether you're implementing a change initiative or not, your ability to perceive high-level dynamics is as important as your attention to details and subtleties.

STEP 6: ADJUSTING AND BALANCING

As you know, Steps 5 and 6 are linked because balancing is also necessary during implementation phase. This is when your team is expected to adopt new skills in a situation where they have diverse change implementation skills and attitudes. The same diversity may exist within your leadership team, increasing the level of difficulty and depending on cultural values, reducing or strengthening the probability that your organization can successfully transition into an IFB organization.

On a closing note, since this entire chapter was dedicated to balance and adjustment, I will say this: When you and your leadership team master what it means to be a changed-based organization, powered by IFB, it is adept at change initiatives as well as facilitating ongoing adjustment and balance.

These skills are the foundation for creating an agile, flexible organization that can remain responsive to known and unexpected events – including crises. This is a powerful potential competitive advantage in a global reality with unexpected twists and turns that can threaten the lifespan of underprepared organizations.

CHAPTER 18

A VISION OF ORGANIZATIONS EMPOWERED BY IFB

If you don't have a vision you are going to be stuck in what you know. And the only thing you know is what you have already seen.

—Iyanla Vanzant, lawyer and inspirational speaker

Change-based organizations are adaptive institutions with values that support growth, creativity, and flexibility. Their core values include (but are not limited to) change as a constant, interconnectivity, flow, balance, and the Pillar of Trust. While this book concentrates on helping you build a change-based organization through your leaders, IFB principles work best when they are embraced, mastered, and exhibited by all players in the organizational ecosystem.

In other words, IFB is a shared responsibility because depending on the state of your culture, integrating and sustaining IFB principles may require significant cultural change if the core values of your organizational culture vary greatly from the core principles of an IFB organization.

To initiate changes in behavior, some organizations invest in developing leaders first, then middle management and other team members. These organizations create a training hierarchy that mimics the organizational hierarchy and depending on the timing of your learning activities, this can be a waste of resources since neurological studies reveal mindset changes don't take root as an outcome of training, they happen as a result of behavioral change (action).

In IFB organizations, leaders delegate authority to enable employees who are open to learning and growth. IFB leaders have confidence in their team members, and trust is reciprocated. They trust employees to be competent and to have the best interests of the organization at heart. Employees wake up in the morning with enthusiasm, not a hollow sense of obligation motivated by basic survival instincts. Thanks to their individual Pillars of Trust, they are more likely to be inspired, passionate, and free to create in respectful, safe environments.

I don't want to paint the picture that the IFB Model can create some type of utopian workplace. My vision is one where when the model is implemented effectively, the organization will grow with the potential for numerous positive side effects, namely:

- It can evolve organizations into learning organizations, leading to continuous organizational improvement.
- Leaders can continuously develop the skills they need in a modern workplace.
- It can stimulate collaboration.
- It can set the stage for innovation and proactive collaboration in organizations that value these qualities.
- It can improve engagement.
- It can strengthen internal and external communication.
- It can help leaders and employees build valuable alliances.
- It can help organizations to become flexible and agile.

Start a Movement at Work: Operation Cultural Liberation

I envision formal and informal leaders collaborating to shape an empowered movement at work—one that will free cultures from unproductive dynamics that hinder employees from expressing themselves. I would like to see more executives who can authentically engage members of their teams while implementing and sustaining IFB—not as an edict or a directive, but as a movement that engages employees at all levels.

I call this movement Operation Cultural Liberation, and each organization can have its own version of it founded on the principles of IFB. Town hall meetings, social media, collaboration, shared goals, creativity, cultural change, trust, freedom, assessments, personal growth, and yes, even fun—all fall under the umbrella of Operation Cultural Liberation. This movement can be used to organize and introduce IFB changes and build support because in addition to executives, employees who are most passionate about social reengineering and cultural change can step into leadership roles through the movement.

Engagement and connection are the hallmarks of Operation Cultural Liberation. The movement starts within the walls of your organization, so effective communication skills and processes are vital. There are many available corporate social media and *social engineering* applications available to help establish your movement.

Whatever your software application preference, this can be the start of something transformational. Blogs, social media messages from executives, and gamification are all tools that can fuel an interactive cultural change portal that can be especially engaging for millennials.

Operation Cultural Liberation is open to the imagination of your entire team. There is no one right way to go about starting a movement like this that can help you enhance your culture, once you integrate the principles from the Pillar of Trust and IFB Model you can add compatible values. Here is a short list of some of the qualities you can integrate into your vision for cultural change using Operation Cultural Liberation:

- empowerment
- caring about others
- achieving harmony through diversity
- collaboration
- agility
- innovation

Empowerment

Power is an interesting topic. When unproductive power dynamics are embedded within a culture, there are often systems in place to preserve those structures. Some people despise the games of office politics while others are exhilarated by them. Duplicitous behavior, corruption, favoritism, and status are all hallmarks of an unproductive political model.

One goal of Operation Cultural Liberation is to overshadow personal power agendas with shared team goals. When goals are shared, and team members cultivate healthy work relationships based on trust, coworkers are more concerned about collaborating to achieve team goals than jockeying for power—especially when leaders reward team members based on merit and not political criteria. They build relationships and networks that support the team and they can resolve conflict skillfully. Team members who possess a "we" disposition have well-developed skills that reflect the Pillar of Trust and support interconnectivity and flow.

No two empowered organizations are alike, but there are common characteristics that inspire empowerment and engagement. Mutual trust and respect are essential, and employees within empowered organizations are emotionally committed to the organization and its goals. They exhibit productive social and emotional skills, understand urgency, and are results oriented.

Empowered teams know how to distribute power so no one person is viewed as having more of an advantage than others. Empowered leaders focus on the well-being of their teams and they have discretionary decision-making authority that allows them to competently adjust where necessary. They naturally work toward sustaining safe psychological space, supporting healthy work relationships that culminate in mutual growth and support. These leaders know reasonable decisions will be supported by their reporting executives and the board, and mistakes will be treated as learning opportunities, not natural disasters.

Empowered IFB leaders build teams that automatically anticipate the needs of their clients, board members, vendors, and other stakeholders. They find creative ways to expand and enrich these relationships, and they are aware of themselves and the needs of others. These leaders are agile and creative, and they encourage these same qualities in their coworkers. Empowered leaders can express appreciation to their team members because they don't feel diminished in any way. They are simultaneously empowered and empowering.

Caring about Others

There are leaders who tend to take everything personally. If an employee disagrees with an opinion or decision, the divergent view is perceived as a personal affront, not just a different view. These leaders tend to view members of the team as being either for them or against them.

When an organizational culture is on the path to liberation and leaders are using the IFB framework, leadership has a broader definition than managing a team of people and leaders are not limited by black and white thinking—their thinking taps into a full palette of colors. They are inclusive, and they genuinely care about employees without sacrificing their boundaries or overstepping into the abyss of codependence. They know how far to go and stand for integrity, collaboration, engagement, change as a constant, trust, and all the other values the IFB Model represents.

Achieving Harmony Through Inclusion

In my IFB vision of the future, executives and managers don't frame diversity as a potential source of conflict. In cultures liberated by IFB, leaders perceive inclusion as an opportunity to grow by tapping into and integrating unique, insightful perspectives. These leaders aren't threatened by creative tensions introduced by differences, they are energized by them

Sometimes leaders attempt to maintain harmony through equitable treatment of staff. In various jurisdictions, fairness and equality are defined by law, but this is not the only source of definition. Other sources include your code of conduct and organizational and

HR policies. In an environment where diversity is valued, equal treatment may or may not be the fair response.

Inclusion is about respecting differences; therefore, in my vision for IFB organizations even though teams have their challenges, coworkers are open-minded and respectful of each other's differences. Leaders have growth, mental models that expand their capacities to listen without judgment. Inclusion and trust are central to the achievement of harmony and are necessary cultural competencies when your intention is to realize the highest possible standards of interconnectivity, flow, and balance.

Collaboration

The IFB Model supports actions that predispose organizations toward collaboration among team members, between teams, and between internal and external stakeholders. The IFB Model promotes improved and sustained collaboration, as well as systems and structures that support it.

In my vision for collaboration, the IFB Model is not limited to building collaboration within an organization. IFB can be also used in complex situations to clarify, resolve, and create new internal and external structures that consider the people aspects of new projects and challenges in balanced, considered ways.

Agility

Organizational agility exists when an organization is highly adaptive in an ever-changing environment. For instance, when resource challenges arise, agile organizations are adept at doing more with less — unlike organizations that allow resource shortages to create imbalances. Agility also counts when unexpected events happen that have a significant effect on the organization.

My vision of IFB organizations includes teams skilled at detecting imbalances, accurately analyzing them, and creating and executing plans to bring the business into balance. This constant balancing activity sharpens the competencies needed to facilitate organizational flexibility and agility over the long term.

Innovation

My vision for IFB organizations is that they will be predisposed to innovation in all its forms: new products and services, advanced problem-solving skills, or blue ocean strategies. A strong Pillar of Trust is one prerequisite for innovation, but so are the right people, the right skills, the right culture, and the right leadership. I would like to see organizations powered by IFB achieve the right balance between critical tensions.

IFB Learning

My vision for IFB learning is that it will become universal, continuous learning model that adheres to the interconnectivity, flow, and balance framework. Because behavior changes mindsets, I envision using the IFB model to socially reengineer organizations using relationship and network restructuring along with other changes, to stimulate behavioral change that shifts mindsets and helps teams to evolve.

There is power in the crowd and this is evident with crowdfunding and other types of innovative sourcing. I believe crowds can teach us, providing live, relevant data and moving in relevant directions of interest, always on the cutting edge. Creating a movement within your organization is one way to harness the power of the crowd and tapping into the energy and excitement of the crowd also stimulates creativity and supports the emergence of a new type of leader—taking the organization down the paths of learning and progress.

Social Engineering

My vision of IFB extends beyond organizations. My dream is for the model to be used to socially reengineer towns, cities, countries, in addition to organizations of all kinds. As a discipline, social engineering involves influencing attitudes and social behaviors on a large scale. Over time, I'd like the IFB Model to be used to help governments eradicate corruption and build cultures based on integrity, transparency, and collaboration.

In time, I also envision the IFB Model being used to help address complex social issues such as poverty; it can also be useful for redesigning failing industries and making positive changes in how political systems work. Once the versatility of the model is understood, there are no limits to its applications. In the words of Walt Disney, "We keep moving forward, opening new doors, and doing new things because we're curious, and curiosity keeps leading us down new paths." I invite you to create new paths using IFB!

GLOSSARY

action plan: A focused, disciplined, and thoughtful approach to achieving organizational goals.

active listening: The ability to paraphrase information from another party and use probing questions to gain a better understanding of what is communicated.

balance: A state of equilibrium or equipoise; equal distribution of weight, amount, etc.; something used to produce equilibrium; counterpoise; mental steadiness or emotional stability; habit of calm behavior, judgment, etc. In a business context, balance involves consideration of strategic priorities, such as vision, mission, and core values.

balance wheel: A tool that highlights the important components of an organization allowing decision-makers to determine their satisfaction with those components and assign priority levels to them so they can take balancing action.

blame: A self-preservation tactic based on fear; the antithesis of integrity and being held accountable for one's own actions.

boundary spanner: A role developed by Southwest Airlines. These workers manage the flow of information to ensure that the right information is received by the right people at the right time.

change-based organization: An organization where leaders and employees treat change as a constant phenomenon. Leaders within these organizations don't limit their definition of change to discrete initiatives.

channels of communication: Are made up of human beings and use various modalities to facilitate movement of information throughout an organization vertically, horizontally, and even diagonally.

climate: In an organization, climate encompasses institutional memory, accountability, emotion, behavior, communication, reward, trust, organizational structure, connectedness, and leadership.

coach: A person who helps a learner to develop or achieve specific goals. In a business context, leaders provide performance coaching to help direct reports improve their performance.

collaboration: Working together to create something new in support of a shared vision.

communication loop: At an interpersonal level, a communication loop is the process by which information flows between two or more people. Within a corporation a healthy communication loop exists when information flows in a loop: top-down and bottom-up.

competency: The knowledge, skills, and abilities that enable a person (or organization) to act effectively in their respective role.

consequential thinking: The ability to understand the consequences or secondary results of one's actions.

control: To exercise restraint or direction over, dominate, command; to hold in check, curb. It can be a cultural feature that can be quite dominant when transactional activity is highly valued.

cooperation: Important in networks where individuals exchange relevant information and resources in support of each other's goals, rather than a shared goal. Something new may be achieved as a result, but it arises from the individual, not from a collective team effort.

coordination: Sharing information and resources so that each party can accomplish their part in support of a mutual objective. It is about teamwork in implementation, not about creating something new.

corporate governance: Corporate governance is the framework of rules and controls that boards use to operate.

critical thinking: Exercising or involving careful judgment in evaluating a situation.

culture: An organizational culture is the collective behavior of people within an organization and the meaning that people attach to those behaviors. Culture includes the organization's vision, values, norms, systems, symbols, language, assumptions, myths, traditions, policies, procedures, beliefs, and habits.

decision-maker: An organizational leader with the authority to effect change and implement policy.

dyad: In a sociological context, a dyad refers to communication or interrelationship between two people.

drivers of flow: The force behind movement/flow. Drivers of flow include trust, integrity, competence, and emotion — all forces that propel a single type or multiple types of flow.

emotional competence: A thorough understanding of various emotions and emotional responses experienced by oneself and others.

emotional intelligence: A form of social intelligence that involves the ability to monitor your feelings and emotions and those of other people, discriminate among them, and use this information to guide your thinking and actions.

empathy: The ability to experience the thought, feelings, conditions and emotions of another party. It is a connective skill that can support trust building and healthy networks.

empowerment: Facilitation the initiative and creativity of others by sharing information and rewarding desired behaviors so employees can make decisions to solve problems and improve performance.

engagement: A characteristic of the relationship between an organization and its employees. An "engaged employee" is one who is fully absorbed by and enthusiastic about their work and so takes positive action to further the organization's reputation and interests.

feedback loop: The continual cycle of communication that occurs when interconnectivity and flow are occurring. Information flows in a loop, facilitating flow in multiple ways.

flow: Moving steadily or intermittently.

force: The cause of motion or change.

freedom: The power or right to act, speak, or think as one wants, the state of not being imprisoned or enslaved, or the state of not being subject to or affected by something undesirable.

heart: The center of the total personality, especially with reference to intuition, feeling, or emotion.

hierarchy: Any system of persons or things ranked one above another.

high-performing relationships: A relationship between two or more people that is very productive. Individuals within the relationship find a way to operate at full capacity, creating synergies.

influence: The ability to use the tools of persuasion to get a desired result from an individual or party.

institutional memory: A collective set of facts, concepts, experiences, and know-how held by a group of people.

integrity: Adherence to moral and ethical principles, soundness of moral character, honesty. It also refers to the state of being whole, entire, or undiminished.

interconnective infrastructure: The interconnective infrastructure is a relationship substructure within the IFB Model that is comprised of interpersonal relationships, communication, organizational structures, and strategy. Each component is connected to all others affecting both flow and balance.

interconnectivity: A state or condition of being connected. This means bringing together or bringing into contact, so a real or notional link is established.

Interconnectivity, Flow, and Balance (IFB) Model: A framework for transforming environments into trust-based, engaged networks. The IFB system can be used to improve the performance of for-profit or nonprofit organizations through trust-based social reengineering. The IFB Model is not limited to the confines of organizational applications; other groups like families and communities can also benefit from its application because it not only improves performance (however performance is defined) but also has a built-in balancing mechanism that is always turned on when the model is operating as designed.

ivory tower: An ivory tower exists when persons who are responsible for leading are not connected to or concerned with practical realities that affect the people they lead. From the standpoint of the team, the leader has no idea who they are, what they bring to the table, and how to best support them. The ivory tower is synonymous with disconnection, and the antithesis of the IFB Model.

low-performing relationships: Relationships between two or more people that are performing below expectations and may or may not have the potential to operate more productively.

mentoring: An employee developmental system under which a senior or more experienced individual (the mentor) is assigned to act as an advisor, counselor, or guide to a junior or trainee. The mentor is responsible for providing support to, and feedback on, the individual in his or her charge.

mindfulness: A person's ability to hold their awareness in the present and live in the moment without preoccupying themselves with the past or future (these preoccupations can be sources of stress). Mindfulness doesn't preclude experiences of emotion. Mindful people are aware of emotions but do not allow them to cause judgment or distraction.

mindset: Your mindset is a mental framework that informs your emotions and actions. It is influenced by your environmental conditioning and innate proclivities. Two examples of mindset are fixed and growth. When people possess a fixed mindset, change is difficult. The old ways prevail. As a result, they don't spend time developing themselves. Conversely, people with growth mindsets are dedicated to learning and development.

morale: The mental and emotional disposition of a group regarding tasks and functions of group operation.

office politics: The use of one's individual or assigned power within an organization for obtaining advantages beyond one's legitimate authority.

organizational chart: A visual depiction of the configuration of the roles, relationships, and responsibilities within an organization. An organizational chart can be designed based on strategic priorities and interpersonal considerations. They provide insight into a company's culture as various types of chart designs facilitate specific cultures. For example, hierarchical structures support control cultures that rely heavily on stability and policy compliance.

organizational ecosystem: In an organizational ecosystem, everything relates with other parts of the system. People interact with each other and with structures like policies and procedures. Organizational ecosystems also extend beyond the boundaries of an organization, encompassing external stakeholders.

organizational structure: The arrangement of lines of authority, communication, and duties of an organization. Organizational structure determines how roles, power, and responsibilities are assigned, controlled, and coordinated. Multiple tools support organizational structure: organizational charts, job descriptions, policies, procedures, and delegated authorities, to name a few.

performance management: A system that evaluates the performance of employees to gauge progress toward predetermined goals.

Pillar of Trust: This is specific to the IFB Model. It is a developmental framework that can be used by leaders to build a trust-based environment. The Pillar of Trust supports quality relationships, and by extension, strengthens IFB implementations and the performance of the organization. Each Pillar of Trust has three distinct components: integrity, a "we" disposition, and self-mastery.

policies and procedures: Together, they establish the structure within which all activities take place. Policies are a set of principles, rules, and guidelines formulated or adopted by an organization to reach its long-term goals and are typically published in a booklet or other widely accessible form. Procedures are the specific methods employed to express policies in action in day-to-day operations of the organization. Together, policies and procedures ensure a point of view held by the governing body of an organization is translated into steps that result in an outcome that is compatible with that view.

power: The capacity or ability to direct or influence the behavior of others or the course of events.

power structures: These are formal and informal systems of influence that are driven by personal or team goals. Sometimes both systems of influence coexist within a single group or team.

reframing: Cognitive reframing is a psychological technique that consists of identifying and then disputing irrational or maladaptive thoughts. Reframing is a way of viewing and experiencing events, ideas, concepts, and emotions in new ways, and of finding more positive alternatives.

relational coordination: A term coined by Southwest Airlines that describes coordination carried out through relationships of shared goals, shared knowledge, and mutual respect. Relational coordination isn't just a morale-boosting nicety for employees. It accounts for dramatic differences.

relationship: An interconnective factor that facilitates flow. Relationships can exist between people or between groups, or they can exist between people and processes, processes and processes, etc. Myriad relationships are possible.

relationship architecture: The configuration of relationships that exists within an organization, family, or group. The organizational structure is the formal structure, but the informal network of relationships can be quite different and extend across the organization and into the external environment.

relationship intelligence: Encompasses emotional intelligence. It involves understanding how to connect appropriately and manage relationships and networks. Knowing how best to strengthen or maintain healthy relationships. Persons who demonstrate relationship intelligence understand why relationships and networks exist, how they operate, why they perish and how they are powered.

relationship map: A visual representation of relationships that illustrates the connections and why those connections exist.

safe space: An area or forum where a marginalized group doesn't face mainstream stereotypes and marginalization, or in which a shared political or social viewpoint is required to participate in the space. The term safe psychological space is used interchangeably.

self-awareness: Conscious knowledge of one's own character, feelings, motives, and desires.

self-management: Management of or by oneself; the taking of responsibility for one's own behavior and well-being.

self-mastery: The capacity to manage your feelings and emotions especially when difficult or unexpected circumstances throw you off course.

self-regulation: The ability to act in your long-term best interest, consistent with your deepest values.

silo: Isolation of one department from others. This dynamic leads to inefficiency due to impaired communication and a lack of collaboration.

situational awareness: The ability to identify, process, and comprehend the critical elements of information about what is happening to the team regarding the mission. More simply, it's knowing what is going on around you.

social engineering: In the context of teams, social engineering involves facilitating goals by developing your team members' people skills and changing organizational structures in ways that positively affect them.

social responsibility: The obligation of an organization toward the welfare and interests of the society in which it operates.

stakeholder: A person with an interest or concern in something, especially a business.

stretch project: A project designed to push the envelope and develop a person's internal abilities and confidence.

SWOT: An initialism for strengths, weaknesses, opportunities, and threats. It is a planning methodology used to analyze strengths, weaknesses, opportunities and threats and can be applied to individuals, teams, organizations, and other groups.

talent development: An organization's attempt to develop the highest quality staff members.

value system: A set of consistent personal and cultural values used to determine ethical integrity.

voice: A way for a person to shape their environment. It involves stating one's beliefs, objections, and so forth bravely and firmly.

WhatsApp: A messaging application (software) used on mobile devices.

BIBLIOGRAPHY

Arbabisarjou, Azizollah, Maede-Sadat Raghib, Narges Moayed, and Shekoofeh-Sadat Rezazadeh. "Relationship Between Different Types of Intelligence and Student Achievement and Purpose." *Life Science Journal* 10, no. 7s (2013): 128–33.

Baker, Dr. Tim. *The End of the Performance Review: A New Approach to Appraising Employee Performance.* Hampshire, England: Palgrave Macmillan, 2013.

Breene, Timothy R., Paul F. Nunes, and Walter E. Shill. "The Chief Strategy Officer." *Harvard Business Review* 85, no. 10 (October 2007): 84–93.

"Corporate Social Responsibility Report 2014–2015." Nathaniel Litchfield & Partners.

Csíkszentmihályi, Mihály. *Flow: The Psychology of Optimal Experience.* New York: Harper Collins, 1990.

Dweck, Caroline. *Mindset: The New Psychology of Success; How We Can Learn to Fulfill Our Potential.* New York: Ballantine Books, 2008.

"Employee Job Satisfaction and Engagement: The Road to Economic Recovery." *SHRM Report,* May 2014.

"Employee Satisfaction vs. Employee Engagement: Are They the Same Thing?" ADP Research Institute White Paper, 2012.

Freedman, Joshua. "The Business Case for Emotional Intelligence." Six Seconds white paper, 3rd ed., 2010.

Gallup Report. "State of the American Workplace: Employee Engagement Insights for US Business Leaders." 2013.

Gareth, R., and Jennifer M. George. "The Experience and Evolution of Trust: Implications for Cooperation and Teamwork." *Academy of Management Review* 23, no. 3 (July 1998): 531–46.

Geirland, John. "Go with the Flow Interview with Mihaly Csikszentmihalyi." *Wired* 4, no. 9 (September 1996). https://www.wired.com/1996/09/czik.

Gladwell, Malcolm. *The Tipping Point: How Little Things Can Make a Big Difference.* New York: Little Brown and Company, 2006.

Gottfredson, Linda. "Mainstream Science on Intelligence." *Wall Street Journal*, December 13, 1994.

Gracian, Balthasar y Morales. *The Art of Worldly Wisdom.* Translated by Joseph Jacobs. New York: MacMillan & Co., 1892.

Hanson, Kenneth. *Essene Book of Everyday Virtues: Spiritual Wisdom from the Dead Sea Scrolls.* San Francisco: Council Oak Books, 2006.

Hoffer Gittell, Judy. *The Southwest Airlines Way: Using the Power of Relationships to Achieve High Performance.* New York: McGraw-Hill, 2005.

"Holacracy Constitution V 4.0." HolacracyOne, 2013.

Kamal, Yousuf, and Moriom Ferdousi. "Managing Diversity at Workplace: A Case Study of HP." *ASA University Review* 3, no. 2 (July–December 2009): 157–70.

Kim, W. Cha, and Renée Mauborgne. *Blue Ocean Strategy.* Boston: Harvard Business School Publishing, 2005.

Krznaric, Roman. *How Should We Live? Great Ideas from the Past for Everyday Life.* New York: BlueBridge Books, 2013.

Logan, T. Collins. "Compassion and Codependence." San Diego: Integral Lifework Center.

Mosely, Eric. "The Power of the Crowdsourced Performance Review." *Compensation and Benefits Review* 45, no. 6 (2014): 320–23.

Nietzsche, Friedrich. *Twilight of the Idols*, accessed November 23, 2017, https://en.wikiquote.org/wiki/Twilight_of_the_Idols.

"OECD Principles of Corporate Governance 2004." OECD Publications Service, 2004.

Senge, Peter M. *The Fifth Discipline: The Art and Practice of the Learning Organization.* New York: Doubleday Books, 1990.

Spinoza, Baruch. *Tractatus Theologico-Politicus.* Hamburg: Henricus Künraht, 1670.

ENDNOTES

[1] Peter Tyrer, "Personality Disorders in the Workplace," *Occupational Medicine* 64, no. 8 (December 2014): 566–68, https://doi.org/10.1093/occmed/kqu113.

[2] Sree Rama Rao, "Lateral and Informal Communication," *Cite Management Article Repository of Cite.co* (August 25 2014), http://www.citeman.com/4973-lateral-and-informal-communication.html.

[3] John Geirland, "Go with the Flow: Interview with Mihaly Csikszentmihalyi," *Wired* 4, no. 9 (September 1996).

[4] Albert Einstein, "Appeal to Several Hundred Prominent Americans in a Plea for $200,000 to Promote a New Type of Essential Thinking," telegram from the Emergency Committee of Atomic Scientists Chaired by Albert Einstein and the Federation of American Scientists, May 24, 1946.

[5] Paul Zak, *Trust Factor: The Science of Creating High Performance Companies* (New York: AMACOM, 2017).

[6] "Organizational Vitality Report," Six Seconds, accessed June 13, 2018, https://www.6seconds.org/2017/08/17/the-neuroscience-of-trust-2/.

[7] Dr. Jason Jones, "How Character Can be Built," accessed June 13, 2018, http://drjasonjones.com/how-character-can-be-built.

[8] Peter M. Senge, *The Fifth Discipline: The Art and Practice of the Learning Organization* (New York: Doubleday Books, 1990).

[9] Joshua Freedman, "The Six Seconds EQ Model," (2010), accessed June 16, 2018, https://www.6seconds.org/2010/01/27/the-six-seconds-eq-model/

[10] Ibid.

[11] John R. P. French Jr. and Bertram H. Raven, "The Bases of Social Power," in Dorwin Cartwright, *Studies in Social Power* (Ann Arbor: Research Center for Group Dynamics, Institute for Social Research, University of Michigan: 1959), 150–67.

[12] Jesse Lyn Stoner, "Cooperation, Teamwork and Collaboration," Seapoint Center for Collaborative Leadership, accessed September 2, 2014, http://seapointcenter.com/cooperation-teamwork-and-collaboration/.

[13] Doug Macnamara, "The Real Work of Governance," Banff Executive Leadership Inc., accessed September 7, 2017, https://www.cmc-global.org/content/real-work-governance.

ABOUT THE AUTHOR

As a consultant, author, speaker, trainer, executive coach, and advanced emotional intelligence practitioner, Yvette Bethel understands the people side of organizations and how to effectively bring together the corporate vision of business with the know-how of staff. She helps organizations take the necessary steps to resolve strategic people issues.

Yvette is a Fulbright Scholar who put her acquired skills to good use with more than twenty years' experience in a Fortune 500 company prior to founding her consulting firm, Organizational Soul, in 2006.

Yvette realizes that businesses operate using the same universal principles of interconnectivity, flow, and balance. Everything in business is connected: people, policies, and strategies. When leaders are encouraged to connect with their strengths and develop skills that can transform situations, a natural balance that supports optimal performance emerges. Balance is a process, not an event. It fluctuates, influenced by change both within the workplace and the external environment.

Yvette developed the proprietary **Interconnectivity, Flow, and Balance**[SM] (IFB[SM]) framework to help leaders who desire a cutting-edge roadmap that can help them navigate cultural transformation and organizational strengthening. This system is based on a foundation of integrity and trust and is the impetus for the movement to transform conventional practices into redefining ones.

OTHER PRODUCTS BY YVETTE BETHEL

The Trust Style Inventory is a validated psychometric assessment created in partnership with Six Seconds, the largest global emotional intelligence network, to help you diagnose the prevailing trust styles of your team. The self-assessment can provide insights into how individuals trust so together, you can identify opportunities to strengthen trust and build healthy work relationships.

Available: November 30, 2018 •
Publishers: Six Seconds & Organizational Soul Ltd. •
www.orgsoul.com | www.6seconds.org

E.Q. Librium: Unleash the Power of Your Emotional Intelligence; A Proven Path to Career Success helps you develop your ability to use your Emotional Quotient (EQ) to achieve self-regulation in emotionally charged situations. When you build your capacity to stabilize your emotions internally, you can better position yourself to achieve your career goals. The more you develop your skills to navigate your emotions, the more effective you will be at managing yourself, particularly when there are diverse personalities at play.

Publication Date March 28, 2012 • Distribution: Ingram •
Publisher: Organizational Soul Ltd • 232 pages
Amazon | Barnes and Noble | iTunes
www.orgsoul.com

The USA Best Book Award–Winning companion **Getting to E.Q. Librium** activity book is designed to improve your emotional quotient. The introspective exercises help you to recognize your emotions, navigate those emotions, and then respond to emotionally charged situations in a self-regulated way.

Publication Date March 28, 2012 • Distribution: Ingram •
Publisher: Organizational Soul Ltd • 160 pages
Amazon | Barnes and Noble
www.orgsoul.com

The Games People Play at Work interactive video simulation is an emotional intelligence–based simulation that both educates and entertains by immersing learners in a work environment where they are immediately challenged to navigate personalities and situations.

Distribution: www.thegamespeopleplayatwork.com •
Production: The Kennedy Group •
Publisher: Organizational Soul Ltd •
www.thegamespeopleplayatwork.com
www.orgsoul.com

Made in the USA
San Bernardino, CA
13 December 2018